MISCELLANEA EVANGELICA (II)

CHRIST'S MIRACLES OF FEEDING

MISCELLANEA EVANGELICA (II)

CHRIST'S MIRACLES OF FEEDING

BY

EDWIN A. ABBOTT

Honorary Fellow of St John's College, Cambridge
Fellow of the British Academy

Cambridge:
at the University Press
1915

CAMBRIDGE UNIVERSITY PRESS
Cambridge, New York, Melbourne, Madrid, Cape Town,
Singapore, São Paulo, Delhi, Tokyo, Mexico City

Cambridge University Press
The Edinburgh Building, Cambridge CB2 8RU, UK

Published in the United States of America by Cambridge University Press, New York

www.cambridge.org
Information on this title: www.cambridge.org/9781107600195

© Cambridge University Press 1915

First published 1915
First paperback edition 2011

A catalogue record for this publication is available from the British Library

ISBN 978-1-107-60019-5 Paperback

PREFACE

THIS treatise—a chapter in a forthcoming volume of Diatessarica to be entitled The Law of the New Kingdom—is here published in advance, separately, in the hope that it may receive criticism resulting in corrections and improvements, and that it may reach some who would not be likely to read the larger and more expensive work.

Additional evidence is alleged in it for the conclusion—arrived at in previous parts of Diatessarica—that where Luke alters or omits what is in Mark, John as a rule intervenes to support or explain Mark. But its main object is to investigate what may be called Christ's Doctrine of Bread. It gives reasons for believing that the Eucharist of the Last Supper was the outcome and climax of earlier meals that were not only eucharistic but also altruistic. They expressed a divine Law of giving and receiving. They reinforced, in a material emblem with a spiritual application, Isaiah's precepts to Israel, "Break thy bread and draw out thy soul to the hungry," as conditions to be fulfilled by every human being that desires to receive for his own hungry soul that bread which is broken for him by the Son of Man.

EDWIN A. ABBOTT.

Wellside, Well Walk
Hampstead, N.W.
12 July 1915.

CONTENTS

CONTENTS

REFERENCES

(i) *a.* References to the first nine Parts of Diatessarica (as to which see pp. 196—7) are by paragraphs in black Arabic numbers :—

> **1— 272** = *Clue.*
> **273— 552** = *Corrections of Mark.*
> **553—1149** = *From Letter to Spirit.*
> **1150—1435** = *Paradosis.*
> **1436—1885** = *Johannine Vocabulary.*
> **1886—2799** = *Johannine Grammar.*
> **2800—2999** = *Notes on New Testament Criticism.*
> **3000—3635** = *The Son of Man.*
> **3636—3999** = *Light on the Gospel from an ancient Poet.*

(i) *b.* References to the Sections of the Tenth Part of Diatessarica, entitled *The Fourfold Gospel*, are by pages. The three Sections now completed are :—

> (Section 1) *Introduction.*
> (Section 2) *The Beginning.*
> (Section 3) *The Proclamation of the New Kingdom.*

(ii) The Books of Scripture are referred to by the ordinary abbreviations, except where specified below. But when it is said that Samuel, Isaiah, Matthew, or any other writer, wrote this or that, it is to be understood as meaning *the writer, whoever he may be, of the words in question*, and not as meaning that the actual writer was Samuel, Isaiah, or Matthew.

(iii) The principal Greek MSS are denoted by ℵ, A, B, etc.; the Latin versions by *a*, *b*, etc., as usual. The Syriac version discovered by Mrs Lewis on Mount Sinai is referred to as SS, *i.e.* "Sinaitic Syrian." It is always quoted from Prof. Burkitt's translation. I regret that in the first three vols. of Diatessarica Mrs Lewis's name was omitted in connection with this version.

(iv) The text of the Greek Old Testament adopted is that of B, edited by Prof. Swete; of the New, that of Westcott and Hort.

(v) Modern works are referred to by the name of the work, or author, vol., and page, *e.g.* Levy iii. 343 *a*, *i.e.* vol. iii. p. 343, col. 1.

ABBREVIATIONS

Aq. = Aquila's version of O.T.

Brederek = Brederek's *Konkordanz zum Targum Onkelos*, Giessen, 1906.

Burk. = Prof. F. C. Burkitt's *Evangelion Da-mepharreshe*, Cambridge University Press, 1904.

Chr. = *Chronicles*.

Clem. Alex. 42 = Clement of Alexandria in Potter's page 42.

Dalman, *Words* = *Words of Jesus*, Eng. Transl. 1902; *Aram. G.* = *Grammatik des Jüdisch-Palästinischen Aramäisch*, 1894.

En. = Enoch ed. Charles, Clarendon Press, 1893.

Ency. = *Encyclopaedia Biblica*, A. & C. Black, 1899.

Ephrem = Ephraemus Syrus, ed. Moesinger.

Etheridge = Etheridge's translations of the Targums on the Pentateuch.

Euseb. = the Ecclesiastical History of Eusebius.

Field = Origenis Hexaplorum quae supersunt, Oxford, 1875, also Otium Norvicense, 1881.

Gesen. = the Oxford edition of Gesenius.

Goldschm. = *Der Babylonische Talmud*, 1897—1912, ed. Goldschmidt.

Goodspeed = Goodspeed's *Indices*, (i) *Patristicus*, Leipzig, 1907, (ii) *Apologeticus*, Leipzig, 1912.

Hastings = Dictionary of the Bible, ed. Hastings (5 vols.).

Hor. Heb. = *Horae Hebraicae*, by John Lightfoot, 1658—74, ed. Gandell, Oxf. 1859.

Iren. = the treatise of Irenaeus against Heresies.

Jer. Targ. or Targ. Jer. (abbrev. for Jerusalem Targum), or Jon. Targ. (*i.e.* Targum of Jonathan, abbrev. for the Targum of Pseudo-Jonathan) = the Targum of Pseudo-Jonathan on the Pentateuch, of which there are two recensions—both quoted (*Notes on N.T. Criticism*, Pref. p. viii) by ancient authorities under the name "Jerusalem Targum." The two recensions are severally denoted by Jer. I and Jer. II. On other books, the Targum is referred to as simply "Targ." Jon. Targ., see Jer. Targ.

Justin = Justin Martyr (*Apol.* = his First Apology, *Tryph.* = the Dialogue with Trypho).

K. = *Kings*.

Krauss = Krauss's *Griechische und Lateinische Lehnwörter* etc., Part II, Berlin, 1899.

Levy = Levy's *Neuhebräisches und Chaldäisches Wörterbuch*, 4 vols., Leipzig, 1889; Levy Ch. = *Chaldäisches Wörterbuch*, 2 vols., 1881.

L.S. = Liddell and Scott's Greek Lexicon.

Mechilta, see Wü(nsche).

Onk. = the Targum of Onkelos on the Pentateuch.

Origen is referred to variously, e.g. *Hom. Exod.* ii. 25 = lib. ii. ch. 25 of Hom. Exod., but Orig. on Exod. ii. 25 = the commentary *ad loc.*; Lomm. iii. 24 = vol. iii. p. 24 of Lommatzsch's edition.

Oxf. Conc. = *The Oxford Concordance to the Septuagint*.

Pec. = peculiar to the writer mentioned in the context.

Pesikta, see Wü(nsche).

Philo is referred to by Mangey's volume and page, *e.g.* Philo ii. 234, or, as to Latin treatises, by the Scripture text or Aucher's pages (P. A.).

Pistis = *Pistis Sophia*, ed. Petermann (marginal pages).

Ps. Sol. = *Psalms of Solomon*, ed. Ryle and James, Cambr. 1891.

R., after Gen., Exod., Lev. etc. means *Rabboth*, and refers to Wünsche's edition of the Midrash on the Pentateuch, e.g. *Gen. r.* (on Gen. xii. 2, Wü. p. 177).

Rashi, sometimes quoted from Breithaupt's translation, 1714.

S. = *Samuel*; s. = "see."

Schöttg. = Schöttgen's *Horae Hebraicae*, Dresden and Leipzig, 1733.

Sir. = the work of Ben Sira, *i.e.* the son of Sira. It is commonly called Ecclesiasticus (see *Clue* 20 *a*). The original Hebrew used in this work is that which has been edited, in part, by Cowley and Neubauer, Oxf. 1897; in part, by Schechter and Taylor, Cambr. 1899; in part, by G. Margoliouth, *Jewish Quart. Rev.*, Oct. 1899 (also printed in *About Hebrew Manuscripts* (Frowde, 1905) by Mr E. N. Adler, who discovered the missing chapters).

SS, see (iii) above.

Steph. Thes. = Stephani *Thesaurus Graecae Linguae* (Didot).

Sym. = Symmachus's version of O.T.

Targ. (by itself) is used where only one Targum is extant on the passage quoted.

Targ. Jer., Targ. Jon., and Targ. Onk., see Jer. Targ., Jon. Targ., and Onk., above.

Tehillim = Midrash on Psalms, ed. Wünsche (2 vols.).

Test. xii Patr. = Testaments of the Twelve Patriarchs ed. Charles, 1908 (Gk., Clarendon Press, Eng., A. & C. Black).

Theod. = Theodotion's version of O.T.

Thes. Syr. = Payne Smith's *Thesaurus Syriacus*, Oxf. 1901.

Tromm. = Trommius' *Concordance to the Septuagint*.

Tryph. = the Dialogue between Justin Martyr and Trypho the Jew.

Walton = *Biblia Sacra Polyglotta*, 1657.

Wetst. = Wetstein's *Comm. on the New Testament*, Amsterdam, 1751.

W.H. = Westcott and Hort's New Testament.

Wü. = Wünsche's translation of *Rabboth* etc., 1880—1909 (including *Mechilta, Pesikta Rab Kahana, Tehillim* etc.).

(*a*) A bracketed Arabic number, following Mk, Mt., etc. indicates the number of instances in which a word occurs in Mark, Matthew, etc., *e.g.* ἀγάπη Mk (0), Mt. (1), Lk. (1), Jn (7).

(*b*) Where verses in Hebrew, Greek, and Revised Version, are numbered differently, the number of R.V. is given alone.

(*c*) In transliterating a Hebrew, Aramaic, or Syriac word, preference has often, but not invariably, been given to that form which best reveals the connection between the word in question and forms of it familiar to English readers.   Where a word is not transliterated, it is often indicated (for the sake of experts) by a reference to Gesen., *Thes. Syr.*, Levy, or Levy *Ch.*

CHRIST'S MIRACLES OF FEEDING

[Mark vi. 29—44, viii. 1—9, viii. 14—21]

§ 1. *The complexity of the evidence*

THE study of Christ's miracles of feeding is complicated by Jewish peculiarities not only of thought but also of expression. The former often can be briefly explained; the latter often cannot.

For example, the Feeding of the Five Thousand challenges some kind of comparison (such as we find in the Fourth Gospel) with the giving of the manna in the wilderness[1]. Now concerning the latter it is said in Exodus "The people shall go out and gather (lit.) the word of the day in its day[2]." That is to say, the amount necessary for the day was to be gathered on that same day. It was also to be eaten on that same day. None of it was to be left till next morning[3].

According to the texts of our English Versions, the Lord's Prayer, instead of saying "Give us *the bread of the day in its day*," says "Give us *this day our daily bread*," or "Give us *day by day our daily bread*[4]." But these appear to be Christian

---

[1] Jn vi. 31.

[2] Exod. xvi. 4. The Heb. for "word" often means "thing" or "matter." LXX omits it, τὸ τῆς ἡμέρας εἰς ἡμέραν, Vulg. "quae sufficiunt per singulos dies." Aq. inserts αὐτῆς after ἡμέραν.

[3] Exod. xvi. 19.

[4] Mt. vi. 11 τὸν ἄρτον ἡμῶν τὸν ἐπιούσιον δὸς ἡμῖν σήμερον, Lk. xi. 3 τὸν ἄρτον ἡμῶν τὸν ἐπιούσιον δίδου ἡμῖν τὸ καθ᾽ ἡμέραν. The pres. imperat. denotes continuous action. A.V. marg. in Lk. has "for the day" instead of "day by day." R.V. marg. in both has "*Gr.* our bread for the coming day" instead of "our daily bread."

attempts to render in Greek some Aramaic expression corresponding to the Hebrew of Exodus. For Origen tells us that the Greek for "daily," *epiousios*, did not exist till it came into use in the Lord's Prayer. It is a word of irregular formation and doubtful meaning of which he gives two interpretations, (1) "sufficient for our existence," (2) "fit for future [time]," that is, "fit for the next world[1]." Matthew makes the prayer one for a special giving and for a special day, "*Give* (aorist) us *to-day*"; Luke makes it a prayer for continuous giving for every day, "*Give* (pres.) us [*continually*] *day by day*[2]."

The Jews themselves differed in their interpretations of the passage in Exodus. R. Joshua said that they were to collect from one day to the next as one does from the sabbath-preparation-day to the sabbath itself; R. Eleazar denied this[3]. In a prayer of this kind, "the bread of the day" might have meanings varying with the time of day when it was uttered and with the time from which one reckoned "the day" as beginning, whether at sunrise as in nature, or at midnight as among the moderns, or at sunset as among the Jews. There are good reasons for concluding that, in the Lord's Prayer, the Greek word that we render "*daily*" meant "*belonging to the day that is now coming on*," which would be specially appropriate to a prayer uttered in the early morning. But the conclusion could not easily be reached without studying the ancient precept in Exodus[4].

---

[1] See Origen *De Orat.* § 27.

[2] Comp. Lk. ix. 23 "take up his cross *daily*," where the parall. Mk viii. 34, Mt. xvi. 24 omit "daily."

[3] See *Mechilt.* on Exod. xvi. 4.

[4] In Exodus (xvi. 13, 14) the manna comes with "the morning" and "the dew." See Steph. *Thes.* iii. 1460 for passages shewing that ἡ ἐπιοῦσα, sometimes without ἡμέρα, means the day that is "coming on" and will arrive in a few hours or minutes, where αὔριον, "the morrow," would sound too formal. Also comp. Prov. xxvii. 1 (Heb.) "Boast not thyself of (lit.) [the] day [that is] to-morrow (LXX τὰ εἰς αὔριον), for thou knowest not what *a day* (LXX ἡ ἐπιοῦσα) may bring forth." Here, and here alone, the LXX has

Passing to the Gospels we find that whereas in Mark (followed by Luke) Jesus is described as sending out the

---

ἡ ἐπιοῦσα with Heb. equiv. (in Prov. iii. 28 it is corrupt) and the meaning is declared by Rashi to be "*to-day*" ("forsitan *hodie* accidet aliquid mali quod aboleat cogitationes de die crastino"); Walton also renders the Targ. יומא as "hodierna dies." R. Eleazar said (*Mechilt.* on Exod. xvi. 4) "He that hath what he shall eat *to-day*, and saith, 'What shall I eat to-morrow?' is of little faith." From ἐπιοῦσα there appears to have been constructed an irregular adj. ἐπιούσιος meaning "belonging to the coming day." In ἐπιοῦσα, "*on-coming*," ἐπὶ means "*on*"; but in many compound words it means "*fit*," as in ἐπιτερπής, "*fit* to please," and ἐπιούσιος may possibly have conveyed to those who first used it a duplicated meaning, "*fit* (or, *sufficient*), for the *on-coming* day."

'Επιέναι occurs in LXX elsewhere only in Deut. xxxii. 29 εἰς τὸν ἐπιόντα χρόνον, Heb. "their latter-end (אחריתם)," Aq. εἰς ἐσχάτην αὐτῶν, and 1 Chr. xx. 1 ἐν τῷ ἐπιόντι ἔτει, Heb. "at the time of the return of the year," Vulg. "post anni circulum," Syr. "anno sequenti," A.V. "after the year was expired."

These variations may be illustrated from Jas. ii. 15 τῆς ἐφημέρου τροφῆς, R.V. "*of daily food*," on which Field says "More correctly, '*of the day's supply of food*,' as distinguished from τῆς καθ' ἡμέραν τροφῆς." These two renderings, in effect, correspond to Matthew's and Luke's renderings of the petition for bread in the Lord's Prayer. And it is probable that the original Aramaic of that petition is best represented by Matthew, and is based on the precept about the manna "the word *of the day in its day*," that is, "the day's supply in the same day."

Field (on Jas. ii. 15) quotes from Menander a line contrasting the life that is ἐφήμερος, i.e. "*dependent on the day's supply*," with the life that has περιουσία, i.e. "*superabundance*." From this it follows that ἐπιούσιος, *when meaning* ἐφήμερος, might suggest a popular contrast with περιούσιος, so that, as the latter implied "*above* sufficiency," the former might mean "*fit for* sufficiency."

Some confusion of this kind might be facilitated by the Hebraized use of οὐσία to mean (Levy i. 43 *b*) "*property*" in various senses.

But while attempting to do justice to minor causes of this variety of interpretation, we must not be diverted by them from keeping in view the main and almost sufficient cause, namely, that Christ's precept originally referred to the saying in the Law, "the word of the day in its day"; and the same ambiguity that varied the interpretation of the clause in the Law has also varied its interpretation in the Gospel.

I—2

Apostles with the precept "take no bread," Matthew omits the prohibition, and the Didaché limits it ("no bread except [to suffice] till a lodging is found for the night")[1]. The only other Marcan instance of "bread" in words of Christ is in the saying "It is not fit to take the children's bread and cast it to the dogs[2]." Reasons have been given for thinking that these words may have belonged, in the original tradition, to the disciples, and that they have been assigned to Jesus by error[3]. But in any case they are metaphorical and do not clearly shew what is beneath the metaphor[4].

We may fairly say that we do not find in Mark a single instance where Jesus is described as inculcating a doctrine of Bread. And yet we know, not only from the Lord's Prayer, but also from other passages in Matthew and Luke, as well as from copious discourses in John, that such a doctrine must have existed. Mark seems to hint at some hidden truth or mystery when he says concerning the disciples, shortly after the Feeding of the Five Thousand and the Walking on the Waters, "For they understood not in the matter of the loaves, but their heart had been hardened (*or*, made callous[5])." But he does not tell us what the mystery was.

---

[1] These passages will be found discussed in Section IV of *The Fourfold Gospel* under Mk vi. 8. Here they are mentioned merely to shew the necessity of discussing verbal detail in Mark.

[2] Mk vii. 27. This statement refers only to ἄρτος sing. Mk viii. 17 has the pl., and the literal rendering is "ye have not *loaves*."

[3] See *Son* 3353 (iv) *a* foll.

[4] The woman's desire was that Jesus should heal her daughter. How this healing could "take the bread of the children" away from the children is not clear, unless the meaning was that Christ's energy was limited, and that, if part of it were bestowed on Syrophoenicians, less would remain for Jews. More probably "*take and cast*" is rhetorically used for "*cast*," i.e. give it to the dogs as well. This is not the sort of saying that one would assign to Jesus even as a beneficent trial of the woman's faith.

[5] Mk vi. 52 οὐ γὰρ συνῆκαν ἐπὶ τοῖς ἄρτοις, ἀλλ' ἦν αὐτῶν ἡ καρδία πεπωρωμένη. On πώρωσις, "callousness," see *Proclamation* p. 362 foll.

4

These considerations should prepare us for a more than usually patient and laborious investigation of Mark's words and phrases in connection with Christ's feeding of the multitudes, while we attempt to ascertain what was the nature of this "callousness of the heart" and what was the nature of the truth "in the matter of the loaves," which truth, in consequence of the "callousness," the disciples "understood not[1]."

There will be the usual temptation to explain everything from one cause. And the cause to which many facts appear to point will be found to be poetic metaphor. But there is also the possibility of error arising from antedating post-resurrectional acts and words of Christ[2]. And we shall have to remember that even in pre-Christian days there was already established the homely but sacred meal connected with the *Kiddûsh*, or Sanctification of the Sabbath[3]. It may be taken as certain that Jesus, in some form, celebrated the *Kiddûsh* on many occasions with His disciples; and it is probable that on some occasions He extended it to the sanctification of other days, and admitted strangers to the meal. Such celebrations, when related in the language of poetic metaphor—and with allusions to such admissions of thousands at a time into the Church as are described in the Acts of the Apostles—might account for much that could not be explained as the result of metaphor alone.

---

[1] I dismiss, as unworthy of consideration, the notion that it meant that the disciples ought to have learned from the multiplication of the loaves that Jesus could do whatever He liked, and therefore that they were culpably foolish and faithless in being astonished that He could walk upon water.

[2] See "Post-resurrectional" in Indices of *Son* and *Proclamation*, and see *Proclam.* pp. 1, 56–7 concerning a miraculous draught of fishes, placed by Luke before, but by John after, Christ's resurrection.

[3] On the *Kiddûsh*, see *The Religion and Worship of the Synagogue* (Oesterley and Box) p. 346 foll.

There are no less than seven accounts of miraculous feeding in the Gospels:—(1) the Feeding of the Five Thousand, related by four evangelists, (2) that of the Four Thousand, related by two, (3) that of the seven disciples (after Christ's resurrection) related by one. Mark (followed by Matthew) besides giving two of these accounts, adds a comment[1]. He represents Jesus as referring to two of the miracles thus: "When I brake the five loaves among the five thousand, how many baskets (*cophinoi*) full of broken pieces took ye up?....And when the seven among the four thousand, how many full baskets (*sphurides*) of broken pieces took ye up[2]?" Here Jesus is described as distinguishing, not only the two actions and the numbers affected by them, but even the two kinds of "*baskets*" used on the two occasions.

Philo, in his treatise on the Feast of the Baskets—meaning the baskets of the firstfruits mentioned in Deuteronomy—says that it extended over about half the year, being "at two seasons[3]." He appears to mean the "season" of the corn harvest (including the barley harvest which came first in late spring) and the "season" of "fruits," strictly so called, which extended to the autumn. The Hebrew for the "basket" mentioned in Deuteronomy is different from that used by

---

[1] Mk vi. 29—44, after describing (*a*) what immediately followed the death of John the Baptist, describes (*b*) the Feeding of the Five Thousand; Mk viii. 1—9 describes (*c*) the Feeding of the Four Thousand; Mk viii. 14—21 describes (*d*) Jesus as reproaching the disciples for not learning what they ought to have learned from these two actions. These Marcan passages, with their parallels, will be found below, (*a*) p. 14, (*b*) pp. 67, 81, 95, 113, 134, 146, (*c*) pp. 61, 67, 81, 95, 113, 134, 146, (*d*) pp. 8—9.

[2] Mk viii. 19—20, Mt. xvi. 9—10, omitted by Luke.

[3] See Philo ii. 298 foll. *De Fest. Coph.* § 3 where he says that the song of the baskets (καρτάλλων) is sung δυσὶ καιροῖς ὁλοκλήρῳ μέρει ἡμίσει τοῦ ἐνιαυτοῦ. He is referring to Deut. xxvi. 2—4 καὶ ἐμβαλεῖς εἰς κάρταλλον...λήψεται ὁ ἱερεὺς τὸν κάρταλλον. The LXX omits "*all*" in "*all* the fruits of the land," but Philo seems to assume that its inclusion is implied.

Jeremiah, speaking of the vintage, "as a grape-gatherer into the *baskets*[1]." This suggests that something more than a mere literal difference between two kinds of "*baskets*" may be intended in the two Marcan narratives of feeding—possibly some allusion to the firstfruits of the cornfields and to those of the vineyards and orchards, taken metaphorically as applicable to the ingathering of converts into the Church of Christ.

§ 2.   *Traces of metaphor underlying the narratives about the "baskets"*

The last-quoted words of Jesus about the two kinds of "baskets" follow a warning in Mark (and a similar one in Matthew) addressed by Jesus to the disciples, "And he charged them, saying, Take heed, beware of the leaven of the Pharisees and the leaven of Herod." This the disciples take literally, saying "We have no loaves." Jesus rebukes them for their literalism, reminding them of the *cophinoi* and the *sphurides* and saying "Do ye not yet understand?" In Mark the connection is obscure. But it is made clearer by Matthew, who represents Jesus as saying "How is it that ye do not perceive that I spake *not to you concerning loaves*? *But beware of the leaven of the Pharisees and Sadducees.*" Afterwards Matthew adds "Then understood they how that he bade them *not beware of the leaven of loaves, but of the teaching of the Pharisees and Sadducees.*"

This, though clear, leads us to think of metaphorical loaves as well as metaphorical leaven. If the "leaven" is the formal teaching by which the Pharisees vitiated the Law, then it would seem that the "loaves," metaphorically regarded, are the Law itself. In that case, might not the "five loaves" be the five books of the Law "broken up" and explained to the multitude, piece by piece?

---

[1] Jer. vi. 9, so R.V. txt, Targ., LXX, Rashi, and Jerome. In Deut. xxvi. 3, Jer. Targ. has (Etheridge) "baskets, hampers, and paper cases."

This will be considered later on. Meanwhile we must add that there is a difficulty in the mention of a perplexity about "leaven" at a time of the year when, according to Synoptic chronology, no question of leavened or unleavened bread could arise. The Passover and the Feast of Unleavened Bread were not then at hand. Why should the disciples suppose that their Master warned them against literal "leaven," at a season when literal leaven was quite lawful? It is not surprising that Luke omits all the Mark-Matthew tradition about "loaves." He retains merely a warning against "leaven" as given below[1].

---

[1] In the parallel passages printed below, and for the most part in others printed in footnotes, R.V. text is followed (with a very few occasional deviations indicated by brackets) as being convenient for rapid reference enabling the reader to take a broad view of the subject under consideration. But in the detailed study of the Greek text, R.V. text is frequently departed from.

Mk viii. 14—21 (R.V.)

(14) And they forgot to take bread (*lit.* loaves); and they had not in the boat with them more than one loaf.
(15) And he charged them, saying, Take heed, beware of the leaven of the Pharisees and the leaven of Herod.
(16) And they reasoned one with another, saying, We have no bread (*lit.* loaves).
(17) And Jesus perceiving it saith unto them, Why reason ye, because ye have no bread (*lit.* loaves)? do ye not yet perceive, neither understand? have ye your heart hardened?
(18) Having eyes,

Mt. xvi. 5—12 (R.V.)

(5) And the disciples came to the other side and forgot to take bread (*lit.* loaves).
(6) And Jesus said unto them, Take heed and beware of the leaven of the Pharisees and Sadducees.
(7) And they reasoned among themselves, saying, We took no bread (*lit.* loaves).
(8) And Jesus perceiving it said, O ye of little faith, why reason ye among yourselves, because ye have no bread (*lit.* loaves)?
(9) Do ye not yet perceive, neither remember the five loaves of the five thousand, and how

Lk. xii. 1 (R.V.)

In the meantime, when the many thousands of the multitude were gathered together, insomuch that they trode one upon another, he began to say unto his disciples first of all, Beware ye of the leaven of the Pharisees, which is hypocrisy.

8

Besides the Lucan omission of all that part of Mark which connects "leaven" with the feeding of the two multitudes, it will be seen below that there is a remarkable lacuna in Matthew. He omits "they had not in the boat with them more than one loaf." The omission is not surprising. Though Mark often deals in picturesque superfluities, few of his details are so apparently superfluous as this—if taken literally. But, if we can regard it as an ancient symbolical tradition, inserted here as if it were literally true, then it may become both intelligible and interesting. Paul speaks of *"one loaf, one body"* in connection with *"the loaf that we break"* in the Christian Eucharist[1]. John also describes Jesus, after the Resurrection, as feeding seven disciples on a fish and *"a loaf[2]."* It seems a reasonable supposition that Mark has here preserved, out of

---

Mk viii. 14—21(R.V.) *contd.*	Mt. xvi. 5—12 (R.V.) *contd.*	Lk. xii. 1 (R.V.)
see ye not? and having ears, hear ye not? and do ye not remember? (19) When I brake the five loaves among the five thousand, how many baskets† full of broken pieces took ye up? They say unto him, Twelve. (20) And when the seven among the four thousand, how many basketfuls† of broken pieces took ye up? And they say unto him, Seven. (21) And he said unto them, Do ye not yet understand?	many baskets† ye took up? (10) Neither the seven loaves of the four thousand, and how many baskets† ye took up? (11) How is it that ye do not perceive that I spake not to you concerning bread (*lit.* loaves)? But beware of the leaven of the Pharisees and Sadducees. (12) Then understood they how that he bade them not beware of the leaven of bread (*lit.* loaves), but of the teaching of the Pharisees and Sadducees.	

† N.B. "Baskets," when first mentioned = *cophinoi*, when next mentioned = *sphurides.*

[1] 1 Cor. x. 16—17.
[2] Jn xxi. 9, 13. On the sing. "*loaf*," see *Son* **3422** *i.*

9

place, a symbolical tradition of weighty and solemn meaning,
of which he has misunderstood the weight and importance.
This hypothesis is at all events more probable than to suppose
that Mark has preserved, in its place, a literal detail that never
had any importance at all. Matthew's rejection of it may then
be explained because he believed it to be out of its right place,
and so wrongly placed as to give a false impression which he
could not correct. If this hypothesis is accepted, the Marcan
detail of the "one loaf" may fairly be regarded along with its
Johannine counterpart, as an instance of Johannine Intervention, where John has given the right place and the right
interpretation to a tradition misplaced and misunderstood by
Mark.

Now let us return to Luke's omission of the connection of
"leaven"—called by him "the leaven of the Pharisees, which
is hypocrisy"—with the miraculous feeding. Does John fail
to intervene? It might be assumed that he does fail since he
nowhere mentions either "leaven" or "unleavened." But he
mentions "Passover," that is, in effect, the Feast of Unleavened
Bread. And, what is more, he speaks of "the Passover *of the
Jews*," and "the Passover, *the feast* [*so called*] *of the Jews*," in
such a way as to suggest that he contrasts "the Passover of
the Jews" with "the Passover of Christians." This he does
repeatedly[1]. He does not indeed expressly contrast the
material "leaven" cast out by the Pharisees with the spiritual
"leaven" that they retained, but he does imply this distinction.

This we shall see if we put ourselves in the position of
Christians of the first century. They would certainly apply
Pauline language to the Lord's last Passover. "He kept it,"
they would say, "on the Cross, or rather He was our Passover
on the Cross, so that we might '*keep the feast not with old leaven
but with the unleavened bread of sincerity and truth*'; but the rulers

---

[1] Jn ii. 13, xi. 55 τὸ πάσχα τῶν Ἰουδαίων, vi. 4 (W.H.) ⌜τὸ πάσχα⌝,
ἡ ἑορτὴ τῶν Ἰουδαίων.

of the Jews, His murderers, they kept it in what the Apostle Paul called '*the leaven of malice and wickedness*[1].'" Now John, toward the conclusion of his Gospel, expresses the same thought, not indeed in words, but (as often) in dramatic action. His Gospel lays ironical stress on the scrupulousness with which the rulers of the Jews, on the morning of the Crucifixion, at the very time when they were constraining Pilate to destroy Jesus by judicial murder, "entered not into the palace." Their reason was "*that they might not be defiled*, but might eat the passover[2]." They duly "*ate*" their "*passover*," but it was "the passover of the Jews." They cast out their leaven. But they *were* "*defiled*"—with the leaven of malice and wickedness.

In the light of these later Johannine utterances let us consider whether John perhaps desired to express something more than a mere chronological fact, when he prefixed to his account of the Feeding of the Five Thousand the words "Now *the Passover, the feast of the Jews*, was at hand. Jesus, therefore, lifting up his eyes, and seeing that a great multitude cometh unto him, saith unto Philip, Whence are we to buy bread, that these may eat[3]?" This was immediately after the murder of John the Baptist. Many a Galilaean in those days would regard John as a shepherd of Israel; and Mark tells us that Jesus had compassion on the multitude because they were "as sheep

---

[1] 1 Cor. v. 8.

[2] Jn xviii. 28. See also Jn xi. 55 "Now *the passover of the Jews* was at hand: and many went up...*to purify themselves*," on which Origen says (Lomm. ii. 372) "The multitude did not know how to purify themselves. Wherefore, while fancying that they were offering '*their own Passover*' as a service to God, they were so far from 'purifying themselves' that they became more accursed than they were before...." Origen says, and quotes passages to shew, that (*ib.* 371) "We must not suppose the Passover of the Lord to be also *the Passover of the Jews*; for the Passover according to the Law [of God] is that of the Lord, but the Passover of those who break the Law (τῶν παρανόμων) is *that of the Jews*."

[3] Jn vi. 4—5; "bread," *lit.* "loaves."

without a shepherd[1]." The Pharisees, as far as we know, had made no such protest as John the Baptist made against Herod Antipas, nor had they directly or indirectly supported the prophet. They were also plotting the death of Jesus, while professing to be the teachers of the Law, the Word of Life.

Such conduct—combined with a severe enforcement of precepts of purification—was called by Jesus in the Synoptic Gospels "hypocrisy." It was, in effect, "the leaven of malice and wickedness." The Law, as taught by such teachers, was a false parody of "bread." In the Fourth Gospel, Jesus, before the Feeding of the Five Thousand, says, "Whence shall we buy *loaves* that these may eat?" and, later on, in terms of reproach or warning, "Ye ate of the *loaves* and were satisfied[2]." But these are the only Johannine passages where Jesus uses the plural "loaves." A little later He uses the singular, which He frequently repeats, "My Father giveth you *the true bread* out of heaven[3]." It is John's custom to dwell on positives rather than negatives, and on truths rather than falsehoods. In the Synoptic Gospels, Jesus warns His disciples negatively against "the leaven of the Pharisees" (Luke adding "which is hypocrisy"). This is the false leaven, and implies the false bread. In John, a similar warning to the multitude is included in His positive doctrine concerning "the true bread." And the words "Whence shall we buy loaves?" addressed to Philip, may convey the same warning to the disciples, a warning against those many kinds of false foods which one buys at the cost of spiritual health and life, whereas the true bread, the living bread, is bought "without money and without price[4]," coming as a gift to those who are taught by the Giver of all Good to give themselves to Him even as He gives Himself to them.

---

[1] Mk vi. 34. Luke (ix. 11 foll.) omits this. Matthew (xiv. 14 foll.) omits it here, but places it earlier (ix. 36).
[2] Jn vi. 5, 26. [3] Jn vi. 32.
[4] Is. lv. 1, see below, p. 70.

As regards the word "buy," in connection with food or bread, we may note here that the Synoptists use it nowhere except in the Feeding of the Five Thousand[1]. There all the Evangelists have it, but with this important difference, that while the Three ascribe it in various forms ("are we to buy," "that they may buy") to the disciples, the Fourth ascribes it *to Jesus, associating Himself with the disciples—"Whence are we to buy loaves?"* Mark, alone of the Synoptists, has *"buy loaves."* It is highly probable that this Johannine repetition of the Marcan *"buy loaves"* in what seems[2] an entirely different context is deliberate. The probability is increased by the fact that, in the same context, John agrees with Mark, against Matthew and Luke, in mentioning "two hundred pennyworth of loaves," as uttered by a disciple or disciples. These two details, even if they stood alone, would suffice to prove that John had in view Marcan traditions. But they do not stand alone. They are parts of a web of traditions, indicating an unusual abundance of complex evidence, bearing on the Rule of Johannine Intervention, and, ultimately, on the historical fact at the bottom of all these narratives.

---

[1] Ἀγοράζω occurs in Mk vi. 36 with τί φάγωσιν and *ib.* 37 with ἄρτους, in Mt. xiv. 15, Lk. ix. 13 with βρώματα. It occurs also in Jn iv. 8 with τροφάς and vi. 5 with ἄρτους.

[2] "Seems," because it is conceivable that John does not reject, but supplements, the Synoptic traditions about buying. Perhaps he regards Jesus as first overhearing, and then receiving, complaints from His disciples ("How are we to buy?"). These He repeats in a kindly "tempting" of Philip: "Yes, truly, how are we to buy?"

§ 3. *The immediate sequel of John the Baptist's death*[1]

According to Matthew, the Baptist's disciples, after burying their Master, came and *"brought word"* of his death to Jesus,

---

[1] Mk vi. 29—34 (R.V.)   Mt. xiv. 12—14 (R.V.)   Lk. ix. 10—11 (R.V.)

(29) And when his disciples heard [thereof], they came and took up his corpse, and laid it in a tomb.

(30) And the apostles gather themselves together unto Jesus; and they told him all things, whatsoever they had done, and whatsoever they had taught.

(31) And he saith unto them, Come ye yourselves apart into a desert place, and rest a while. For there were many coming and going, and they had no leisure so much as to eat.

(32) And they went away in the boat to a desert place apart.

(33) And [the people] saw them going, and many knew [them], and they ran there together on foot (*or*, by land) from all the cities, and outwent them.

(12) And his disciples. came, and took up the corpse, and buried him; and they went and told Jesus.

(13) Now when Jesus heard [it], he withdrew from thence in a boat, to a desert place apart: and when the multitudes heard [thereof], they followed him on foot (*or*, by land) from the cities.

(14) And he came forth, and saw a great multitude, and he had compassion on them, and healed their sick.

Comp. Mt. ix. 36

But when he saw the multitudes, he was moved with compassion for them, because they were dis-

(10) And the apostles, when they were returned, declared unto him what things they had done.   And he took them, and withdrew apart to a city called Bethsaida.

(11) But the multitudes perceiving it followed him: and he welcomed them, and spake to them of the kingdom of God, and them that had need of healing he healed.

(34) And he came forth and saw a great multitude, and he had compassion on them,

14

who, on "hearing [of it]," withdrew into a desert place. But according to Mark, the Baptist's disciples, "on hearing [of it]," buried him; and the apostles gathered to Jesus and "*brought word*" to Him of all that they had done and taught. Matthew's use of "*bring word*" accords better than Mark's with the usage of N.T. and of Greek in general. The Greek verb "*bring word*," literally, "*bring-message-from*," implies etymologically, and for the most part practically, bringing word from a certain person or place about what the bringers have heard (as a message) from that person, or have seen or heard at that place. It does not often mean simply describe what the describers have themselves done. In that sense, "*declare*" or "*relate*" would be a better word than "*bring word*." Luke, who follows Mark in inserting a coming of "the apostles" to Jesus, says that they "*declared*" to Him "all that they had done[1]."

The text of Mark is liable to suspicion. We do not know whether this is the first or the second instance in which he uses the word "apostles[2]." If it is the first, it comes here with

---

Mk vi. 29—34 (R.V.) *contd.*	Mt. xiv. 12—14 (R.V.) *contd.*	Lk. ix. 10—11 (R.V.)
because they were as sheep not having a shepherd : and he began to teach them many things.	tressed and scattered, as sheep not having a shepherd.	

Jn vi. 1—5 *a* (R.V.). (1) After these things Jesus went away to the other side of the sea of Galilee, which is [the sea] of Tiberias. (2) And a great multitude followed him, because they beheld the signs which he did on them that were sick. (3) And Jesus went up into the mountain, and there he sat with his disciples. (4) Now the passover, the feast of the Jews, was at hand. (5) Jesus therefore lifting up his eyes, and seeing that a great multitude cometh unto him,...

[1] Mk vi. 30 (and Mt. xiv. 12) "brought word (ἀπήγγειλαν)," Lk. ix. 10 "declared (διηγήσαντο)." Luke omits "all that they had taught."

[2] See *Proclamation* p. 394 on Mk iii. 14 (R.V. marg. "some anc. auth. add *whom also he named apostles*").

extreme abruptness; and, even if it is the second and refers to those mentioned by Mark above, "whom also he [*i.e.* Jesus] named apostles," we should expect Mark to say, not that "they *gather* themselves together" to Jesus, but that "they *returned*" —which Luke actually says[1]. In his parallel to Mark's expression "and *when* his disciples *heard thereof*," Matthew omits the "hearing[2]," which Mark may have added (as LXX often adds it) to imply "consequently[3]." But Matthew also omits all mention of the "apostles." This seems best explained from an original and ambiguous "they." This Matthew may have taken as meaning *the persons last mentioned*, namely, the disciples of the Baptist, but Mark as *the persons last mentioned before the digression concerning the death of the Baptist*, namely, the Twelve Apostles. Luke's omission of the Marcan phrase "whatsoever things they had taught" can be best explained by supposing it to be a Marcan amplification for clearness, the original being simply "they brought word of *everything*." This, if "they" were the disciples of the Baptist, would mean "they brought word of the whole story of the Baptist's death[4]." But Mark took it

---

[1] Mk vi. 30 συνάγονται, Lk. ix. 10 ὑποστρέψαντες. Συνάγω, which occurs five times in Mark, is used thrice of multitudes, and once (Mk vii. 1) of Pharisees and scribes, "gathering together" to Jesus. It is not the word we should expect for the return of so small a number as twelve persons, unless it was intended to suggest that they had been sent in different directions (comp. Lk. ix. 6 "everywhere").

[2] Mk vi. 29 καὶ ἀκούσαντες οἱ μαθηταὶ αὐτοῦ ἦλθαν καὶ ἦραν..., Mt. xiv. 12 καὶ προσελθόντες οἱ μαθηταὶ αὐτοῦ ἦραν.... Matthew applies "hearing" to Jesus in the next verse, Mt. xiv. 13 ἀκούσας δὲ ὁ Ἰησοῦς. See next note.

[3] Comp. Josh. ix. 11, 2 K. ix. 13, Esth. iv. 4, Job i. 20 (A), where Heb. has "and [consequently]," and LXX (or v.r.) inserts ἀκούσας.

[4] SS has "they declared to him all that *he did* and *he taught*." Prof. Burkitt says that this is "probably a mere error" of SS, the pronunciation for this being the same as that for "they did and taught." If the scribe of SS attached any meaning to the text it would seem to be this, "the disciples of John recounted to Jesus

CHRIST'S MIRACLES OF FEEDING

as referring to the Twelve. The notion that the Apostles at this critical and busy moment found leisure to bring word to Jesus about *"whatsoever things* they had taught," as well as *"whatsoever things* they had done," is antecedently improbable —at least in this hyperbolical form—and the rejection of it by Luke increases the improbability.

Since these details refer mainly to the Baptist, we cannot expect the Fourth Gospel to intervene although Luke deviates from, or omits, what is in Mark[1].

§ 4. *"And he saith unto them, Come ye...and rest a little,"* in Mark[2]

Matthew and Luke omit these words. But, whereas Luke nowhere has any words of Jesus resembling them, Matthew has an invitation at least so far resembling Mark's that it contains similar words for "come" and "rest": *"Come* unto me...and *I will give-you-rest*...ye shall find *rest* for your souls[3]." The context in Matthew is a paradox, namely, that by taking on oneself a new "yoke," one may find "rest" from a heavy "burden." Ben Sira writes to the same effect about "discipline" or "instruction," saying "Incline thy shoulder and carry her, and loathe not her cords..., for afterward thou shalt find her *rest*[4]." A different aspect of *"rest,"* namely, rest from wanderings, is presented by Jeremiah, "Ask for the

all their Master's last actions and utterances," including those mentioned in Mk vi. 20.

[1] See *Beginning* pp. 66, 68—71, "Non-intervention in matters affecting John the Baptist."

[2] Mk vi. 31 Δεῦτε ὑμεῖς αὐτοὶ κατ᾽ ἰδίαν εἰς ἔρημον τόπον καὶ ἀναπαύσασθε ὀλίγον. SS has here "Come, let us go to *the wilderness*...," but in vi. 32, "they went to *a desert place*." The "desert place" will be discussed in a later section.

[3] Mt. xi. 28—9 Δεῦτε πρός με πάντες...κἀγὼ ἀναπαύσω ὑμᾶς...εὑρήσετε ἀνάπαυσιν ταῖς ψυχαῖς ὑμῶν. The words δεῦτε and ἀναπαύω are common to Mark and Matthew.

[4] Sir. vi. 28 (ed. Schechter and Taylor), "rest," ἀνάπαυσιν, מנוחה.

old paths...and walk therein, and ye shall find *rest*, i.e. *repose*, for your souls[1]." Again another aspect is presented where Isaiah says "This is the *rest*, give ye *rest* to him that is weary." There "weary" corresponds to a Hebrew word meaning faintness caused by hunger, or by thirst, or by wandering, and the LXX has "this is the rest for *him that is hungry*[2]." The Greek words used by Mark and Matthew for "rest" may also mean "refresh" in general, and "refresh with food" in particular. But in the latter sense, "with food" would have to be inserted. Mark does not insert it, and therefore we have no right to assume that he means "refresh yourselves a little [with food]." That interpretation however—besides being suggested by Mark's following words, "for those that were coming and those that were going were many, and *they* (i.e. *the disciples*) *had no leisure so much as to eat*"—appears to be favoured by Origen, who, after quoting Mark and Luke (about the "rows" or "companies" of the Five Thousand), speaks of "*those who were about to refresh-themselves on the nourishment of Jesus*[3]."

If Mark and Matthew took different views of the "rest," or "refreshment," to which Jesus invited His disciples, we can understand why Luke omitted the invitation. Mark places it immediately after the return of the Apostles from their mission; Matthew places it not long after Jesus had "made an end of

---

[1] Jerem. vi. 16, מרגוע, LXX ἁγνισμόν, Aq. [ἀνάψυξιν], Sym. ἠρεμίαν.

[2] Is. xxviii. 12 τοῦτο τὸ ἀνάπαυμα τῷ πεινῶντι. The word rendered πεινᾶν, אוי=διψάω (5), πεινάω (4), ἐκλύω (3)—for which comp. Mk viii. 3, Mt. xv. 32 in the Feeding of the Four Thousand.

[3] Origen *Comm. Matth.* xi. 3 (Lomm. iii. 73) τοὺς ἀναπαυσομένους ἐπὶ ταῖς Ἰησοῦ τροφαῖς. I have not found such an instance in Steph. *Thes.*, nor one parall. to Mt. xi. 28 ἀναπαύσω ὑμᾶς, but there "from your burdens" may be supplied from what precedes. In Aesch. *fragm.* 178, ἀναπαύει, with καματὸν ἵππων, prob. does not mean (as L.S.) "refresh," but (as Steph. *Thes.*) "pausare," "make to cease."

commanding his twelve disciples[1]." Luke in a quasi-parallel passage mentions the return of the Seventy to Jesus with a report about their mission; but he appends no invitation—only a promise, such as the Mark-Appendix places after Christ's resurrection[2]. Later on, in his Gospel, Luke represents Jesus as eating *in the presence of* His disciples, and later still, in the Acts—according to an ancient interpretation of a very difficult passage—as "*eating with them*"; but even there, no invitation on the part of Jesus to the disciples is mentioned in the context[3].

---

[1] Mt. xi. 1. Mt. xi. 2—24 contains digressions about John the Baptist, Chorazin and Bethsaida. Then *ib.* 25—7 contains an acknowledgment of the Father's purpose to reveal His mysteries to "babes." Then follows (xi. 28—30) the promise of "rest" to the weary.

[2] Luke, after the woe pronounced (x. 13 foll.) on Chorazin and Bethsaida, and the return of the Seventy, represents Jesus as saying (x. 19) "I have given you authority...and nothing shall in any wise hurt you" (comp. Mk [xvi. 18] a promise made after Christ's resurrection).

[3] Acts i. 4 συναλιζόμενος, R.V. and A.V. txt "being assembled together with them," marg. "eating (A.V. + together) with them." See *Notes* 2892—5, to which should be added references to the "covenant of *salt*" in Numb. xviii. 19 (comp. Lev. ii. 13) and to the prominence given by Philo (ii. 477, 483—4) to "*salt* (ἅλες)" in his description of the meals taken by the Essenes in common. Aquila used the word συναλίζομαι to mean "take a friendly meal with" in Ps. cxli. 4 "let me not *eat of* their dainties." There LXX has συνδοιάζω, *i.e.* "make one out of two," "be in close companionship" (comp. 1 S. xxvi. 19 "cleave to," Sym. συνδυάζεσθαι). Aquila's instance does not conclusively shew whether he regarded συναλίζομαι as derived (1) from ἁλίζω "collect [a crowd into a small space]" or (2) from ἁλίζομαι "be salted," *i.e.* "fed on salt"—salt being, both for Greeks and for Jews, the symbol of close, friendly, and festive intercourse (Steph. *Thes.* i. 1580 ἅλες "convictus et communio et sodalitatis necessitudo"). Against (1), there is the fact that ἁλίζω appears to be never used with a personal object in the singular, but always of a crowd, army, etc. This important word will come before us again when we discuss the Marcan (ix. 49) doctrine of being "salted with fire" (which Matthew and Luke omit).

This passage in the Acts brings before us, as a possibility worth considering, the hypothesis that Mark, among a number of detached traditions about Eucharistic feeding which he has included in his narrative of the Five Thousand, may have antedated a tradition (about Jesus as inviting His disciples to a sacred meal) which may have been placed after the Resurrection by other Evangelists, and, in particular, by John. In any case, since "Come and rest" is a saying of Jesus mentioned by Mark and omitted by Luke, we are bound to look for something like it in John. And something like it—much more like it than appears at first sight—occurs in the Johannine account of the post-resurrectional feeding of the seven disciples on the one loaf, where Jesus is represented in our Revised Version as saying to the disciples, "Come, break your fast[1]."

Instead of "break your fast," some such phrase as "take-your-morning-meal" would have been a better rendering of the verb *aristân*. It is nowhere used in N.T. except (twice) in this Johannine passage, and in one passage of Luke, where a Pharisee invites Jesus to a morning meal[2]. There, the texts of our English Versions render it "dine." But the Greek word never means "dine." It is constantly distinguished from "dine," and contrasted with "dine[3]."

Returning to John, and rendering the invitation literally,

---

[1] Jn xxi. 12 δεῦτε, ἀριστήσατε. On δεῦτε, "Come!" never used by Luke, but used by Mk-Mt. in the "invitation" now under consideration (and elsewhere), see *Proclam.* pp. 48—9.

[2] Lk. xi. 37 ἀριστήσῃ. R.V. text "dine," marg. "*Gr.* breakfast." The context speaks of the washing of hands. Possibly, among the common people, though not among the Pharisees, the rule was not so strictly observed before "breakfast" than as before the later meal.

[3] See Steph. *Thes.* It can no more mean "dine" than our "breakfasted" could mean "dined." Luke uses the words "*dine*" and "*dinner*" (δειπνεῖν, δεῖπνον) about six or seven times, and the verb "to *breakfast*" only here. In one passage (xiv. 12) "a breakfast or a dinner," he distinguishes the two.

"*[Come] hither! Take-your-morning-meal!*" we perceive that it accords not only with the literal time—the dawn that brought success to the fishermen after the laborious night of failure—but also with the metaphorical or spiritual time, the dawn that was to bring success to the apostolic fishermen casting the net of the Gospel. The meal was their "morning-meal" preparing them to carry forth the Gospel to the world[1]. It appears to correspond both literally and spiritually to the Marcan tradition "Come ye...and rest," omitted by Luke, of which perhaps a version is given by Matthew. As in Mark, so in John, the invitation precedes a meal on bread and fish; but, as in Matthew, the "rest" or "refreshment" is not of the body but of the spirit. Matthew expresses it by "Take my yoke upon you" and "Learn from me"; John expresses it by the words addressed to Peter, and through Peter to the whole assembly of Christians, commanding each in his appointed way to carry the cross, and to serve Christ by serving those for whom Christ died: "Feed my sheep," and "Follow thou me[2]."

§ 5. "*Come ye, [by] yourselves, apart, into a desert place,*"
in Mark[3]

The words "into a desert place" appear to imply, not a desert place meaning a dry and barren waste, but simply "a lonely, quiet, or retired, place." But they are omitted (with the rest of the sentence) by Matthew and Luke, perhaps as being liable to misunderstanding. The words "by yourselves" and "apart" go some way to make the meaning clear, but not quite far enough. The meaning seems to be that in

---

[1] In canonical LXX, ἀριστᾶν occurs only twice as representing Hebrew correctly, (*a*) Gen. xliii. 25 Heb. "eat bread," (*b*) 1 K. xiii. 7 Heb. "support [thyself with food]," R.V. and A.V. "refresh thyself," Heb. סעד and sim. in Targum. The Clementine Heb. rendering of Jn xxi. 12 ἀριστήσατε is סעדו.

[2] Mt. xi. 28—9, Jn xxi. 15—22.

[3] Mk vi. 31.

the general excitement and consternation consequent on the murder of John the Baptist, Jesus perceived that it would be good for the disciples to be alone with Him for a while. To be alone with Him would not be to be really "alone," or "desolate," or "abandoned in a wilderness." Being with the Son, they would be with the Father. Epictetus has a discourse entitled "What is *desertedness* (or, *a desert* (erēmia)) and what kind of person is *deserted* (erēmos)?" It begins thus: "*Deserted[ness]* is a kind of unbefriended state. For he that is *alone* is not necessarily *deserted*, as also he that is in a crowd is not necessarily *undeserted*[1]."

That John recognised this truth is shewn later on when he represents Jesus as saying "Ye shall leave me alone; and [yet] I am not alone, because the Father is with me[2]." He could not indeed represent Jesus as saying to the seven disciples for whom He has prepared the fish and the loaf "Come ye, by yourselves, apart, into a quiet place"—for they were in a quiet place already. But he does succeed in giving us the impression that, before the Feeding of the Five Thousand, Jesus had invited the disciples to accompany Him away from the multitude into a place of quiet. In the description of the man seeking the one sheep that has strayed, where Matthew has "*the mountains*," Luke has "*the desert*." So here, John does not call the place of retirement "*a desert place*" but "*the mountain*," thus: "And a great multitude followed him... and Jesus went up into *the mountain*, and there he sat with his disciples[3]."

In this way John, in effect, reproduces the Marcan "desert place," but without the notion of desertedness. By "sat with

---

[1] Epictet. iii. 13. 1.

[2] Jn xvi. 32.

[3] Jn vi. 2—3, comp. Mt. xviii. 12 "the mountains," Lk. xv. 4 "the desert." The "loneliness" of "the mountain" comes before us afterwards (Jn vi. 15) "Jesus withdrew again into the mountain *himself alone*."

his disciples" he implies that Jesus was not only with them but also was with them in quiet converse. As regards the term "desert place" or "wilderness" used by all the Synoptists in their narratives of feeding[1], it is noteworthy that John does not use any form of it in the narrative itself. But afterwards, in the subsequent comment of the Jews, and in Christ's reply, he twice has "ate the manna *in the wilderness*," that is, *in the wilderness of Sinai*. The Jews seem to say this with unmixed satisfaction, *"our fathers ate."* Jesus adds a note of warning, *"your fathers ate...and died[2]."*

Before passing from the words of Jesus ("come ye...into *a desert place*") we must note that the Syriac Versions have, not "*a desert place*," but "*the wilderness*," *midbar*[3]. This has quite a different meaning. *Midbar* might be applied to a wilderness or open country near any town or district, named in the context; but where no such place is named it always means (in the Bible) the wilderness of Sinai, as, for example, where the Lord bids Moses say to Pharaoh "Let us go...three days' journey into *the wilderness* that we may sacrifice to the Lord our God[4]." Among the reasons why Matthew and Luke omit these words, one may have been a doubt whether they were correctly used. In early poetic accounts of Christ's miracles of feeding, the language of Scripture about the manna in the Midbar of Sinai might be applied to the Christian "table in the wilderness" in expressions sometimes not strictly correct if taken literally. These might naturally be rejected by later Evangelists.

---

[1] Mk vi. 35, Mt. xiv. 15 (sim. Lk. ix. 12) ἔρημός ἐστιν ὁ τόπος, Mk viii. 4, Mt. xv. 33 ἐρημία.

[2] Jn vi. 31, 49.

[3] Mk vi. 31 (SS) "let us go into *the wilderness* (midbar),' but vi. 32 "they went to *a desert place*" and vi. 35 "the *place* is *desert*."

[4] Exod. iii. 18, rep. viii. 27. It is worth noting here that a mention of "three days" (which will be discussed later on, § 17) occurs at the beginning of the Feeding of the Four Thousand.

§ 6. *The concourse of "many," in Mark*

Mark four times uses the word "many" here, thrice in connection with the concourse of "*many*" or "the *great* [lit. *much*] multitude," and once about the "*many* [things]" that Jesus began to teach them[1]. There are several variations in the MSS and Versions. A specimen of these is given below from the Syro-Sinaitic[2], which avoids one or two difficult questions raised by the received text.

It is not difficult perhaps to realise that the disciples might feel not only overcrowded by people continually coming to Jesus, but also harassed by people continually going away. But it is difficult to believe that the multitude, which (according to Matthew) included women and children, "out-went" the boat that contained Jesus—the multitude going round the lake, a distance of about ten miles, and the boat going across the lake, a distance of about four[3].

---

[1] Mk vi. 31—4 "For those that were coming and those that were going (ὑπάγοντες) were *many*,...and *many* saw (εἶδαν) them (αὐτοὺς) going (ὑπάγοντας) and recognised (ἔγνωσαν, marg. ἐπέγνωσαν) [them] (*or*, and they [*i.e.* people] saw them going, and *many* recognised [them]); and on foot from all the cities they ran-together there and outwent them (συνέδραμον ἐκεῖ καὶ προῆλθον αὐτούς). And having come forth [from the boat] he saw a *great* (πολὺν) multitude...and he began to teach them *many* [*things*] (πολλά)."

[2] Mk vi. 31 foll. (SS) "Many were going and coming unto him... and many saw them and recognised them and went by land after him from all the cities. And when they came and he saw a great multitude...and he had begun to teach them." SS alters "those coming and those going" into "going and coming unto him," thus emphasizing the arrivals rather than the departures, or perhaps using "going and" pleonastically (as it is often used in English); it substitutes "went after him" for "ran-together"; it omits "outwent them"; it substitutes "they came and he saw" for "he came forth [from the vessel] and saw."

This important version had not been discovered when W.H. discussed the variations of Mk vi. 33 in W.H. Intr. p. 95 foll.

[3] Prof. Swete says *ad loc.* "Across the Lake from *Tell Hum* or *Khan Minyeh* is scarcely more than four miles; by land the distance

24

Luke seems to imply, by omitting all these Marcan details, that they seemed to him either unimportant, or difficult, or both, and that the one important fact was that "the multitudes followed" Jesus—how "they followed" being a matter of detail that might be neglected. Perhaps Luke, in this respect, is imitating Matthew, who also accepts "the multitudes followed" as a convenient summary of Mark's diffuse statements[1]. But Luke deviates from Matthew as well as from Mark by omitting the words "And, having gone forth [from the boat] he saw a great multitude[2]." They do not seem very important, and, even if John had nothing whatever corresponding to them, though we should have to confess that the law of Johannine Intervention failed here, it would not seem a very serious failure. But John has in the context something that appears to correspond to them, only modified by a suggestion of symbolism, as follows: "After these things Jesus went away beyond the sea of Galilee [the sea] of Tiberias. Now a great multitude was following him, because they were [constantly] seeing the signs that he was doing on the sick. But Jesus went up to the mountain, and there sat with his disciples. Now the passover was near—the feast of the Jews

---

to the upper part of Batîhah could hardly be above ten (Sanday, *Fourth Gospel*, p. 120) unless they went by road and crossed the Jordan by the bridge." He adds "If there was little wind, it would be easy to get to the place before a sailing boat." But if there was so "little wind" that they could not cover "more than four miles" while a crowd including women and children covered "ten," would they not have at once used their oars, which Mark (vi. 48) and John (vi. 19) describe them as using on their return?

[1] Mt. xiv. 13 καὶ ἀκούσαντες οἱ ὄχλοι ἠκολούθησαν αὐτῷ, Lk. ix. 11 οἱ δὲ ὄχλοι γνόντες ἠκολούθησαν αὐτῷ. Mark does not use ἀκολουθέω here. His view is that the multitude went round the lake before Jesus so as to meet Him when He landed—which would not naturally be described as "following."

[2] Mk vi. 34, Mt. xiv. 14 (identical in order as well as in words) καὶ ἐξελθὼν εἶδεν πολὺν ὄχλον.

[so called]. Jesus therefore, *lifting up his eyes and beholding that a great multitude was coming to him*, saith unto Philip...[1]."

It will be noted that here, while first accepting the Matthew-Luke prosaic summarizing word, "*followed*," John adds a form of the Mark-Matthew tradition that Jesus "*beheld*" this "*great multitude*." That this is symbolical is indicated by the contextual "lifting up of the eyes"—an act thrice attributed to Jesus by John and always as a symbol[2]. It is also attributed thrice in Scripture to Abraham. The first Abrahamic instance is where the Patriarch "lifted up his eyes" and beheld the three divine Persons to whom he ministered and gave bread; the second is where he saw the mountain on which he was to offer up his son; the third is where he saw the ram that was to be Isaac's substitute[3]. It is a commonplace in Jewish tradition that whatever Abraham did in service to God, God has done, or will do, in return, to Abraham's seed. It would therefore be appropriate that before the Feeding of the Five Thousand, who represented the congregation of Israel, the Son of God should "go up into the mountain" and "*lift up his eyes*," and "behold that a great multitude was coming unto him."

---

[1] Jn vi. 1—5. This implies that Jesus was on the spot and receiving the multitude (as Lk. ix. 11 "he welcomed them"), not that the multitude was on the spot awaiting Jesus whom they "outwent" (as Mk vi. 33). In Mk vi. 33 προῆλθον αὐτούς, "they outwent them," "*they*" may mean (1) Jesus and the disciples, or (2) the multitude (and "*them*" is similarly ambiguous). The former meaning of "*they*" is the more consistent with the circumstances; taking the short cut across the lake, Jesus and the disciples easily "outwent" the multitude. Then, some hours afterwards, Jesus received and welcomed those who persistently followed Him. Mark's use of προέρχομαι with accus. is noteworthy (see Steph. *Thes.*). In Lk. xxii. 47 it is used of Judas "*going before*" the soldiers as their guide.

[2] See *Joh. Voc.* **1608** (quoting Philo) and *Joh. Gr.* **2616—7** on Jn vi. 3—5. The other instances are xi. 41 (at the tomb of Lazarus), xvii. 1 (before "Father, the hour hath come"). Once Jesus uses the phrase as a precept, iv. 35 "Lift up your eyes," *i.e.* to the harvest in the heavens.   [3] Gen. xviii. 2, xxii. 4, 13.

Whatever may have been the historical reality, the Evangelist contemplates it as including a vision. The Son, the Sacrifice, the Bread of Life, who in old days came to Abraham and received Abraham's bread, now "beholds" the children of Abraham coming to Him in need of bread. Visibly, they are five thousand Jews from northern Palestine; but invisibly they are the seed of Abraham as a whole, invited to enter the circle of that large family of nations which was to be blessed with the blessing pronounced on Abraham. As Abraham gave bread to the Son, so the Son gives bread to Abraham's children. And as Abraham offered up Isaac to God, so the Son of God, in the sign of the bread that followed, signified that He Himself was purposing to offer Himself up for Abraham's children in accordance with the will of the Father in heaven.

If this instance stood alone, the hypothesis of Johannine Intervention here would not be a very probable one; but when taken with many other instances of which some few are certain and many others are highly probable, it acquires considerable probability. And this is greatly increased by the drift of Jewish traditions concerning Abraham and his relation to the Messiah. In a Gospel that assigns to Jesus the words "Abraham rejoiced to see my day, and he saw it and was glad[1]," it is obvious that we must expect to find thoughts about Abraham latent under many of the acts and utterances of Him to whom these words are assigned. We may safely assert that the actual words are John's, not Christ's, but we shall not be so safe in making such an assertion about the thoughts.

This proof of intervention is quite irrespective of the correctness of the Marcan or the Johannine tradition. Even if Mark is quite wrong, it will still be true that John, believing Mark to be right in a certain sense, has intervened to shew that sense. What that "sense" might naturally be will be perceived from such a prophecy as that of Amos, "I will send a

---

[1] Jn viii. 56. See *Joh. Gr.* 2097, 2688—9.

27

famine in the land, not a famine of bread, nor a thirst of water, but of hearing the words of the Lord; and they shall wander from sea to sea, and from the north even to the east; they shall run to and fro to seek the word of the Lord[1]." Jesus Himself seems to allude to this prophecy in the words "Many shall come from the east and the west"—where Luke adds "and from the north and the south"—"and shall sit down with Abraham and Isaac and Jacob in the kingdom of heaven[2]." Also a prophecy of Daniel, interpreted by Irenaeus as referring to Christ, says "Many shall run to and fro and knowledge shall be increased[3]." This, when combined with the prophecy of Amos, might originate just such traditions as Mark has thrown together about the concourse of "many" to Christ's teaching, and to the banquet that He provided for those who suffered from a "famine" for "hearing the words of the Lord." The hypothesis of such an origin would give a satisfactory explanation of Mark's diffuse traditions and Luke's omissions. "Mark,"

---

[1] Amos viii. 11—12.

[2] Mt. viii. 11, Lk. xiii. 29. The occasions on which these parallel sayings were uttered are quite different. Origen, quoting the Gospels, has (*Comm. Rom.* ii. 14, Lomm. vi. 148) "ab oriente et occidente *et a quatuor ventis terrae.*" Does this mean "and [indeed, not only from east and west, but also, as Luke says] from the four winds of the world"? The Targum on Amos viii. 12 has "from the sea to *the west* (מערבא) and from the north to the east." *Sabbath* p. 138 *b* (ed. Goldschmidt) quotes Amos "From sea to sea from east (ממזרח) and from west (וממערב)" with no note. On Zech. ix. 10 "from sea to sea," the Targ. says "from the sea even to the west," but Kimchi "from the South Sea which is called Red, to the North Sea which is called Ocean." These variations may have influenced Christian traditions about the concourse to Jesus. Some might take "from sea to sea" as "from the sea of Galilee to the Mediterranean," *i.e.* the parts about Tyre and Sidon. Luke would not interpret "sea" as referring to the sea of Galilee since he always calls it "lake."

[3] Dan. xii. 4 LXX ἕως ἂν ἀπομανῶσιν οἱ πολλοὶ καὶ πλησθῇ ἡ γῆ ἀδικίας. But Theod. ἕως διδαχθῶσιν πολλοὶ καὶ πληθυνθῇ ἡ γνῶσις (הדעת) (see *Clue* 7, 90—1), and so Iren. iv. 26. 1 "quoadusque discant multi et adimpleatur agnitio."

we may say, "recorded a historical fact (that is, the Concourse) in the language of poetry based on prophecy—not knowing the nature either of the language or of its basis—and left the old traditions just as they were without making them fit together; Luke omitted them; John penetrated to the old poetical purpose underlying Mark and expressed it in a new symbolism."

In a comment on Mark's narrative of the first concourse to Jesus attention was drawn to the apparent allusiveness of the Marcan "great number," as pointing to expressions in Genesis concerning the seed of Abraham[1]. But in that Marcan narrative we may trace also the influence of Amos (variously interpreted) in suggesting the regions of the world from which believers were to draw near to the Messiah[2]. The same influences may be traced in Mark's narrative of a second concourse. The Hebrew use of the somewhat rare verb *"run-to-and-fro,"* applied to those hungering and thirsting after truth by Amos, and to *"many"* by Daniel[3], may very well explain Mark's perplexing accumulation of verbs of motion, commented on above— *"coming and going," "running together,"* and *"outstripping"* —all omitted by Matthew and Luke.

This recognition of Mark's allusiveness, in connection with a prophecy about *"many,"* will come before us again when we consider such Marcan words of Jesus as "to give his life a ransom for *many,"* and, "this is my blood which...is shed for *many*[4]." Both of these sayings appear to be based on words of Isaiah: "By his knowledge shall my righteous servant justify

---

[1] *Proclamation* p. 376, quoting Mk iii. 7—8 πολὺ πλῆθος...πλῆθος πολύ.

[2] Amos viii. 12, mentioning the "north," may explain why Mark (*Proclamation* p. 375) followed by Matthew, inserts "Galilee," as representing the "north" (besides being the "Galilee of the Gentiles" mentioned by Isaiah). Luke vi. 17 omits "Galilee."

[3] Amos viii. 12, Dan. xii. 4 "run-to-and-fro" (Gesen. 1001—2).

[4] Mk x. 45, xiv. 24 parall. to Mt. xx. 28, xxvi. 28, omitted in parall. Lk. xxii. 27 and *ib.* 20 (see W.H.).

many...he bare the sin of *many*[1]." Both are adopted by the parallel Matthew but omitted by the parallel Luke.

Are we to infer that in both these passages Mark has been induced by the influence of prophecy to attribute to Jesus sayings that He did not really utter, which Luke has consequently omitted? Without anticipating the discussion of these Marcan traditions in their order, we may note here, as to the first of them, that the parallel Luke introduces, as words of Jesus, "he that sitteth at meat" and "he that serveth," and represents Jesus as saying "I am among you as he that serveth[2]." Now John represents Jesus as actually "serving" while the disciples sit at meat—and serving in such a way as to suggest a picture of the Saviour of the world wiping off the stains of sinful men upon Himself[3]. This points to a Johannine intervention between Mark and Luke, as if John said: "It is true that Mark has added, to the actual words that Jesus uttered, words that He did not utter. But he added

---

[1] Is. liii. 11—12. Of רבים, freq. = "*many* [*men*]," Gesen. 913 *a* gives, as the first instance, Exod. xxiii. 2 (*bis*) "Thou shalt not follow *a multitude* (so R.V. and A.V.) to do evil, neither shalt thou speak in a cause to turn aside after *a multitude* (A.V. *many*) to wrest [judgment]," LXX οὐκ ἔσῃ μετὰ πλειόνων ἐν κακίᾳ· οὐ προσθήσῃ μετὰ πλήθους ἐκκλῖναι μετὰ πλειόνων ὥστε ἐκκλεῖσαι κρίσιν. On this, Rashi says "Sunt hujus textus expositiones sapientum Israëlis, sed sermo Scripturae eis non convenit...." But it does not appear to be disputed that the Heb. "*many*," in a suitable context, may mean "*the many*," or "*the majority*."

[2] Lk. xxii. 27 τίς γὰρ μείζων, ὁ ἀνακείμενος ἢ ὁ διακονῶν ;...ἐγὼ δὲ ἐν μέσῳ ὑμῶν εἰμι ὡς ὁ διακονῶν.

[3] Jn xiii. 4 foll. See *Notes* 2963—4 shewing that Origen (on Jn xiii. 5) quotes Luke xxii. 27 with a reminiscence of Mk x. 45 "He who said 'I came not as the guest but as the attendant'...He Himself puts water in the basin." Origen also (Lomm. ii. 401) connects the Saviour's "wiping off" on Himself the filth from the feet of the disciples with Is. liii. 4 (comp. Mt. viii. 17) "He beareth our infirmities." See *Son* 3276 *a* where the belief is expressed that this representation was not a dramatic fiction, but was based on tradition.

them to explain what Jesus *meant* by 'ministering': Luke, rejecting those additional words, has left the saying of Jesus in such a context as to lead his readers into a misunderstanding of His 'ministering.' It was not waiting at table, handing this dish or that. It might rather be described as a washing of the feet before the repast. And indeed the Saviour did this kind of service for His disciples, wiping off on Himself the defilements that could not but from time to time befall them in the course of their pilgrimage through the impurities of this present world[1]."

§ 7. *"They had no leisure so much as to eat," in Mark*[2]

It is of course possible that this Marcan tradition meant, from the first, nothing more than this, that the disciples had literally "no leisure" to eat enough for their simple wants; that Mark inserted it in this sense; and that Matthew and Luke omitted it—influenced perhaps in part by the fact that Jesus seemed to have summoned them at an early hour of the morning[3], before the time had come for a regular meal—because they thought it hyperbolical. Or Matthew and Luke may have omitted it as being unimportant from a spiritual point of view.

---

[1] On Gen. xviii. 4 "let a little water be fetched and wash your feet," Rashi says that as the water is fetched by Abraham's "servant" "per aliquem qui mittitur," i.e. *Sheliach*, or *Apostle* (*Proclamation* pp. 391, 395), so God recompenses Abraham's children by a messenger ("legatum"), namely, Moses. But *Gen. r.* ad loc. sees a divine recompense of water proceeding not only from Moses (Numb. xxi. 17) who gives water to drink, but also from God (Is. iv. 4, Ezek. xvi. 9) who Himself purifies Israel with water (sim. more fully in *Numb. r.*, on Numb. vii. 48, Wü. pp. 348—9).

[2] Mk vi. 31 οὐδὲ φαγεῖν εὐκαίρουν, D ουδε φαγειν ευκαιρος (i.e. εὐκαίρως) ειχον, a "nec cibum poterant capere," SS (lit.) "and there was not for them place even bread to eat."

[3] Mk vi. 30—35 shews that a great deal took place between the summons of Jesus and the advent of evening, so that the summons must have been early.

But there are so many instances where Mark's apparently unimportant little phrases about certain subjects, and particularly about the Doctrine of Bread, are much more important than they seem, that this phrase invites investigation. Its insertion in an early Gospel would become intelligible if it originally described the disciples as being unable to "eat their bread" at a common meal with such "gladness and singleness of heart[1]" as characterized the meals taken by them in company with Jesus. Such meals would partake of the nature of a religious service. The omission of the phrase by Matthew and Luke would, by itself, oblige us to discuss it; and the fact that it refers to bread (not indeed here mentioned but certainly implied by the word "eat") makes the discussion all the more necessary.

The Marcan verb "*have-leisure*," literally "*have-good-season*," occurs nowhere else in the Gospels nor in LXX. Codex D substitutes a phrase with a corresponding adverb meaning "*in-good-season*." This adverb occurs in Ben Sira "Be not thou hindered from paying a vow *in-good-season*[2]"; and the corresponding adjective occurs in the Psalms "These wait upon thee that thou mayest give them their meat *in-due-season*[3]." These passages vaguely suggest that in the beginnings of the Christian Church forms of the word might be associated by some with the Eucharist, or with Christ's "breaking of bread" before the Eucharist was formally instituted. But the verb, though proscribed by the Grammarians as a barbarous equivalent of the legitimate phrase "have leisure[4]," is used by Luke (in the

---

[1] Acts ii. 46 "breaking bread at home they did take their food with gladness and singleness of heart."

[2] Sir. xviii. 22 μὴ ἐμποδισθῇς τοῦ ἀποδοῦναι εὐχὴν εὐκαίρως. It occurs nowhere else in LXX.

[3] Ps. civ. 27 τὴν τροφὴν αὐτοῖς εὔκαιρον (v. r. εἰς καιρον, εν ευκαιρια, εις ευκαιρον). This is the only instance in canon. LXX, but in 2 and 3 Macc. εὔκαιρος occurs five times.

[4] "Have leisure," σχολὴν ἄγω, or σχολάζω. See Steph. *Thes.*

Acts) concerning the Athenians: "Now all the Athenians and the strangers sojourning there (lit.) *were-wont-to-have-good-season* for nothing else except to say or hear something of more than usual novelty[1]." Luke obviously means, by his use of the imperfect tense in such a context, not that the Athenians really *had* no leisure, but that they *would habitually make* no leisure. They habitually said "*We have no leisure* for this or that." But if they had spoken the truth they would have said "We are not disposed to do this or that[2]." Mark, like Luke, uses the verb in the imperfect tense. Is it not possible, then, that Luke rejected the word here in his Gospel because it seemed to him to suggest that the disciples were like the Athenians, restlessly *refusing to "find leisure"* for something for which they ought to have "found leisure"?

This supposition Luke might deem incredible. But the Fourth Gospel indicates that there was a spirit of restlessness among the Five Thousand, which extended to the disciples, including ultimately almost all but the Twelve; and if we consider these indications along with the recent execution of John the Baptist by Herod, we shall perceive that there may be nothing absurd in the supposition that the Twelve themselves were restless and unsettled and not disposed to "find leisure" for "eating bread" in the presence of their Master with the "gladness and singleness of heart" to which He was gradually accustoming them[3].

---

and (preferably) Wetstein on Mk vi. 31, quoting *Etymol.*, *Moeris*, *Thomas*, and *Phrynichus*.

[1] Acts xvii. 21 εἰς οὐδὲν ἕτερον ηὐκαίρουν ἢ λέγειν τι ἢ ἀκούειν τι καινό-τερον. It was not only to be "new" but "newer [than usual]." And their first object was to "say" something of this kind, their second, to "hear" it.

[2] Comp. Acts xxiv. 25, where Felix *says*—in answer to Paul's "reasoning" about "righteousness" and "the judgment to come"— "When I get a [suitable] season (καιρὸν) I will call thee unto me"; but he *means* "I am not disposed to listen to reasoning about 'righteousness,' I want money."

[3] Acts ii. 46.

The first intimation of this is in the exclamation of those who have fed on the loaves and fishes, "This is of a truth the prophet that cometh into the world," where it is added that Jesus perceived that they proposed "to take him by force to make him a king[1]." Jesus reproaches them thus, "Ye seek me, not because ye saw signs, but because ye ate of the loaves[2]." They prefer "the meat that perisheth" to "the meat that abideth unto eternal life[3]." Jesus does not reproach the Twelve thus. But He implies that one of them (Judas Iscariot) deserved such a reproach ("one of you is a devil"); and to all of them He says "Will ye also depart[4]?" These would-be king-makers might be called—in the language of Matthew and Luke describing Christ's Temptation—instruments of the Tempter, tempting Jesus to pay Satan homage; and perhaps that thought underlies the Johannine saying "one of you is a devil."

If the disciples, amid the political excitement and concourse consequent on the death of John the Baptist, shewed some disposition to favour the views of the multitude, who wished to make their Master a king, that would explain not only Mark's brief and obscure mention of "want of leisure to eat," but also John's long and emphatic comment on the necessity of "eating," and on the impossibility of doing God's work without the sustenance of God's Bread, the "living" Bread, God's Word, God's Son.

Summing up the evidence as to the Marcan phrase about "leisure to eat," we find that the conclusion is doubtful as to its precise allusion and as to the reasons why Luke omits it. But there is a fair probability that it contains, or might be regarded in early times as containing, some allusion to the Hebrew thought of food as God's "seasonable" gift and to the expression of this by the LXX in the Psalmist's

---

[1] Jn vi. 14—15.　　　[2] Jn vi. 26.
[3] Jn vi. 27.　　　[4] Jn vi. 67—70.

language about God as giving food to His creatures "in its season[1]." Further, there is evidence enough to justify our accepting, as a working hypothesis, the supposition that under Mark's original there was latent an obscure Eucharistic meaning. This, if existent, is wholly lost by Matthew and Luke, who omit the Marcan phrase, but not by John, who attempts to elicit and to expound it[2].

§ 8. *"To a desert place apart," in Mark and Matthew*

It will be observed below that instead of "to a desert place" —where we should rather expect a "solitary" or "retired" place—Luke has *"to a city called Bethsaida[3]."* Mark himself mentions Bethsaida later on, immediately after the Feeding of the Five Thousand and before the Walking on the Waters. There, however, he describes the disciples, not as coming back *from* Bethsaida (as we should have expected from Luke's account) but as coming *to* Bethsaida, and the parallel Matthew

---

[1] See Ps. civ. 27, cxlv. 15, and the comment (in *Gen. r.*, on Gen. i. 3, Wü. p. 11) on Prov. xv. 23 "a word *in its season*, how good it is!" where it is maintained that the "word" is "*Light*," which God uttered "in its season" when He said, "Let there be *Light*!" and He saw that the Light was "good." The Lord's Prayer, and the Sermon on the Mount, and the Temptation, all point to the conclusion that Jesus taught that the Father in heaven is the Giver of every good thing, and of each in "its season," which is also "His season." The Eucharist includes this lesson.

[2] Comp. 1 Cor. xi. 20 συνερχομένων οὖν ὑμῶν ἐπὶ τὸ αὐτὸ οὐκ ἔστιν κυριακὸν δεῖπνον φαγεῖν. The various renderings of these words, and the interpretations of modern commentators, shew how other early Eucharistic traditions might be misunderstood.

[3]
Mk vi. 32	Mt. xiv. 13	Lk. ix. 10
And they went away in the boat to a desert place apart.	Now when Jesus heard it he withdrew (ἀνεχώρησεν) from thence in a boat to a desert place apart....	And he took them and retired (ὑπεχώρησεν) apart to a city called Bethsaida.

omits "Bethsaida," while the parallel Luke omits both "Beth-saida" and the whole of the narrative that follows[1].

These facts indicate some early confusion about "Beth-saida." Instead of this name the Curetonian Syriac in Luke has "a desert place," while the Sinaitic Syrian has "to the gate of a city called Bethsaida[2]." Codex D has "village" instead of "city." The Latin and other versions mostly omit "city" and insert "desert place." One way of explaining not only these variations, but also Luke's inconsistency in "came *to* Bethsaida" and "we are here *in a desert place*," would be to suppose that Luke has mistaken *Beth Saida*, a poetic phrase meaning House of Provisioning, for the "city" of that name. The same Psalm that represents Israel as exclaiming "Can God prepare a table in the wilderness[3]?" says "He rained

---

[1] Mk vi. 45	Mt. xiv. 22	Lk. ix. 18
And straightway he constrained his disciples to enter into the boat, and to go before [him] unto the other side *to Beth-saida*....	And straightway he constrained the disciples to enter into the [*or,* a] boat, and to go before him unto the other side....	And it came to pass, as he was praying alone (καταμόνας) ....

Lk. ix. 18, which follows Luke's Feeding of the Five Thousand, is printed here to shew Luke's divergence at this stage from Mark and Matthew.

Mk vi. 47, Mt. xiv. 23, and Jn vi. 15 agree with Luke ix. 18 in representing Jesus as "alone (μόνος)" after the Feeding of the Five Thousand, but they mention it in their preface to the Walking on the Waters, which Luke omits.

[2] In Lk. ix. 10 (Curet.) "and he *took* (דבר) them apart-by-them-selves and went to a place [that was] desert," the verb "*took*" in the form מדבר (*e.g.* 1 S. xix. 14 (Targ. and Syr.) "to *take* (מדבר) David") might be regarded as meaning (מדברא), *midbar*, the regular word for "*wilderness*" in Hebrew and Aramaic. Walton's Syr. has "in locum desertum Bethsaidae," and *a, b, e* and *Brix.* all insert "locum desertum" without "urbs" or "vicus."

[3] Ps. lxxviii. 19 Heb. "in the wilderness," but LXX, here and *ib.* 15, quite contrary to rule, has ἐν ἐρήμῳ, omitting the article. Contrast Exod. v. 1, vii. 16, viii. 20, 28 etc., and perhaps a hundred more instances, all ἐν τῇ ἐρήμῳ. The Heb., when unpointed, might mean "the" or "a" wilderness. Israelites, when described in poetry as

down manna upon them to eat, and gave them of the corn of heaven..., he sent them *provision* to the full[1]." Now the Hebrew for "*provision*" is there *Saida*. Poetically therefore it might be said that God in bringing Israel into the wilderness where He rained manna on them, brought them to "a *house*, or *place, of provision*," that is, "*Bethsaida*."

This view is confirmed from Greek sources. The Greek for "*provision*" is literally "*supplying with corn*," *episitismos*. This word applies exactly to the supply of manna. For manna was, as the same Psalm says, "*corn* from heaven," not "bread," but of the nature of "*corn*," since it had to be ground and seethed to make it eatable[2]. *Episitismos* in LXX always corresponds to the Hebrew "*Saida*." It is used, in Genesis, of Joseph supplying "*provision*" from Egypt to his brethren, and, in Exodus, of the inability of Israel to supply themselves with "*provision*" for their journey into the wilderness[3]. The instance in Exodus would make the word peculiarly appropriate in the Psalm which represents God as making for Israel in the wilderness that "*provision*" which Israel could not make for themselves in Egypt. Similarly, we shall presently find Luke, alone among the Evangelists, representing the disciples as saying to Jesus, "Send away the multitude...that they may find *provision (episitismos)*[4], because we are here *in a desert*

---

being new to the wilderness of Sinai, might speak of it as "a" wilderness, but afterwards as "the" wilderness.

[1] Ps. lxxviii. 25 "provision," צֵידָה, ἐπισιτισμός (R.V. "meat").

[2] Ps. lxxviii. 24 "corn (דָגָן)." LXX renders this word elsewhere 37 times (Tromm.) by σῖτος, but ἄρτος only here—a mistranslation. On the grinding and seething of the manna see Numb. xi. 8. The mistranslation ("bread") is repeated by unbelieving Jews in Jn vi. 31. Jesus implies in His answer that it was *not* (ib. 32) "the true bread out of heaven." It should be noted however that "*the bread* of the mighty" is mentioned in Ps. lxxviii. 25.

[3] Gen. xlii. 25, xlv. 21, Exod. xii. 39, ἐπισιτισμός here and elsewhere (11 times in Heb. LXX and alw. = צֵידָה, Saida).

[4] Lk. ix. 12 ἐπισιτισμός (R.V. "victuals"). It does not occur elsewhere in N.T.

place." The coincidence is not likely to be accidental, especially since *episitismos* does not occur anywhere else in N.T. It is reasonable to believe that there is an allusion to Exodus, and to the "provision" of manna in the wilderness.

According to this view, Luke is right in retaining this word *episitismos*, unique in N.T., but wrong in duplicating it as "Bethsaida," and in placing "Bethsaida" at the beginning of the narrative. It should have come at the end. The disciples say, in effect, as the representatives of Israel, "We are in the wilderness. We are unable to *make provision* for the people. Send them away that they may *make provision* for themselves." Jesus replies by "*making provision.*" Accordingly, after the gathering of the fragments, the conclusion of the narrative should have been: "Thus did the Lord lead His people that were in the wilderness into *a place of provision,* i.e. *into Bethsaida.*" As a fact, Mark places a mention of Bethsaida in that position, though not in suitable context[1]. Matthew omits "Bethsaida," and it is very probable that it is an error of Mark. If so, it is similar, and yet dissimilar, to that of Luke. Mark, like Luke, has perhaps confused a poetic phrase with a proper name. But unlike Luke, Mark has placed the name at the end of the narrative, whereas Luke (less correctly) has placed it at the beginning.

The Johannine equivalents to "desert place" or "wilderness" in the Feeding of the Five Thousand have been touched on above. As to Bethsaida John cannot be expected to intervene. As a rule, he avoids Synoptic names, being the only Evangelist that does not use the name "Gennesaret," and that does use "Tiberias." Bethsaida he mentions only in connection with Philip, who is "from Bethsaida[2]."

---

[1] Mk vi. 45 "unto the other side *to Bethsaida,*" Mt. xiv. 22 om. "*to Bethsaida.*"

[2] Jn i. 44, xii. 21. W.H. marg. has Bethsaida in Jn v. 2, but that is the name of a pool.

§ 9. *"In the boat," in Mark*[1]

Mark, having previously told us that Jesus ordered that a boat should be constantly ready[2], now calls it naturally *"the boat."* Matthew, not having made this statement, calls it *"a boat*[3].*"* Luke does not mention it here, and rather implies that Jesus quietly withdrew on foot, and that the multitudes followed Him on foot afterwards, when they became aware of His departure[4]. John suggests the same thing at the beginning of his narrative, and afterwards suggests it again, or indirectly affirms it, with curious detail. First he says that Jesus (R.V.) *"went away to the other side of* (A.V. *went over*) the sea of Galilee[5]"*; then he says that, after the Feeding, when the disciples came down to the sea for the purpose of going to Capernaum, they "entered into *a boat.*" He does not here say *"the boat,"* which would have clearly meant the boat in which they had come. And yet afterwards he says that "the multitude saw...that there was *no other boat* there, save [*only there had been*] one, and that Jesus entered not with his disciples into *the boat,* but that his disciples had gone away alone—howbeit there came (*or,* had come) [*other*] boats from Tiberias...[6]." These

---

[1] Mk vi. 32.

[2] Mk iii. 9. See *Proclamation* p. 377 suggesting that in the early Galilaean Church there may have been sometimes a play on the two words—almost identical in Aramaic and Syriac—*"boat"* and *"teaching."*

[3] Mt. xiv. 13.

[4] Lk. ix. 10—11 ὑπεχώρησεν...οἱ δὲ ὄχλοι γνόντες ἠκολούθησαν αὐτῷ. One would not infer from these words that Jesus "withdrew" by sea and the multitudes "followed" by land.

[5] Jn vi. 1 ἀπῆλθεν πέραν. Nonnus adds "in a ship (νηὶ πολυκλήιδι ταμὼν ἀντώπιον ὕδωρ)." If that had been the meaning, it would have been easy to make it clear by substituting διεπέρασεν or διῆλθεν for ἀπῆλθεν. Διαπερᾶν is used in Mk v. 21, vi. 53, Mt. ix. 1, xiv. 34 about crossing the Lake, and διέρχεσθαι in Mk iv. 35, Lk. viii. 22. The text of Jn suggests that Jesus passed into the translacustrian region without going across the Lake.

[6] Jn vi. 16, 22. R.V. "save one," though literal, is misleading.

statements—which can hardly be explained as originating from Johannine symbolism or dramatic picturesqueness—may perhaps be explained by supposing that there were very early differences of tradition about the manner in which Jesus and the disciples passed to, and returned from, the translacustrian scene of the Feeding of the Five Thousand[1]. Later on, at the conclusion of the Feeding of the Four Thousand, we shall find Mark saying that Jesus crossed to "the parts of Dalmanutha," whereas Matthew says that He crossed to "the borders of Magadan," and there are reasons for thinking that both of these names are not real place-names but phrases mistaken for place-names, such as *"their haven"* or *"the parts [of the] opposite [coast]*[2]." If that is probable it strengthens the probability that, in the present Lucan passage, "Bethsaida" is not a place-name, but a phrase mistaken for a place-name, *"House of Provision*[3]."

---

[1] In John, some mention of these details might seem necessary to explain how it came to pass that many of the Five Thousand, immediately after the miracle on the eastern side of the Lake, were addressed by Jesus in Capernaum, on the western side.

[2] Mk viii. 10, Mt. xv. 39. As regards "Dalmanutha," see *Corrections* **498** *g, h*, which gives as alternatives (1) the emphatic form of the Talmudic word for "harbour"—a Hebraized form of λιμήν—preceded by the relative *d-*, so as to mean "belonging to the harbour," (2) a transliteration, in Mark, of the preceding word "parts" (μέρη, מנותא). But it should have been added that, against the second explanation, Prof. Dalman says (and gives evidence to shew) that (*Words* p. 66) "τὰ μέρη with the meaning of 'district' is a pure Graecism, quite incapable of being literally reproduced in Aramaic." In Ps. cvii. 30 "the *haven* of their desire," the Syr. has, for "haven," a form of λιμήν (*Thes. Syr.* 1952, comp. 1941) common in Syriac. This favours the hypothesis called (1) above.

[3] Comp. Macar. p. 85 "For He satisfied five thousand, having caused them to lie down *in the desert as if it were a Megalopolis* (ὡς εἰς μεγαλόπολιν κατακλίνας τὴν ἔρημον)."

§ 10. *Signs of conflation in Mark*

Writing of Christ's eastward passage together with the dis-ciples across the Lake, Mark describes the people as "*knowing*" them and as "*running together* from all the cities." In the following verse he omits the Matthew-Luke tradition that Jesus "healed" the people, but inserts—what Matthew and Luke do not contain—that He "taught" them[1]. Later on, writing of Christ's westward return across the Lake, Mark—as we shall presently find—says again that people at Gennesaret "*knew*" Him, and that they "*ran about*" or "*ran round*[2]." And there he adds, at great length, that the sick were healed by Jesus in the "market-places[3]." Later still, after the Feeding of the Four Thousand, Mark describes Jesus as coming to "Dalmanutha." This name—non-occurrent elsewhere inside, or outside, the Bible—has been shewn to be explicable as an allusion to the Psalmist's "*haven*" in "*the haven* of their desire[4]," a Hebrew word that occurs nowhere else in the Bible but is frequent in Aramaic, meaning "open place," "street," "market-place." Something of the nature of a *harbour* is suggested in the tradition peculiar to Mark "they moored-to-the-shore[5]."

---

[1] Mk vi. 33—4.

[2] Mk vi. 54—5 περιέδραμον, "ran about," occurs nowhere else in N.T. In LXX it occurs twice and in both cases=Heb. שׁוט (the word quoted above, pp. 28—9, from Amos and Daniel). The second instance of LXX περιτρέχω is Jerem. v. 1 "*Run ye to and fro* through the streets of Jerusalem...and seek in the broad places thereof if ye can find a man, if there be any that doeth justly...and I will pardon her."

[3] Mk vi. 56 ἀγοραῖς. Mt. xiv. 35 ("they brought to him all the sick") omits "market-places."

[4] See note above, p. 40, on Ps. cvii. 30 "haven (מחוז)." Levy iii. 70 gives the word as = (1) "city," (2) *Machos*, the name of a place, (3) any enclosed place. Levy *Ch.* ii. 23 gives it as freq. = "*town with market-place*," and also "*market-place*," as in Lam. ii. 19 (Targ.).

[5] Mk vi. 53 "...unto Gennesaret *and moored-to-the-shore* (καὶ

It is necessary to look forward here to these later Marcan passages in order to take a collective view of Mark's whole narrative. For if we find clear signs of reiteration in the employment of one word of prophetic use, such as *"run-to-and-fro,"* we ought to be prepared to find them in other words. And if they are found, then we must recognise that all this Marcan account of the sequel of the Baptist's death must be regarded as coming from sources quite different from those of the narrative of the death itself. In that narrative there is diffuseness but little or no room for prophetic allusion, and there are few or no signs of Marcan "conflation." But here we seem to be in an altogether different atmosphere, so that we may expect continuous conflations such as might be exemplified in many LXX renderings, and especially in Daniel[1]. The influence of this consideration extends beyond the Feeding of the Five Thousand to its sequel. This, in all the Evangelists but Luke, contains a description of Christ appearing to the disciples in their boat while, as Matthew says, it was being *"sorely tried* (literally, *tormented) by the waves"*; but Mark, besides saying that the disciples themselves were being *"sorely tried* (literally, *tormented)"* adds that they were *"in the act of rowing"*; and John, too, describes the disciples as *"rowing[2]."* Now the regular Hebrew and Aramaic word for *"row"* is the same as that which we have been commenting on above, as meaning *"run-to-and-fro"*

προσωρμίσθησαν)," Mt. xiv. 34 "unto Gennesaret." Προσορμίζω does not occur in LXX nor again in N.T. Delitzsch renders Mark *"and they drew near to the dry land,"* the Clementine transl. has *"and they drew near the shore of the sea."* D, SS, *a, b,* and Corb. omit it. Steph. *Thes.* vi. 1974 quotes figurative uses of it from Demosth. p. 795, 14 πρὸς οὓς αὐτὸς ἔχωσας λιμένας (misericordiae)...πρὸς τούτους μὴ προσορμίζου, and from Philostr. p. 717.

[1] See *Clue* 127 on Dan. iv. 19, also 105—111 on 2 S. xxiv. 19—20 compared with 1 Chr. xxi. 19—20, and 95 foll. on "Longer Conflations."

[2] Mk vi. 48, Mt. xiv. 24, Jn vi. 19.

in Amos and Daniel[1]. And the question will come before us whether John is here deliberately intervening in favour of Mark—against Matthew, who omits the word *"rowing,"* and still more against Luke, who omits the whole of the story about *"rowing"*—and, if so, in what sense whether symbolical or otherwise.

§ 11. *"On foot," in Mark and Matthew*[2]

Why does Luke omit *"on foot"*? One reason may be that in Hebrew, "a multitude following [a leader] *at his feet"* may be confused with "a multitude following *on their feet*[3]." But another reason may be that Luke did not perceive a latent allusion in the Marcan phrase, which he consequently deemed superfluous.

Mark is describing a miracle akin to that of the Manna, which speedily followed the departure of Israel from Egypt. And the description of that departure contains the first mention of the phrase *"on foot"* to be found in our English Version of the Bible: "about six hundred thousand [that were] *on foot*[4]." There the Hebrew adds "the men [of military age], besides children[5]." Rabbi Ishmael explains that "children" includes

---

[1] Jon. i. 13 (Heb.) has the exceptional word חתר "dug [into the sea]," but the Targ. has שׁוט, which is used of "rowing" in Heb. of Is. xxxiii. 21, Ezek. xxvii. 8, 26.

[2] Mk vi. 33, Mt. xiv. 13. R.V. marg. *"by land."* Delitzsch *"on their feet."*

[3] *Clue* 75—6 contains an attempt to explain Mk vi. 33, Mt. xiv. 13 thus. See 2 S. xv. 16—18 (*bis*) ברגליו, Walton "in pedibus suis," (*semel*) ברגלו, Walton "in pede suo," R.V. (*ter*) "after him," Targ. (*ter*) "cum illo," LXX (1) τοῖς ποσὶν αὐτῶν, (2) πεζῇ v. r. πεζοί, (3) τοῖς ποσὶν αὐτῶν. Comp. Jer. xii. 5 "thou hast run with the *footmen*," LXX "thy *feet* run."

[4] *"On foot,"* so R.V. here (Exod. xii. 37), but the same Heb. is rendered *"footmen"* in Numb. xi. 21 "Six hundred thousand *footmen* (רגלי) [are] the people...." See below, § 31.

[5] Exod. xii. 37 "the men [of military age]" *ha-gebârîm*, Rashi "men above 20 years old." The first instance of *geber* is in Exod. x. 11 "Go now, *the men* [among you]...," where Moses has

"women," and Rabbi Jonathan adds "the aged[1]"—additions that may illustrate the words added by Matthew alone at the conclusion of both the Miracles of Feeding, "besides women and children[2]."

In the Fourth Gospel there is nothing on the surface to indicate Johannine intervention in favour of Mark here. On the contrary John rather seems to favour Matthew-Luke by himself saying, as they do, that the multitude "followed" Jesus[3]. He does not add *"on their feet"*; although, later on, he certainly implies that they did not come by boat and leaves us to infer that they came on foot[4]. The picture he gives us is of Jesus on a mountain, first looking down and seeing that the multitude that had been following Him is now approaching, and then descending to give them food. If therefore "foot" is to enter at all into the Johannine picture, it would seem that we are to think of the crowd as down below at the feet of Jesus, somewhat as the Song of Moses says concerning Israel at Sinai, "They sat down *at thy feet*, [everyone] shall receive (*marg.* received) of thy words[5]."

But John goes on to say "Now the passover, *the feast of the Jews*, was nigh[6]." And it is at all events worth noting that both in New Hebrew and in Aramaic the word "*foot*" is very frequently used to denote "*a feast*," and especially one of the three great feasts. Possibly therefore John may be following a tradition that explained "*on foot*" as "*at the feast*," to which

---

asked (x. 9) that "young" and "old" may go; Rashi explains that Pharaoh is refusing to let the children go.

[1] See *Mechilt.* on Exod. xii. 37. Jer. Targ. on Exod. xii. 37 adds "*none riding on horses* except the children"—apparently intended to explain antithetically the phrase "*on foot*" applied to the men.

[2] This addition is contained in Mt. xv. 38 as well as Mt. xiv. 21. See below on Mk vi. 44, p. 146 foll.

[3] Jn vi. 2, Mt. xiv. 13, Lk. ix. 11 "followed."

[4] See above, p. 39.

[5] Deut. xxxiii. 3 LXX ὑπὸ σέ, Aq. τοῖς ποσί σου.

[6] Jn vi. 4.

John added an explanatory context indicating that it was "*the passover*[1]."

It is not contended that the Johannine "passover" is proved to represent the Marcan "on foot." The evidence is not sufficient for that. But, in view of the multitude of positive proofs of the rule of Johannine Intervention, the evidence is sufficient here for at least a negative conclusion—it is not proved that the rule fails, and there is nothing unreasonable in the supposition that the rule holds[2].

§ 12. "*He had compassion*," *in Mark and Matthew*[3]

The verb here rendered "*had compassion*" means literally "*had [the] bowels [of his compassion opened]*[4]." In the Healing of the Leper Mark alone used this word[5]. Here Matthew follows Mark in using it, but Luke does not[6]. It is therefore a case where we should expect Johannine intervention.

If we ask why Luke omitted it here, we shall find that it cannot well be because the word is unknown in the LXX and in literary Greek; for Luke uses it elsewhere thrice, and once

---

[1] See Levy iv. 424—5, which shews that this meaning of "*foot*" was very common, and that the double meaning of the term was sometimes played upon. The phrase "*in the foot of*" also meant (ib.) "*on account of*," so that "they followed *on account of* Jesus [and His signs]" (comp. Jn vi. 2) might be expressed by "*at the feet of* Jesus." "*Foot*" is also thus used in Aramaic (Levy *Ch.* ii. 406 *a*). Gesen. 290 *b* renders חגג (LXX ἑορτάζω) not "feast," but "make-pilgrimage," "keep a pilgrim-feast."

[2] It is not contended that John is right. Further reasons will be given below (§ 31) for thinking that Mark's tradition alluded to the phrase "*on foot*," or "*footmen*," connected with the exodus of Israel from Egypt.

[3] Mk vi. 34, Mt. xiv. 14.

[4] Comp. the use of the noun in 1 Jn iii. 17 A.V. "shut up *his bowels [of compassion]*," R.V. "*his compassion*," τὰ σπλάγχνα αὐτοῦ.

[5] Mk i. 41, on which see *Proclam.* pp. 252 foll.

[6] Mk vi. 34, Mt. xiv. 14 parall. to Lk. ix. 11 ἀποδεξάμενος αὐτούς.

about Jesus[1]. But it may be explained by his other contextual variations from Mark. Mark states, as the reason for compassion, "They were as sheep that had no shepherd," and then "He began to teach them many things"—as though the whole multitude were spiritually shepherdless and pitiably ignorant of spiritual things. Later on, Mark says about the disciples, "They understood not [the truth] about the loaves, but their heart was callous[2]"—as though, even by the disciples, some latent spiritual truth, underlying the sign of the Feeding, had been overlooked. All this is omitted by Luke. It would not suit his comparatively prosaic and passionless representation: "Having received (or, welcomed) them, He proceeded to speak to them about the kingdom of God, and to heal those that needed tendance[3]." Apparently Luke did not see that the occasion was one that called for a feeling so strong as to need the Marcan word to describe it.

Passing to John, we perceive that in accordance with Mark's brief observation—but at much greater length, and not in his own words but in words attributed to Jesus—he lays stress on the spiritual meaning of the Feeding, which not only the multitude but also almost all the disciples misunderstood. But neither here nor elsewhere in his Gospel does he mention "bowels of compassion." Can we say, then, that he implies it either here or elsewhere?

It will seem probable that he does, if we bear in mind the Johannine habit of dramatizing and ask ourselves how John would dramatically represent Jesus as *"having-bowels-of-compassion."* The Johannine Epistle says, about Him, "Hereby know we love, because *he laid down his life for us,* and we

---

[1] Lk. vii. 13 (of Jesus at Nain), x. 33, xv. 20 (all peculiar to Luke).

[2] Mk vi. 52, not in the parall. Mt. xiv. 33. Luke omits the whole narrative (the Walking on the Water).

[3] Lk. ix. 11 ἀποδεξάμενος αὐτοὺς ἐλάλει αὐτοῖς περὶ τῆς βασιλείας τοῦ θεοῦ καὶ τοὺς χρείαν ἔχοντας θεραπείας ἰᾶτο.

ought to *lay down our lives* for the brethren.   But whoso hath
the world's goods, and beholdeth his brother in need and *shutteth
up his bowels* from him, how doth the love of God abide in
him[1]?"   The "*shutting up of the bowels*" of compassion, then,
is the Johannine opposite of Christ's sacrifice, or "laying down
life" for others.   It follows that the "opening, or free action,
of *the bowels of compassion*" would be the Johannine equivalent
of Christ's "*laying down His life for the brethren.*"   Now though
the word "*bowels*" is not mentioned in the whole of the Fourth
Gospel, yet the thing—*that is to say, a yearning compassion for
the hunger and the thirst of the sinful world*, and a longing to
lay down life that the world may live—is implied, not only in
the words "The bread that I will give is my flesh, for the life
of the world," but in the whole of the doctrine of the gift of
His flesh and blood, enunciated "in synagogue, as he taught in
Capernaum[2]."

If this view is correct, John is expressing dramatically and
symbolically a moral and sacrificial view of the Feeding of
the Five Thousand of which there is no trace in Luke.   Mark
and Matthew suggest it twice, first, by saying that Jesus "*had
compassion,*" and later on, in the Feeding of the Four Thousand,
by representing Jesus Himself as saying "*I have compassion.*"
John seems to attempt to make us feel that in this "sign"
Jesus is (so to speak) "*doing compassion,*" i.e. symbolically
offering up Himself, as a sacrifice for men.   In the Epistle to
Philemon Paul calls Onesimus first his "*child*" and then his
"*bowels,*" and *The Testaments of the Patriarchs* represents
Joseph as saying to his brethren "Pity the *bowels* of Jacob our
father," meaning "Pity his *beloved son*[3]."   Philo also represents

---

[1] 1 Jn iii. 16—17.

[2] Jn vi. 51—9.

[3] Philem. 10, 12, *Test. XII Patr. Zab.* ii. 2.   Comp. *ib. Neph.* iv. 5
"until there shall come the *bowels* (σπλάγχνον) of the Lord, a man
doing righteousness."

Jacob as calling Joseph "*my bowels*[1]." Thus there was a connection, for Jews in the first century, not at first perceptible to us, between "*compassion*" and "*a son*," or rather "*a dear son*," "*a son specially beloved*."

If this connection is obscure to us it must have been much more obscure to Greeks in the first century. For to them the word "bowels," though conveying often the notion of some strong inward feeling, more often implied depth of resentment than depth of love[2]. It was therefore an appropriate task for the Fourth Evangelist to make this connection clear. He himself certainly believed that the Sign of the Five Thousand was a sign of God's love in sending down His Compassion incarnate in Jesus Christ to give Himself as the living bread for the life of men. This he found hinted at in the Marcan tradition about "bowels of compassion," but only hinted at— and so obscurely that Luke passed it over in word and neglected it in thought. To remedy this defect John may have adopted "*Son*"—meaning "a Son uniquely beloved, or only-begotten" —as a Hellenic paraphrase for the Hebrew "*bowels of compassion*[3]." At all events he represents Jesus as teaching in the synagogue at Capernaum a consistent doctrine such as might be based on this paraphrase.

In conclusion we may naturally ask what induced Mark to use—if not to invent—this unprecedented Greek verb (unprecedented at least so far as researches of modern commentators go) to express Christ's compassion. Might he not have used

---

[1] Philo ii. 45 rhetorically represents Jacob as saying that the wild beasts, in devouring Joseph, devour τῶν ἐμῶν σπλάγχνων.

[2] See Steph. *Thes.* which alleges, as exceptional uses, σπλάγχνον "de utero," of fatherhood in Soph. *Oed. T.* 1066, and of motherhood in Pind. *Ol.* vi. 43 and Aesch. *Sept.* 1031.

[3] Comp. *Test. XII Patr. Lev.* iv. 4, where the text has "The Lord shall visit all the Gentiles *in His bowels* [*of compassion*]," but several versions have, as a Christian modification, "*in the bowels* [*of compassion*] *of His Son*."

the verb "pitied," frequent in LXX and thrice used by himself[1]? It is hardly enough to say Mark wanted to express abundant or extreme pity, for he could have added adverbs (as he adds them elsewhere) to express this[2].

It is reasonable therefore to look back to O.T. for some Biblical instance of a phrase implying "bowels of compassion." A notable one—almost the only one outside the prophets— occurs in Genesis, where it is said of Joseph that "*his bowels did yearn upon his brother*[3]." The context describes Joseph's brethren as coming to buy corn from him. Jewish Christians from a very early date would naturally accept Joseph as a type of Christ; and Joseph, giving food to his brethren in Egypt, might represent one aspect (a rudimentary one) of Jesus giving food to His brethren in the wilderness[4]. Then the compassion of Jesus for the multitude, whom He fed as His little ones, might be likened in early Christian poetry to the "bowels of compassion" of Joseph—who was himself called "the bowels of Jacob," as we have seen above—"yearning" for his beloved brother Benjamin, "the little one" among the Twelve. Thoughts of this kind may well have been in the mind of those who originated early Christian songs and poetic traditions concerning Christ's acts of compassion for the hunger and thirst of the multitudes.

---

[1] Ἐλεεῖν, of which there are about 150 instances in O.T.

[2] E.g. σφόδρα, λίαν, περισσῶς.

[3] Gen. xliii. 30 (where the marg. gives only 1 K. iii. 26 (apart from prophecy)). I have found no ancient comment on the rather curious use of "lift up the eyes" in the context (*ib.* 28—9) "And they [*i.e.* Joseph's brethren]...made obeisance. And he [*i.e.* Joseph] *lifted up his eyes*, and saw Benjamin his brother."

[4] See Jerome on Ps. cv. 21 "He made him [Joseph] lord of his house." Jerome explains "house" as "the Church acquired by [His] blood."

§ 13. *"They were as sheep not having a shepherd," in Mark and Matthew*[1]

The mention of a shepherdless flock comes appropriately here in Mark, because it follows the account of the execution of John the Baptist whom many Jews had been regarding as their "shepherd." Matthew places it earlier, between what may be called a Circuit of Healing and the Mission of the Twelve[2]. Luke nowhere inserts it. Textual grounds may suffice perhaps for a partial explanation of his omitting it here[3]. But Luke will be found also to omit, much later on, another Mark-Matthew tradition about "the shepherd"—the quotation, attributed to Jesus, "I will smite the shepherd and the sheep shall be scattered[4]." We must therefore not ignore the possibility that Luke may have been influenced by some doubt as to the utility of this tradition for his readers. The conception of a king as a shepherd is both Hebrew and Homeric. Yet it was liable to philosophic scoffing such as Epictetus addresses to Homer's Agamemnon: "What then are you? A '*shepherd*' in truth. For you weep like *the shepherds* when a wolf snatches one of their sheep[5]."

---

[1] Mk vi. 34, comp. Mt. ix. 36.

[2] Mt. ix. 35 "And Jesus went about all the cities and the villages, teaching...and preaching...and healing all...sickness." This is parall. to Mk vi. 6 "And he went about the villages round about, teaching." Neither Mk vi. 6 nor the parall. Lk. xiii. 22 (which adds "journeying to Jerusalem") makes any mention of "healing." Mt. ix. 36 proceeds "When he saw the multitudes, he was moved with compassion (ἐσπλαγχνίσθη) for them because they were...as sheep not having a shepherd." Then follows (Mt. ix. 37, x. 1) the injunction to pray for "labourers" for "the harvest," and the Mission of the Twelve.

[3] See below, § 15.

[4] Mk xiv. 27, Mt. xxvi. 31, om. by Lk. xxii. 39 foll. The quotation in the Gospels differs from the Heb. of Zech. xiii. 7. There are special reasons why Luke might omit it. See *Son* (Index "Shepherd").

[5] Epict. iii. 22. 35 "*snatches* (ἁρπάσῃ)," comp. Jn x. 12 "the

The Fourth Gospel, whether consciously alluding to such jibes or unconsciously using language that meets them, vindicates at all events the character of the ideal shepherd. It admits that the ideal has not been reached, and that all who have come forward hitherto, representing themselves as true shepherds, have been, as compared with the true Shepherd, "thieves and robbers[1]." But it claims for the Good Shepherd a very different part. The thief (it says) comes to "steal" and to "destroy"; the wolf comes to "snatch"; the hireling "fleeth"; but the Good Shepherd comes, not only to give food to the sheep, but also, by "laying down his life" in conflict with "the wolf," to save them from being "snatched."

John has in mind the thought of the false king, the king of Babel, the hunter or "snatcher" of the souls of men, the wolf[2]. The true king is He who, as Paul says, "being in the form of God, counted it not a [*prize-for-*]*snatching* to be on an equality with God, but emptied himself, taking the form of a servant[3]." Yet the Jews in Jerusalem accused Jesus, in effect, of doing this very thing, "making himself equal with God[4]," that is to say, "*snatching*" at it as a "*prize*." And what are we to say to the fact that the only other Johannine mention of "*snatching*" comes at the conclusion of the Feeding of the Five Thousand, in a passage implying the complete failure of the multitude to understand the spiritual meaning of the sign: "They were about to come and *snatch him* [*away*] to make him king[5]"? Is it a mere accident that the sheep of Israel, whom Jesus

---

wolf *snatcheth* (ἁρπάζει) them." Perhaps one of Luke's reasons for omitting the tradition of Mk vi. 34 was that he thought it attached too great importance to the recent death of John the Baptist.

[1] Jn x. 8, see *Joh. Gr.* **2361—2**.

[2] Philo ii. 41—42, 90 contrasts "shepherding" which is the fit training for a king, with "hunting" which is the training for war.

[3] Philipp. ii. 6 "a [prize-for-]snatching (ἁρπαγμόν)."

[4] Jn v. 18.

[5] Jn vi. 15. Ἁρπάζω occurs in Jn, elsewhere, only in x. 12, 28, 29 (the Good Shepherd and the comment on it).

came to save from *"the snatcher,"* are here described as themselves desiring to *"snatch [away]"* their Shepherd that they
may convert Him into a "king" after their own hearts—a
veritable wolf? In imputing to John a deliberate choice of a
peculiar phrase to describe a fact we do not impugn the fact
itself. The fact in the present instance—the attempt to make
Jesus a king—may be accepted as historical because of its
antecedent probability, although no other Evangelist mentions
it; but the choice of the word to express the fact may not
improbably have been suggested by the Johannine sense of
irony.

§ 14. *"Shepherd"* (sing.) *nowhere mentioned by Luke*

Both Matthew and Luke mention an owner of sheep as
follows:

Mt. xviii. 12 (R.V.)	Lk. xv. 4 (R.V.)
How think ye? if any man have a hundred sheep, and one of them be gone astray, doth he not leave the ninety and nine, and go....[1], and seek that which goeth astray?	What man of you, having a hundred sheep, and having lost one of them, doth not leave the ninety and nine...., and go after that which is lost, until he find it?

The man's conduct seems open to censure—especially in
Luke's version, which represents him as "leaving to themselves"
or "abandoning[2]," the ninety-nine sheep. At all events
opponents of Christianity might object to such a human shepherd as the type of the divine Shepherd. Perhaps some might
say he was no true shepherd. Readers of Philo would know
that he distinguishes the "cattle-feeder" from the "shepherd"
as follows, "Now to those who allow their beasts to fill themselves with what they desire in a promiscuous mass we must

---

[1] R.V. "leave the ninety and nine and go unto the mountains,"
W.H. "leave the ninety and nine on the mountains and go."

[2] Lk. xv. 4 καταλείπει, comp. Mt. xviii. 12 ἀφήσει.

give the name of 'cattle-feeders,' but that of 'shepherds' on the other hand to those who give them what is needful and only what is exactly suitable[1]." The man who "abandoned" his ninety-nine sheep (it might be urged) did not discharge the duty of a shepherd and was not worthy of the name.

Jerome gives two explanations of the parable. Some think (he says) that the Shepherd is the incarnate Son descending to save the one wandering sheep below, the human race (in which case the ninety-nine would be, presumably, the angels in heaven); others think that the ninety-nine are those whom He called "just persons that need no repentance[2]." In the latter case, the parable is still open to the jibe of Celsus, who asked "what evil" these just persons had done to incur the punishment of being abandoned[3]. It is only a prosaic or captious spirit that would take literally this "abandonment" of the safe and unwandering sheep, but still the Fourth Evangelist might naturally feel that there was room for another exposition of the tasks of the Good Shepherd in which He might be described as performing one task without neglecting another[4].

Luke, in his only mention of "flock," calls it a "little one" and connects it with "kingdom," "Fear not, little *flock*; for it is your Father's good pleasure to give you the *kingdom*[5]"; and again, in his parallel to the Marcan passage that speaks of "teaching" and "sheep without a shepherd," Luke mentions

---

[1] Philo i. 306 "cattle-feeders," κτηνοτρόφους.

[2] Lk. xv. 7.   [3] Orig. *Cels.* iii. 62.

[4] Philo, besides quoting Numb. xxvii. 16 foll. from LXX "sheep that have no shepherd," with the paraphrase (i. 307) χωρὶς ἐπιστάτου καὶ ἡγεμόνος, also alludes to it (i. 170) δίχα ἐπιστάτου καὶ ἡγεμόνος, without quoting it. Such a condition he calls (*ib.*) ὀρφανίαν (comp. Jn xiv. 18).

[5] Lk. xii. 32 τὸ μικρὸν ποίμνιον, on which see *Son* **3440** *b* quoting Clem. Alex. 953, who uses Lk. and Mt. xviii. 10 μικρῶν to illustrate Christ's doctrine of "little ones." This would make good sense, "*flock of the little-ones*," i.e. flock of the children of the New Kingdom.

53

"*kingdom*[1]." Somewhat similarly in one of the Psalms, where the Hebrew has "he *shepherded* them," and the R.V. "he *fed* them," the Targum has "he *reigned* over them[2]." Such variations of rendering are all justifiable. But they imply preferences of this or that aspect of "*shepherding*."

Luke seems to like the royal aspect. John, if he does not dislike, at all events avoids it. He represents Jesus as using the word "*kingdom*" on only two occasions, namely, in dialogues with Nicodemus and Pilate, both of whom misunderstand it[3]. Also, in John, the flock is not called "little," though it is divided, at the close of his Gospel, into three classes, one of which consists of "little-sheep[4]." In the Parable of the Good Shepherd we are told that the sheep are of more than one fold, though they will all be brought together so as to make "one flock, one shepherd[5]."

§ 15. "*And he began to teach them many things*," *in Mark*

The parallel Matthew-Luke makes no mention of "teaching," but Matthew mentions "curing," and Luke has "welcoming" and "speaking about the kingdom of God" and "healing[6]." An explanation of these variations is afforded by the hypothesis of an original Hebrew verb "*to shepherd*." Mark has given us a hint of this in his negative phrase above discussed ("sheep not having a *shepherd*"). But we have now to note that the Hebrew verb "*to shepherd*" occurs more frequently in the Bible than might be supposed. The English Version does not reveal it, because "shepherding" includes various actions such as feeding and tending, which may be expressed in English

---

[1] Mk vi. 34, Lk. ix. 11.   [2] Ps. lxxviii. 72.

[3] See *Joh. Voc.* **1685** *a* quoting Jn iii. 3, 5, xviii. 36.

[4] Jn xxi. 15—17 (txt doubtful).

[5] Jn x. 16.

[6] Mk vi. 34 ἤρξατο διδάσκειν αὐτοὺς πολλά, Mt. xiv. 14 ἐθεράπευσεν τοὺς ἀρρώστους αὐτῶν, Lk. ix. 11 ἀποδεξάμενος αὐτοὺς ἐλάλει αὐτοῖς περὶ τῆς βασιλείας τοῦ θεοῦ, καὶ τοὺς χρείαν ἔχοντας θεραπείας ἰᾶτο.

by their several verbs "feed," "tend," etc. This is the first and probably the principal cause of variation. A second cause is the accidental similarity of the Hebrew verb *"shepherd"* to forms of the verb meaning *"know"* or *"cause to know"* (i.e. *"teach"*).

This second cause has been discussed in a previous treatise[1]. One of the instances there given deserves to be repeated here because it illustrates both causes at the same time: "The lips of the righteous [man] shepherd many[2]." Here "to *shepherd*" may mean "to *guide*," or "*tend*," as well as "*feed*," but LXX has confused it with "*know*," meaning "[*come to*] *know*," i.e. "learn." Moreover the LXX renders "many" (the Hebrew *rab*) as though it meant "great" or "lofty," and renders the whole sentence "The lips of the righteous [*come to*] *know* lofty [things]." This suggests an explanation of the phrase in our Marcan context "*and many knew* [*them, or him*]," as being an error for "*and he caused-to-know many*," i.e. either "*he taught many* [*persons*]," or "*he taught* [*them*] *many* [*things*]"—which is, in substance, the phrase at the heading of this section.

More important than this verbal cause is the cause placed first above—namely, the Hebrew thought and stream of tradition about God's "*shepherding*." Jacob illustrates it when he begins his career at Bethel, praying that the Lord would guide him, guard him, and feed him[3]; and he expressly mentions the word when he closes his career in Egypt, invoking

---

[1] See *Son* **3437** *c—d*, which refers to *Clue* **5, 7**, and **90**, and deals with Mk vi. 34 and the parall. Mt.-Lk. from the verbal point of view.

[2] Prov. x. 21 (R.V.) "*feed* (ירעו)," LXX ἐπίσταται, "*learn*," or, "[*come to*] *know*," leg. ידעו. Targ. retains the Heb. in רעין (Aram.); but in the sense "*treat-as-friends*" (Walton, "*placant*"), Aq. ποιμαίνουσι "*they shepherd*," Field "*pascunt* (i.e. *erudiunt*)." In Job xxxii. 7, the causative "*make to know*" ידיעו, i.e. "*teach*," is rendered by LXX "*know*."

[3] Gen. xxviii. 20 "If God will be with me, and will keep me in this way that I go and will give me bread to eat...."

"the God that *shepherded* me all my life long unto this day[1]."
Moses implied "*shepherding*" when he besought the Lord to
appoint a successor to himself "that the congregation of the
Lord be not as sheep that have no shepherd[2]." And all his
life testified that he too, like Jacob, recognised that the good
shepherd on earth was the type of the Shepherd in heaven,
the God that had guided Israel out of Egypt and guarded and
fed them in the wilderness; to whom the Psalmist appealed
as Shepherd of Israel and of whom the Psalmist said "The
Lord is *my shepherd*, I shall not want[3]."

This last sentence is one of the very few quoted from the
Psalms by Philo, who speaks of it ecstatically as a song that
should be sung by every man that loves God, and above all by
the Cosmos, or Universe, which is the "flock" of the living
God who governs all things like a shepherd and a king[4]. Poets,
he says, are wont to give to kings the title of shepherds of the
people; but the Lawgiver (that is, Moses) gives this title only to
the wise, who are real kings[5]. Elsewhere Philo declares that—
however men may laugh at the notion—the only way of be-
coming a perfect king is to become an adept in the science of
shepherding[6].

---

[1] Gen. xlviii. 15—16 "The God that hath *shepherded* me all my
life long unto this day, the Angel that hath redeemed me from all
evil...." *Gen. r. ad loc.*, assuming that "*shepherding*" means
nourishing, says that it is a greater work (as in Ps. cxlv. 16) to
"*shepherd*" than to "*redeem*," the former being the act of "God,"
the latter of "the angel," and that the "shepherding" is as difficult
as the cleaving of the Red Sea.

[2] Numb. xxvii. 17.

[3] Ps. lxxx. 1, xxiii. 1. Comp. Hos. iv. 16 "The Lord will *shepherd*
them, i.e. Israel," R.V. "*feed*," Targ. "deducet," LXX νεμήσει,
Is. xl. 11 "Like a shepherd his flock shall he *shepherd*," and sim.
Targ., LXX ποιμανεῖ.

[4] Philo i. 308.

[5] Philo i. 306.

[6] Philo ii. 90 καί μοι δοκεῖ... μόνος ἂν γενέσθαι βασιλεὺς τέλειος ὁ τὴν
ποιμενικὴν ἐπιστήμην ἀγαθός.

In a very different strain, yet to the same effect, the Jewish comment on "The Lord is my shepherd" declares that the "shepherd" includes the three characters of Father, Shepherd (as Guide and Guardian), and Brother, and it adds a very early tradition that, although the occupation of the shepherd with his staff and scrip is commonly believed to be one of the meanest on earth, David "knew better." David argued thus: "Jacob called the Lord a Shepherd, saying 'The God that *shepherded* me all my life long'; therefore I, too, will call Him *a Shepherd* and will say 'The Lord is my *Shepherd*[1].'"

The longest of the historical Psalms leads up to the shepherding of Israel as its climax. It tells us how Israel wandered in the wilderness, "led" by God's "cloud" and "fire," and receiving from Him "manna," or "corn of heaven," and "bread" and "meat to the full," and "flesh." All these gifts—which imply guidance and food such as a shepherd gives—were yet to no purpose for Israel because "their heart was not right with him[2]." But the last three verses describe how Israel was finally "*shepherded*" by God's chosen representative: "He chose David also his servant and took him from the sheepfolds...to *shepherd* Jacob his people and Israel his inheritance; so he *shepherded* them according to the integrity of his heart and guided them by the skilfulness of his hands[3]."

---

[1] See *Tehill.* on Ps. xxiii. 1 (Wü. pp. 209—10) giving several traditions on "my shepherd." The first tradition of all is a comment on "*my*" (in "*my* shepherd"). It begins from Cant. ii. 16 "My beloved is *mine* and I am *his*," and passes to Exod. xx. 2 "I am Jehovah, *thy* God," Is. li. 4 "*my* nation."

[2] Ps. lxxviii. 14—37. In *ib.* 52 "he led forth his people *like sheep* and guided them in the wilderness *like a flock*," we are brought to the thought of the sheep, but not to the word "shepherd."

[3] Ps. lxxviii. 70—72. This is quoted in *Exod. r.* on Exod. iii. 1 "And Moses was *shepherding* the flock," where it is said that Moses (as also David afterwards) divided the sheep into three classes (comp. Jn xxi. 15 foll.) according to age, so that he might feed them suitably. We are also told that Moses, finding a lamb that had

Returning to the Synoptic tradition under consideration, we see that Mark's "began to teach them many things," though cold and inadequate in itself, becomes less inadequate if regarded in the light of the Marcan context, which depicts Jesus as compassionating the multitude because they were "as sheep without a shepherd." Luke's text, which mentions "welcoming" and "healing" as well as "speaking about the kingdom of God," is more adequate than the tradition of Mark ("to teach them many things") taken by itself, but misses the thought of "compassion" and all the deep pathos implied in Hebrew traditions about the divine Shepherd to whom Israel says, "My beloved is mine and I am his[1]."

John may be said to combine the Marcan "teaching" with the Lucan "welcoming". and " healing "—only expressing the latter in a more vivid and passionate way. As to "teaching," he says—at the end of Christ's long discourse about the meaning of the Feeding of the Five Thousand—"These things said Jesus...as he *taught* in Capernaum[2]." But in the discourse itself, he declares in effect that, under this sign, the Shepherd of Israel was revealing Himself as purposing to give His own "flesh" and "blood," to be "living bread," food and life for the flock. This doctrine Jesus sets forth in such a form that Peter, despairing of finding any other shepherd like Him, exclaims, "Lord, to whom shall we go? Thou hast words of eternal life[3]." Thus John places before us two characters, briefly hinted at in Mark—the character of the Teacher and the character of the Compassionate Shepherd. The latter he

---

strayed away through thirst, took it on his shoulder to bring it back to the flock. Whereupon God said "Thou hast shewn compassion in leading sheep of flesh and blood. By thy life! thou shalt also shepherd my sheep, the flock of Israel."

[1] Cant. ii. 16.

[2] Jn vi. 59. Διδάσκω, in Johannine narrative, occurs elsewhere only in vii. 14, 28, viii. 20.

[3] Jn vi. 68.

does not intend to describe or even to mention till later on[1]. But he suggests it here, in anticipation, to the minds of those who meditated on the goodness of God towards Israel in preparing a table for them in the wilderness.

§ 16. *"When the day was now far spent," in Mark*

At this point the Four Gospels diverge[2]. The difference resembles one already discussed in the narrative of Christ's first public acts of healing, where Mark says that "it had become late" and the sun "[had] set," Matthew that "it had become late," but Luke that the sun was still "setting[3]." Here Mark's expression is "an advanced hour," a comparatively rare phrase[4]. Matthew uses the more ordinary Greek expression "*evening*." This however does not seem applicable to a time before the miracle but to one after it. And such an application John seems to give it when he says further on "When *evening* came his disciples went down to the sea[5]"; Mark also himself says that "when *evening* had come," the disciples were rowing "in the midst of the sea[6]."

Luke says, "*The day began to incline* (or, *decline*)," an expression that does not recur in N.T. except in his Gospel after the Resurrection, where he uses the perfect "Abide with us, for it is toward evening and *the day has now inclined[7].*"

---

[1] Jn x. 11 foll.

[2] Mk vi. 35 καὶ ἤδη ὥρας πολλῆς γενομένης (marg. γινομένης), Mt. xiv. 15 ὀψίας δὲ γενομένης, Lk. ix. 12 ἡ δὲ ἡμέρα ἤρξατο κλίνειν.

[3] *Proclamation* p. 213 foll. on Mk i. 32, Mt. viii. 16, Lk. iv. 40.

[4] Wetstein on Mk vi. 35 quotes Dion. Hal. *Ant.* ii. 54 ἐμάχοντο καὶ διέμενον ἄχρι πολλῆς ὥρας...ἀγωνιζόμενοι ἕως ἡ νὺξ ἐπιλαβοῦσα διέκρινεν αὐτούς. Steph. *Thes.* quotes Polyb. v. 8. 3, and Joseph. *Ant.* viii. 4. 3. Thucydides uses πολλή with νύξ.

[5] Jn vi. 16 ὡς δὲ ὀψία ἐγένετο.

[6] Mk vi. 47 καὶ ὀψίας γενομένης ἦν τὸ πλοῖον ἐν μέσῳ τῆς θαλάσσης. This implies a time subsequent to that implied by John.

[7] Lk. xxiv. 29 πρὸς ἑσπέραν ἐστὶν καὶ κέκλικεν ἤδη ἡ ἡμέρα.

CHRIST'S MIRACLES OF FEEDING

The "day," or the sun, is said to "incline" not only in Greek and Latin but also once in Hebrew[1], and it may "incline" toward "afternoon" as well as toward "evening." Luke, by saying "*began to incline*" here and "*has inclined*" elsewhere, seems to intend to emphasize "*began*" here, so as to mean "*incline toward afternoon.*" In the story of Emmaus there are reasons for thinking that Luke is imitating the language of the LXX[2]. But there are no such reasons here. It seems probable that Luke is here using an expression, frequent in Greek and Latin, and capable of meaning with slight modifications "afternoon" or "evening," by which he corrects an error of Mark's in such a way that a Greek reader of the Gospels might say: "Mark has taken '*when the day was inclining*' for '*when the day had inclined*' and has paraphrased it in the latter sense. Luke has restored the original phrase, leaving his readers to give it its correct sense."

Some Hebrew original like "between the two evenings"— used about the sacrifice of the Paschal Lamb—might explain the Synoptic variations. Such an original has already been suggested as capable of explaining the Synoptic variations in the accounts of Christ's first public healing[3]. Still more appropriately would it explain them here. For in that earlier narrative there was nothing that pointed to the Passover. But there is much of that nature here. It is antecedently probable that the Galilaean Church would use expressions likening the Feeding of the Five Thousand to the Eucharist or to a prophetic sign of the Eucharist, a preliminary type of a Christian Passover.

---

[1] Judg. xix. 8 (R.V.) "tarry ye *until the day declineth*," (A.V.) "they tarried *until afternoon* (marg. *till the day declined*)." Gesen. 640 *a* gives practically no other instance. Steph. *Thes.* iv. 1651 gives instances from Greek and Latin. The "declining" may be toward "evening" or toward "afternoon."

[2] Comp. in Judg. xix. 7 ἐβιάσατο, and in Lk. xxiv. 29 παρεβιάσαντο, as well as the rare κλίνει ἡμέρα.

[3] See *Proclamation* p. 213 foll.

John himself tells us that "the Passover of the Jews" was "near[1]." No doubt he means us to take this literally. But it would be characteristic of him to intend us also to take it as suggesting something more: "And another 'passover' was also 'near,' the Passover of the Christians." As the sacred Lamb of the Jewish Passover was slain for the sins of Israel "between the two evenings," so the same hour might be regarded in early Galilaean traditions as appropriate for Christ's announcement of the sign of the Eucharistic Sacrifice which He was destined to offer up as the Passover for the sins of the whole world.

§ 17. *"They continue with me now three days," in Mark and Matthew*[2]

The Feeding of the Four Thousand, in several of its expressions, gives to Christ's act a more personal note than is found in the Feeding of the Five Thousand[3]. It is more like Isaiah's description of the considerate Shepherd of Israel gently leading the flock[4]. Moreover Mark's preceding context

---

[1] Jn vi. 4.

[2] Mk viii. 2, Mt. xv. 32. It will be convenient to discuss the Feeding of the Four Thousand here, as a parallel to the Feeding of the Five Thousand, in order to compare and contrast the two.

[3] Mk viii. 1—3 (R.V.)

(1) In those days, when there was again a great multitude, and they had nothing to eat, he called unto him his disciples, and saith unto them,

(2) I have compassion on the multitude, because they continue with me now three days, and have nothing to eat:

(3) And if I send them away fasting to their home, they will faint in the way; and some of them are come from far.

Mt. xv. 32 (R.V.)

And Jesus called unto him his disciples, and said, I have compassion on the multitude, because they continue with me now three days and have nothing to eat: and I would not send them away fasting, lest haply they faint in the way.

[4] Is. xl. 11. Comp. Mk viii. 2 foll. "I have compassion" as compared with vi. 34 "he had compassion." And see Mk viii. 3 "If I send them away fasting...they will faint in the way; and

appears to be influenced by the language of Isaiah, describing the healing and safe guidance of ransomed Israel, returning to Jerusalem across the wilderness[1]. This should prepare us to find traces of prophetic and poetic influence in the narrative that follows. Accordingly we find Jesus describing the multitude as "fasting," or "hungry," and as likely to "faint in the way," very much as the Psalmist says of the redeemed of Israel, "gathered" from the four quarters of the world, "They wandered in the wilderness in a desert *way...hungry* and thirsty, *their soul fainted in them*[2]." "Gathering" is not so easily applicable to the Exodus from Egypt[3] as it is to the gathering of the scattered captives of Israel predicted by Isaiah, or to the gathering of the spiritual Israel contemplated in early Christian traditions[4]. To the latter there would apply the words in Mark (but not in Matthew) "*and some of*

---

some of them are come from far." There is nothing like this in the earlier narrative.

[1] Mk vii. 37 "He maketh even the deaf (τοὺς κωφοὺς) to hear and dumb [folk] (ἀλάλους) to speak," Mt. xv. 31 "They saw dumb [folk] (κωφοὺς) speaking...and blind [folk] (τυφλοὺς) seeing; and they glorified the God of Israel." In Mark, the preceding context describes the healing of (Mk vii. 32) κωφὸν καὶ μογιλάλον, i.e. "deaf and *stammering*." Μογιλάλος, "*stammering*," occurs nowhere in the Greek Bible except here and Is. xxxv. 6 τρανὴ δὲ ἔσται γλῶσσα μογιλάλων, Heb. "and the tongue of *the dumb* shall sing." Ibn Ezra reduces this to prosaic and non-miraculous fact by calling it "a figurative expression for '*they shall find water everywhere*,'" and contrasting Lam. iv. 4 "the tongue of the suckling cleaveth to the roof of his mouth for thirst." But Mark apparently takes the prophecy as predicting miraculous fact about the healing of a "*stammerer*."

[2] Ps. cvii. 2—5.

[3] See however *Tehill. ad loc.* (Wü. ii. 134) "The Holy One said to the Israelites, 'In Egypt ye were scattered, *and I gathered you in one little hour to Ramses*; and now also are ye scattered into all lands, and as I *gathered* you in ancient days so will I *gather* you in the future,' as it is said... (Is. xi. 12) 'He *shall gather* the dispersed of Judah from the four corners of the earth.'"

[4] Comp. Jn xi. 52 "that he might gather into one (εἰς ἑν) the scattered children of God."

them are come from 'far," applicable to the old remoteness of the Gentiles, illustrated by the language of Isaiah[1].

But we must be on our guard against confining Mark to one Prophecy or one Psalm as his source. The Psalm above quoted does not mention *"three days."* But the account in Exodus on which the Psalm is based, does contain a mention of "three days" ("And they went *three days* in the wilderness and found no water") previously mentioned as the time necessary for a journey to be taken for the purpose of offering a sacrifice to Jehovah[2]. Then, further, if we examine other Hebrew texts, or Jewish traditions about *"three days,"* or *"the third day,"* beginning from the sacrifice of Isaac on Mount Moriah, we shall find that, both in the Bible and in the Midrash and in Philo, as also in the words of Jesus about Himself, a mystical meaning is attached to the phrase[3]. In Philo, the sacrifice of Isaac is connected with that perfect tribute which will be duly paid by the mind, when "perfected," to the "perfecting" God: "When therefore does it duly pay? When it arrives *on the third day* at the place whereof God spoke to it[4]." He goes on to speak of the mind at this stage as passing

---

[1] Eph. ii. 17 "And he came and preached peace *to you that were far off* and peace to them that were nigh," comp. Is. lvii. 19 "Peace, peace, to *him that is far off* and to him that is near."

[2] Exod. xv. 22, comp. *ib.* iii. 18, v. 3, viii. 27.

[3] Gen. xxii. 3—5 "And Abraham rose up early in the morning and saddled his ass, and took two of his young men with him and Isaac his son....*On the third day* Abraham lifted up his eyes and saw the place afar off. And Abraham said unto his young men, Abide ye here with the ass...." The context implies, but does not mention, *"two days,"* preceding. Josephus mentions it, as follows: *Ant.* i. 13. 2 "Now the two servants went along with him *two days*; but on *the third day*, as soon as he saw the mountain, he left those servants that were with him till then in the plain...."

[4] Philo i. 457 (playing on τέλος and its compounds) τελειωθεὶς ὁ νοῦς ἀποδώσει τὸ τέλος τῷ τελεσφόρῳ θεῷ...Πότε οὖν ἀποδίδωσιν; Ὅταν (Gen. xxii. 4) ἐπὶ τὸν τόπον...τῇ ἡμέρᾳ τῇ τρίτῃ παραγένηται....

by distinctions of time and migrating into "the timeless nature[1]."

The very great difference of Philo's language from the simple style of the Gospels must not altogether hide the underlying resemblance of thought between this and the saying of Jesus about being "*perfected on the third day*[2]." The Midrash on the story of Abraham takes as its first illustration the words of Hosea "After *two days* will he cause us to live [again]; *on the third day* he will raise us up and we shall live before him[3]." Then, after enumerating other instances of the phrase, it introduces into the story of Abraham (what Josephus perhaps also implies in his mention of "two days") a distinction between the "servants" who do not accompany Abraham "*on the third day*," and the son who does. Abraham sees the Shechinah over the mountain, and asks his son and his two servants whether they see what he sees. The son says "Yes." The two servants say "No[4]," being only (so to speak) in the second-day stage. To them accordingly it is said "Abide ye here with the ass." But the son (it is implied) having entered the third-day stage, is allowed to go on and to be perfected on the Mount of Sacrifice.

The frequency with which Jesus is recorded in all the Gospels to have used the phrase "on the third day," or some similar expression, about His own resurrection, or about the restoration of the Temple, or about the approach of the Passover, makes it probable that here, in the Feeding of the Four Thousand, it is used in some allusive sense. Perhaps it

---

[1] Philo *ib*. παρελθὼν τὰς πλείους μοίρας τῶν χρονικῶν διαστημάτων καὶ ἤδη πρὸς τὴν ἄχρονον μεταβαίνων φύσιν.

[2] Lk. xiii. 32—3 "I cast out devils and perform cures to-day and to-morrow and *on the third* [*day*] *I am* [*to be*] *perfected* (τελειοῦμαι). Howbeit I must go on my way to-day and to-morrow and *the next* [*day*], for it cannot be that a prophet perish out of Jerusalem."

[3] Hos. vi. 2.

[4] This resembles (I think) something in Wagner's *Parsifal*.

alludes to the precept twice enjoined on Israel at the Giving of the Law, "Be ready *against the third day*[1]." Origen speaks of the Four Thousand as being "*testified to*," in respect of their "abiding by the Lord *for three days*[2]." Clement of Alexandria, writing of Abraham's "seeing *on the third day*," says that "*the three days* are the mystery of the seal[3]." In view of the extracts given above from Scripture, Midrash, Philo, and the Gospels, it would be unwise to dismiss these Christian comments as baseless Christian allegorizing[4]. They all point back to a widespread Hebrew conception of "*the third day*," as being not only a phrase of time but also a phrase of accomplishment, what Philo calls "a timeless nature[5]."

Passing to the Fourth Evangelist we have to consider his attitude, first, toward the Mark-Matthew tradition about a supplementary miracle of Eucharistic Feeding, and secondly, toward this mystical tradition about "three days." As to the first, while nowhere denying that there were, even before the Resurrection, other similar miracles such as the Feeding of the Four Thousand, he turns our attention to something that

---

[1] Exod. xix. 11, 15.

[2] Origen *Comm. Matth.* xi. 19 (Lomm. iii. 123).

[3] Clem. Alex. 690. Comp. Clem. Alex. *Excerpt. Theod.* 988—9 where "baptism" is called ἡ σφραγίς and τὸ τῆς ἀληθείας σφράγισμα, and see Euseb. iii. 23. 8 (quoting from Clem. Alex.) τὴν σφραγῖδα τοῦ κυρίου.

[4] Jerome, however (on Mt. xv. 32), affords an instructive instance of the excesses of the Christian transmutation of Jewish tradition, "Miseretur turbae quia *in trium numero*, Patri, Filio, Spirituique Sancto credebant."

[5] See p. 64, n. 1. Mark (iv. 28) speaks of (1) "the blade," (2) "the ear," (3) "the full corn." John (xii. 24) speaks of the grain of corn (1) falling, (2) dying, (3) producing fruit. Revelation (i. 4) speaks of the IS and the WAS and the COMING. Underlying the whole of the Fourth Gospel there seems to be the conception of (1) the Thought, (2) the uttered Thought, or Word, (3) the influencing Thought, or Spirit. All these are forms of the *thought* of "the third day."

happened after the Resurrection, supplementary, but dis-similar in important details—a quiet and homely little meal, the relation of which to the Synoptic narratives will be discussed as we proceed. As to the second point, the doctrine of "three days," John teaches that it referred to the raising up of what Jesus and the Jews called "this temple," but that it meant "the temple of his body[1]." No doubt, this included (in the Evangelist's judgment) the manifestation of Christ in the body to the disciples after death. But it certainly included also the rising up of Christ's Body in the sense of the Church, the New Temple. In that connection, we should have to use the Philonian phrase again and say that the "three days" had "a timeless nature[2]."

---

[1] Jn ii. 19—21.
[2] On the difficulty of making any confident assertion about the number of Christ's visits to the Temple, see *Introd.* pp. 90—6. John may have desired to impress on his readers, at the very outset of his Gospel, that Jesus regarded the Temple as being a Congregation of human beings, that is to say "sons of men," built up on, and into, one ideal Son of Man, who was also Son of God. As John expounds the Doctrine of Bread before its chronological place, in connection with the Feeding of the Five Thousand, so he may have briefly expressed the Doctrine of the New Temple before its chrono-logical place, in connection with what he believed to be Christ's first public visit to the Temple.

§ 18. *"Buying" or "Whence?"*

In the texts printed below[1] the following are the most remarkable agreements and disagreements. (1) The four narratives of the Five Thousand speak of *"buying,"* though in varying contexts. (2) The two narratives of the Four Thousand omit *"buying"* and ask *"whence?"* (3) John combines *"buying"* with *"whence?"* (4) Mark repeats *"buying"* twice ("that *they may buy,*" "*are we to buy?*"). (5) Matthew has merely "that *they may buy.*" (6) Luke has merely "unless *we are to buy.*" (7) In the Synoptists, *"buying"* (or *"whence"*)

[1] Mk vi. 35—7 (R.V.)

Mt. xiv. 15—16 (R.V.)

Lk. ix. 12—13 (R.V.)

Jn vi. 5—7

Mk vi. 35—7 (R.V.)	Mt. xiv. 15—16 (R.V.)	Lk. ix. 12—13 (R.V.)	Jn vi. 5—7
(35) And when the day was now far spent, his disciples came unto him, and said, The place is desert, and the day is now far spent: (36) Send them away, that they may go (ἀπελθόντες) into the country and villages round about, and buy themselves somewhat to eat. (37) But he answered and said unto them, Give ye them to eat. And they say unto him, Shall we go (ἀπελθόντες) and buy two hundred pennyworth of bread (*lit.* loaves), and give them to eat?	(15) And when even was come, the disciples came to him, saying, The place is desert, and the time is already past ; send the multitudes away, that they may go (ἀπελθόντες) into the villages, and buy themselves food. (16) But Jesus said unto them, They have no need to go away (ἀπελθεῖν); give ye them to eat.	(12) And the day began to wear away ; and the twelve came, and said unto him, Send the multitude away, that they may go (πορευθέντες) into the villages and country round about, and lodge, and get (εὕρωσιν) victuals: for we are here in a desert place. (13) But he said unto them, Give ye them to eat. And they said, We have no more than five loaves and two fishes; except we should go (πορευθέντες) and buy food for all this people.	(5) Jesus therefore lifting up his eyes...saith unto Philip, Whence are we to buy bread (*lit.* loaves), that these may eat? (6) Now this he said tempting (or, trying) him, for he himself knew what he purposed (or, was destined) (ἔμελλε) to do. (7) Philip answered him, Two hundred pennyworth of bread (*lit.* loaves) is not sufficient for them, that each may take a little.

Lk. ix. 14 *a* adds here "For they were about five thousand men," which is parall. to Mk vi. 44, Mt. xiv. 21.

Mk viii. 4 (R.V.)	Mt. xv. 33 (R.V.)
And his disciples answered him, Whence shall one be able to fill these men with bread (*lit.* loaves) here in a desert place?	And the disciples say unto him, Whence should we have so many loaves in a desert place, as to fill so great a multitude?

is uttered by the disciples; in the Fourth Gospel, *"whence"* and *"buy"* are uttered by Jesus identifying Himself with the disciples (*"whence are we to buy?"*).

In these passages, "whence" means "from what possible source," with an assumption that there is no possible source. "Whence," in any sense, is rare in LXX; but in this sense it does not occur more than thrice[1]. The Pentateuch has but one instance. That occurs in a remonstrance of Moses, somewhat similar to the remonstrance of the disciples. Moses pleads that he cannot feed Israel in the wilderness. *"Whence to me flesh,"* he asks, "to give to all this people[2]?" "Whence to me flesh?" means, of course, "Whence could I *get* flesh?" But we might supply other verbs such as *"find,"* or even *"buy."*

Moses adds "Shall flocks and herds be slain for them to *suffice* them? Or shall all the fish of the sea be gathered...to *suffice* them[3]?" *"Suffice"*—a rare word both in LXX and in Gospels—occurs in the Johannine answer to the question *"Whence?"* asked by Jesus. "Two hundred pennyworth of loaves does not *suffice* for them," says Philip, "that each may take a little[4]." This combination of the rare words *'whence"* and *"suffice,"* together with the similarity of circumstances, leads to the conclusion that John has in view, not only the Gospel traditions about the Feeding, but also the remonstrance of Moses. There is also a fair, though slighter, probability that the same remonstrance underlies the Mark-Matthew tradition.

---

[1] "Whence?" in "Whence ($\pi \acute{o} \theta \epsilon \nu$) comest thou?" etc. occurs in Gen. xvi. 8, xxix. 4, etc. But, in the sense "from what possible source?" (implying "there is no possible source") it occurs (in A.V.) only in Numb. xi. 13, 2 K. vi. 27, Nahum iii. 7.

[2] Numb. xi. 13.

[3] Numb. xi. 22, see below, p. 69, n. 3.

[4] Jn vi. 7. ᾿Αρκέω occurs only eight or nine times in canon. LXX and four times in the Gospels.

This hypothesis—of a brief original like that in Numbers "*Whence* [*should there accrue*] to me flesh?" or, still better, one in which "to me" was omitted—might explain the extraordinary Gospel variations as to "*buying*." No verb being in the original, evangelists would have to supply one—such as "*get*," "*find*," or "*buy*." Compare the Mark-Matthew "that they may *buy* food," parallel to the Lucan "that they may *find* provision (R.V. get victuals)." This may be illustrated from Proverbs "A scorner seeketh wisdom and [*doth*] *not* [*find it*]," where "*find*" is supplied by the LXX and English Versions[1].

In the Feeding of the Four Thousand, Mark's parallel to Matthew's (lit.) "*Whence to us so many loaves as to fill* so great a multitude?" is "*Whence shall one be* (SS *art thou*) *able to fill with loaves* these men[2]?" This indicates that the original had no definite personal pronoun. Also the Syro-Sinaitic of Mark has "*find*" for "be able." These small links of verbal evidence connect the Gospel narratives both with one another and with that in Numbers which represents Moses as twice asking, in the Hebrew text, "shall it be *found* for them[3]?"

From "finding" to "buying" is a transition of thought that may be illustrated from Job and Isaiah. Job asks "Where shall wisdom *be found?*" and proceeds to speak of "*the price*"

---

[1] Prov. xiv. 6. Comp. 1 S. xxvi. 18 (A.V.) "What evil [*is*] in my hand?" LXX εὑρέθη ἐν ἐμοί, Job xii. 12 (A.V.) "With the ancient [*is*] wisdom," (A) εὑρίσκεται, Prov. v. 4 (Heb.) "Her end [*is*] bitter," LXX εὑρήσεις, i.e. "thou wilt find it bitter."

[2] In Mk viii. 4 πόθεν δυνήσεταί τις, SS has literally "*Whence dost thou find* [power]?" *Thes. Syr.* 4147—8 shews that the radical meaning of the word is "find," and it is easy to see that "*I find* [*how*] to do" may mean "*I am able* to do."

[3] Numb. xi. 22 (Heb.) "Shall flocks and herds be slain...and *shall it be found* (LXX ἀρκέσει) for them... (rep.) and *shall it be found* (LXX ἀρκέσει) for them?" i.e. "shall sufficient food be found for them?" No persons are indicated as the finders. See Gesen. 593 *b* and 594 *a* indicating that the literal translation is "and so *one find* [enough] for them," i.e. shall it be found.

as being beyond all silver, gold, and jewels[1]. Isaiah says "Ho, every one that thirsteth, come ye to the waters; and he that hath no money, come ye, *buy* (*shâbar*) and eat; yea, come, *buy* (*shâbar*), without money and without price, wine and milk[2]." The word *shâbar* is not often used for "*buy*." It means "*buy-corn*." Rashi, on Isaiah, says that it is used here as in the words "*to buy corn*"—alluding to the first Biblical use of the word in the description of "all countries" coming "into Egypt to Joseph *to buy-corn*[3]."

This allusion brings out the prophet's meaning: "Egypt sells its corn for a price. But God sells you His corn, the corn of heaven, the Law of Righteousness, without money and without price[4]." The Greek word used in the Gospels for "buying" is the same as that used by the LXX about the buying of corn in Genesis and the wine and milk in Isaiah. Consequently, in any Christian narrative that described the feeding of the multitudes by Christ in a form intended to symbolize the spiritual food of the Eucharist, it would be appropriate to use the word "*buy*" by way of contrast, in such a way as to make it clear that Christ's bread could *not* be "bought"—or, at all events, not bought in the ordinary sense of the word.

But the Synoptic Tradition does not make this clear. It speaks about the Five Thousand as (possibly) (Mark-Matthew)

---

[1] Job xxviii. 12—19.

[2] Is. lv. 1, Targ. "Come, hearken and learn, without price and without money, doctrine that is better than wine and milk."

[3] Gen. xli. 56—7 contains the first Biblical instances of *shâbar*. The causative means "*sell* [*corn*]" and the active "*buy* [*corn*]." A.V. "*sold* unto the Egyptians...all countries came...to *buy* [*corn*]." LXX ἐπώλει... ἀγοράζειν.

[4] Ibn Ezra, on Is. lv. 1, says that wine and milk "serve both for food and drink." He seems to anticipate the objection that *shâbar* ought not to be applied except to that which is eaten. Rashi, on Genesis, says (if the text is genuine) "You must not say that *shâbar* is used only of corn, for it is used also of *wine* and *milk* (Is. lv. 1)."

"going away and buying" or (Luke) "going and finding," and also about the impossibility that the disciples should (Mark) "go away and buy" or (Luke) "go and buy[1]"; but it so distracts us with verbal variations that we are in danger of learning nothing from the words[2]. "They were uttered by the disciples," we may say, "not by Jesus, and the disciples were in the dark, and did not know what they were speaking about."

John, without denying that the disciples used these expressions about "*buying*," and also about the impossibility of finding "*whence*" they might procure food in any way, declares that Jesus Himself used expressions of this nature, and that He did it in a kindly and gentle (we may almost say playful) spirit, "tempting (*or*, trying)" Philip. The Evangelist's view is that Jesus had reasons for choosing this particular disciple—a little slow perhaps, but sure and straightforward—in order to lead him, and through him the rest of the Apostles, towards a higher stage of revelation. It was not the highest but only a higher. "He himself"—John says, in a kind of aside—"knew what he would do," but He did not at present say "what he would do." He merely prepared Philip for expecting at once, and for receiving later on, some mystical

---

[1] "Going away" = ἀπελθόντες. "Going" = πορευθέντες. R.V. makes no distinction here, though rendering the infin. ἀπελθεῖν "go away" in Mt. xiv. 16.

[2] The key to the original is perhaps to be found in the deliberative subjunctive ἀγοράσωμεν, found in Mk, Lk., and Jn, and meaning "*ought we*, or, *are we*, or, *we are*, to buy." "Ought" is expressed in Heb. by (1) the future ("Thou *shalt*, i.e. *oughtest to*, do"), (2) the infin. after "it is" ("*It is* [*fit*] to do," "*it is* [*fit*] for thee to do"). Confusion might arise between "*Is it* [*fit*] to go away and buy?" and "*It is* [*fit*] to go away and buy." The former would be taken as "*Is it* [*fit*] *for us* [i.e. the disciples]?" the latter, as "*It is* [*fit*] *for them* [i.e. the five thousand]." See *Oxf. Conc.* LXX δεῖν, and *e.g.* Ezek. xxxiv. 2 Heb. "Shall [*i.e.* should] they not feed?" LXX οὐ βόσκουσιν (interrogative). The ambiguity might be increased by two datives "[fit] *for us* to buy *for them*."

doctrine about the spiritual Bread. "He himself knew what he would do" means "He knew what He was destined to do on the Cross, buying the Bread of Life for the world at the cost of His blood[1]."

§ 19. *"Two hundred pennyworth," in Mark and John*[2]

Why was this precise sum mentioned by the disciples, or recorded by Mark to have been mentioned by them? Why did Matthew and Luke omit Mark's tradition? Why did John insert it? The question here is not whether John intervenes for Mark, but why?

"Two hundred pence (*or*, denars)" is a sum frequently specified in Talmudic enactments about fines, damages, marriage portions, etc.[3] Also, if a man had an income of less than two hundred denars, he could claim certain exemptions and allowances. It was legally recognised as being, so to speak,

---

[1] For this mystical meaning of the word "buy," ἀγοράζω, John has previously prepared the way by representing the disciples (Jn iv. 8, 32) as leaving their Master alone and going *"to buy"* food in Sychar (which He rejects, telling them that He has food to eat that they know not of). The third and last instance of ἀγοράζω is where Judas Iscariot, going forth to betray the Master whom he has sold, is regarded by some of the disciples (Jn xiii. 29) as being instructed by Jesus to *"buy"* something needed for "the feast [of the Passover]."

But what are we to say as to the plural *"loaves"* ("whence are we to buy *loaves?*") assigned by John to Jesus here and nowhere else except in the reproach (Jn vi. 26) "ye ate of *the loaves*"? Does the Evangelist represent Jesus as speaking, as it were, down to the level of Philip, about the rudimentary food to be provided on this occasion? If so, we may illustrate from the plural (Jn iv. 8) "buy *food(s)* (τροφάς)," unique in N.T., where the "foods" are called by Origen *ad loc.* "suitable foods (τροφὰς) *with the heterodox* (παρὰ τοῖς ἑτεροδόξοις),'' and Ammonius (*ad loc.* Cramer p. 216) sees a warning against "various *foods of luxury* (ἐδεσμάτων).'' Τροφαί is used of "forbidden foods" in 4 Macc. i. 33, iv. 26 (comp. 3 Macc. iii. 7).

[2] Mk vi. 37, Jn vi. 7.

[3] See *Hor. Heb.* on Mk vi. 37. Wetstein is silent.

"a poor man's income[1]." Christ's disciples were poor men. Hence, when exhorted by Jesus to give bread to the multitude, one of them might be supposed to reply "Even if we had the whole of our year's income in our hands, should we go away and spend it all in a single meal—and that, too, insufficient—for this multitude?"

Thus explained, the Marcan tradition becomes intelligible. But, outside Palestine, who would know the explanation? Moreover, even with this explanation, it is not clear, because Mark at this stage has not yet told us the number of the multitude, and does not mention it till the very end of the narrative[2]. This omission may be contrasted with the orderly insertion in the O.T. narrative of the meal given by Elisha to the sons of the prophets. Elisha's servant, receiving "*twenty loaves* of barley," says at once, "What! Shall I set this before *an hundred* men[3]?" Similarly Luke, in his parallel to Mark, lets us know at once the number of the multitude thus "Unless we are to go and buy food for all this people—*for they were about five thousand* men[4]." Without this knowledge, the inadequacy of two hundred denarii is by no means obvious. For a denarius was a labourer's daily wage[5] and could presumably suffice for one simple meal for several labourers. Two hundred denarii might therefore well provide for a single meal for a considerable number, quite large enough to be called a "multitude."

Again, "two hundred denarii" might possibly imply *gold*

---

[1] *J. Pea* viii. 8 (Mishna) and *Sota* 21 *b*. *Hor. Heb.* omits this. So also does Schlatter on Jn vi. 7.

[2] Mk vi. 44.

[3] *Hor. Heb.* on Jn vi. 9 refers to 2 K. iv. 42 and *Chetub.* 105. 2, 106. 9, where "the masters enhance the number of men fed by Elisha to two thousand two hundred" from the Scriptural "one hundred."

[4] Comp. Numb. xi. 13 "Whence should I have flesh to give to *all this people?*" *ib.* 21—2 "The people...are *six hundred thousand* ...shall flocks and herds be slain for them to suffice them...?"

[5] Mt. xx. 2—13.

denarii. In that case—since a gold denarius was worth twenty-five silver denarii—the sum would amount to five thousand silver denarii, that is to say, the daily wage for five thousand men[1]. Then the meaning of the expostulating disciples would be "Are we [so rich that we are] to go and buy bread for two hundred [gold] denarii and to give them to eat [a meal worth a day's wage for each man]?"

This is an improbable supposition. For "denarii," without the epithet "gold," would be taken by all to mean "silver denarii." But difficulties like these may explain, not only why Matthew and Luke omitted Mark's tradition about the denarii, but also why Matthew modified the context by transferring "go away" from the disciples to the multitude ("they have no need to go away"), as indicated above[2], and why Luke inserted at this stage the number of the multitude[3].

John retains Mark's "two hundred pence," but assigns the expression to Philip instead of to the disciples collectively. He does not follow Luke in inserting the number of the multitude

---

[1] See *Son* **3420** *g* referring to Levy i. 399 *b*. Wagenseil's *Sota* p. 552 has an obscure remark about a dower of [200] denarii "ut ita ducenti isti denarii efficiant omnino (?) xxv denarios argenteos, quorum cujusque pondus xxvi grana hordacea." If "each" were written for "altogether (omnino)," this would seem to be a confused statement about denarii of gold, as being each worth twenty-five denarii of silver. The mention of a grain of barley as a standard of weight for denarii is perhaps worth noting, in view of the Johannine mention of denarii and barley loaves in the same context.

[2] See p. 67, comp. p. 71, n. 2.

[3] Another possible cause of corruption can be but briefly indicated. In Greek, the sign of "5000" is ͵Є and the sign of "200" is C', and Є and C are frequently confused. Schlatter (on Jn vi. 7) quotes *Siphr*. Deut. 355 "Oil *for* (ב) *a hundred myriads* do I need"— where ב seems to mean "*for the sake of*," somewhat like Gen. xviii. 28 (Gesen. 90 *b*) "on account of five," but it usually means "*at the price of*." Perhaps "for 200 denarii," in Greek, when "denarii" was denoted by a sign, might be confused with "for five thousand [men]." Or ἀγοράσωμεν δηναρίων with C' might be corrupted into ἀγοράσωμεν δὴ ἀνδρῶν with ͵Є.

here to shew the inadequacy of the sum. But he represents Philip as saying that it would be quite inadequate. As to the "pence," he makes no effort to shew what may have been in Philip's mind, but he seems to suggest, as being in Christ's mind, a very different kind of "buying"—namely, what might be called a "ransoming" of the souls of men at a price above visible "denarii."

The first Biblical mention of "ransoming" the "soul" occurs in connection with the numbering of the Israelites. They are to give "every man a ransom for his soul[1]." The Law proceeds "*This* shall they give...half a shekel." The Jerusalem Targum explains "*this*" by adding "This valuation was shewn to Moses in the mountain as with a *denarius* of fire[2]." In one of the many forms in which this tradition is repeated, it is said that God's words so terrified Moses that he replied "Who can give a ransom for his soul?" It was then (said R. Meir) that God shewed Moses a coin of fire and said "*This* shalt thou give[3]."

The three Synoptists agree that on one memorable occasion Jesus called for a denarius and said to the Pharisees "Whose is this image and inscription[4]?" To this they replied "Caesar's." He then bade them give "to Caesar that which is Caesar's." Presumably that which was "*Caesar's*" meant the denarius. And it was "*Caesar's*" because it was stamped

---

[1] Exod. xxx. 12. In Exod. xxi. 30 (A.V.) "*ransom* of his life (*lit.* soul)," R.V. has "*redemption*" (see context).

[2] Similarly Rashi says "God shewed Moses a coin of fire of which the weight was half a shekel, and said, *This* (istiusmodi) shall the Israelites give."

[3] See *Numb. r.* Wü. pp. 275—6, also *Pesikt.* (Piska II) Wü. pp. 10—21, and *ib.* Wü. p. 76. In some forms of the tradition, it is explained that "this" means "Not what thou didst suppose but what I shew thee," or that the coin was under the throne of God. In *Pesikt.* p. 76, one tradition says that the coin is the sacrificial lamb of Numb. xxviii. 3.

[4] Mk xii. 16 foll., Mt xxii. 18 foll., Lk. xx. 24.

with Caesar's image and name. But, if so, what is the meaning of "*God's*" in the following words, "And to God that which is "*God's*"? Does it imply merely this, "If you give the Roman denarius to pay tribute to Caesar, you are equally bound to give the Jewish shekel—that is, the temple shekel, the shekel with its sacred symbols stamped upon it—to God"?

That is, at first sight, an attractive explanation because it is so simple, and lays down so definite a rule. But, on second thoughts, does it seem like Jesus to lay down definite rules (except in hyperbole such as "turning the cheek" and "walking two miles") without regard to motive? Does not Christ's phrase, "that which is God's," imply a heavenly denarius, so to speak, stamped with God's image and name? And what is this stamp but the impress of the Spirit of the divine Love? This love best represents the divine nature in its relation to men. This love God gives to men that they may pay it back to Him, thereby ransoming themselves from selfishness and sin, and making themselves free for a life of sonship toward the Father in heaven and of brotherhood toward His children on earth.

The Jews, in many of their comments on the "ransom of a man's soul," or on other texts that speak of the soul's "ransom," say, or imply, that the ransom is "almsgiving," which they call technically "righteousness[1]." Sometimes they are careful to add that such almsgiving must be disinterested, or at all events not ostentatious; but frequently they use unguarded hyperbole, such as that "*a farthing given to a poor man* bestows on the giver a vision of the Shechinah," and that "I shall behold thy face in righteousness," in the Psalms, means "I shall behold thy face," after the Resurrection, "*because*

---

[1] Prov. xiii. 8 "The ransom of a man's soul is his riches" is often associated with Exod. xxx. 12—13, and is explained by Rashi as being true "because he *distributes alms*" from his riches.

of alms[1]." Against the identification of "righteousness" with "alms"—which resembles the occasional identification of "charity" with "alms" in modern English—Jesus vehemently protested. But He did not deny, and indeed He emphasized, the helpful and purifying influence of singlehearted almsgiving. Alms rightly given on earth (He taught) reproduced themselves in heaven, so that the perishable coin from "the treasure on earth" procured for the giver an eternal "treasure in heaven[2]."

It is only the Double Tradition of Matthew and Luke that speaks thus of this "treasure in heaven." And there the context contains no mention or implication of the negative aspect, "ransoming," but only of the positive aspect, reward. But both aspects are suggested in the Threefold Tradition about the rich young ruler to whom Jesus says "Sell whatsoever thou hast, and give to the poor, and thou shalt have *treasure in heaven*[3]." According to Matthew, the man needed to be ransomed from himself. He was so fettered in self-satisfaction that he believed he had fulfilled not only the commands of the Decalogue but also the precept "Thou shalt love thy neighbour as thyself[4]." He seems to have been what the Pastoral

---

[1] See *Bab. Bathr.* 10 *a*, and *Tehill.* on Ps. xvii. 15, where Rashi, however, does not thus limit righteousness. Comp. *Hor. Heb.* (on Mt. vi. 1) "They called alms by the name of righteousness," and the passages there alleged to prove this. See also the Heb. of Sir. iii. 30, and xl. 24. In the latter, the editors give an alternative, "*righteousness* (or, *almsgiving*) delivereth above them both."

[2] Comp. Mt. vi. 20 "treasure up treasures...," parall. to Lk. xii. 33 "Make to yourselves purses that wax not old, a treasure in the heavens that faileth not." To this Luke (but not Matthew) prefixes "Sell your goods and give alms."

[3] Mk x. 21 on which see *Beginning* p. 263. There it is pointed out that Mark may have confused "*deceived himself*," ΗΠΑΤΗϹΕΝ ΑΥΤΟΝ, with "*loved him*," ΗΓΑΠΗϹΕΝΑΥΤΟΝ, or that Hebrew confusion may have produced the false impression that Jesus "loved him."

[4] Mt. xix. 19.

77

Epistles call "a lover of self" as well as "a lover of money[1]."
If Jesus perceived that he was "in love with himself[2]," we can
understand why He imposed on him a condition that He knew
the man would fail to fulfil. Through the failure the man
would be at least benefited at once to the extent of having his
self-love disturbed. Hereafter, he might attain to the vision
of the true love, the denarius of fire, the ransom of the soul.

The "denarius" will come before us again when we discuss
the Anointing at Bethany, where Mark—again followed by
John, but not by Matthew—mentions "three hundred denarii"
as the price of the ointment[3]. The above-mentioned "denar"
of the Jerusalem Targum is also latent in Matthew's description
of the *stater*, i.e. "*shekel*," taken by Peter from a fish's mouth
in order to satisfy the claims of the collectors of the *didrachm*,
i.e. "half-shekel[4]." That narrative, whatever may be the
full explanation of its details, adds to the cumulative evidence
that metaphors or allegories based upon the payment of coin
as a "ransom for the soul" would be prominent in the doctrine
of early Evangelists, and that literal statements made about
denarii in Mark would be allegorized by John. Such allegorizing is comparatively rare in the Talmud, but frequent in
the Midrash and poetic Targums, which may often throw light
on the imagery underlying Christ's doctrine. In the present
instance, quite apart from its value as an exemplification of
Johannine Intervention, John's retention of the Marcan
"denarii"—taken with the new Johannine context, which

---

[1] 2 Tim. iii. 2 φίλαυτοι, φιλάργυροι.

[2] I have not found an instance of ἀγαπᾶν ἑαυτόν though φιλεῖν
ἑαυτόν is very common. But Mark might use ἠγάπησεν αὑτόν, "he was
in love with himself," to denote an excess of the habit expressed
by φιλεῖν.

[3] Mk xiv. 5.

[4] Mt. xvii. 24—27 A.V. "*tribute [money]...a piece of money,*"
R.V. "*the half-shekel...a shekel,*" W.H. τὰ δίδραχμα...στατῆρα. On
this, and on Philo's allegorizing of "the half of the shekel,"
which LXX calls "the half of the didrachm," see *Notes* 2999 (x).

allows us to regard it as part of a reply to a mystical utterance
of Christ about "buying"—appears to accord with the Johannine doctrine that God is Love. Man, God's coin, restamped by
the redeeming Son of Man with the divine image that has been
wellnigh obliterated by sin, is to present himself wholly, in
the Spirit of Sonship, to the Father. This sacrifice, and not
the partial and formal sacrifice of almsgiving, constitutes the
real and spiritual ransom by which the sinner is redeemed
from his lower self[1].

If we reject the view that John gave a mystical application
to the Marcan "two hundred denarii," what other view are we
prepared to take of his retention of it? Are we to say that he
retained it simply because it was in Mark, and because he saw
no reason why Matthew and Luke should reject it? In that
case, we must suppose him to have argued to this effect: "It
is desirable to retain as much of Mark's detail as possible.
I do not explain what was Mark's reason for mentioning this
precise sum, but I am able to add that it was *not* (as Mark
supposes) 'the disciples' that mentioned it. It was only
Philip."

This would suggest that Philip's utterances were not held
in much account by the Evangelist. But is that so? Philip
loves the concrete and substantial, perhaps. When Nathanael
argues, in the abstract, that no one can be the Messiah if he is
from Nazareth, Philip appeals to the concrete and substantial:
"Come"—that is, "come to Jesus"—and "see[2]." When
Jesus speaks spiritually about "seeing" the Father, Philip

---

[1] At the same time the Fourth Gospel contains evidence shewing
that its author felt the metaphors of "ransoming" and "buying"
to be inadequate, and desired to supplement them by another
metaphor or (x. 6) "proverb," in which the Good Shepherd is
described as rescuing His sheep from the Wolf at the cost of His
life—yet not by ransoming, but by conquering. See *Son*, Index
"Ransom."

[2] Jn i. 46.

asks for a substantial object of vision, "Shew us the Father[1]." Nevertheless it is to Philip that Providence directs the Greeks to come, saying "We would see Jesus[2]." And it is Philip's materialistic utterance, "Shew us the Father," that draws forth from Jesus the words "He that hath seen me hath seen the Father." The Evangelist seems to suggest that this particular Apostle, even though he did not "see" things like a Rabbi or a Philosopher, was more than once made the instrument of Providence for helping others to "see" things as they are. For that reason (it would seem) Jesus "tempts" him—not for Philip's harm but for the world's good. He was worth "tempting." It was destined that through Philip's reply to Christ's question *"Whence are we to buy?"* the world should be led to reflect on the paradoxical nature of that purchase-money with which the Son of God was to buy for them the unpurchasable Bread[3].

---

[1] Jn xiv. 8. Comp. Exod. xxiv. 10 "and they saw the God of Israel."

[2] Jn xii. 21.

[3] Some may reply "Philip and Andrew are mere *dramatis personae* introduced by the Fourth Evangelist, here as elsewhere, in order to present his own thoughts about Jesus in a dramatic setting." But note what Papias says about the pains that he took to inquire not so much about books as about sayings, and in particular (Euseb. iii. 39. 4) "what had been said by *Andrew* or what by *Peter*, or what by *Philip*, or what by *Thomas*...." Is it not very rash to deny that in the Evangelist's days there were current many things alleged to have been "said by *Andrew, Philip, and Thomas,*" not contained in the Synoptic Gospels, and that he made it part of his business to find a place for them in his Gospel wherever they illustrated the Teaching of Christ? No one disputes that Papias did this. Why should we deny the possibility that the Fourth Evangelist did the same thing?

§ 20. *"How many loaves have ye? Go [and] see," in Mark*[1]

These words are in Mark alone. Their omission by Matthew and Luke may be explained by the difficulty of giving them

[1] Mk vi 37—38 (R.V.)

(37) But he answered and said unto them, Give ye them to eat. And they say unto him, Shall we go and buy two hundred pennyworth of bread (*lit.* loaves), and give them to eat? (38) And he saith unto them, How many loaves have ye? Go [and] see. And when they knew (γνόντες), they say, Five, and two fishes.

Mt. xiv. 16—18 (R.V.)

(16) But Jesus said unto them, They have no need to go away; give ye them to eat. (17) And they say unto him, We have here but five loaves, and two fishes. (18) And he said, Bring them hither to me.

Lk. ix. 13—14 *a* (R.V.)

(13) But he said unto them, Give ye them to eat. And they said, We have no more than five loaves and two fishes; except we should go and buy food for all this people. (14*a*) For they were about five thousand men.

Jn vi. 5—9 (R.V.)

(5) Jesus therefore...saith unto Philip, Whence are we to buy bread (*lit.* loaves), that these may eat? (6) And this he said to(?) prove him; for he himself knew what he would do. (7) Philip answered him, Two hundred pennyworth of bread (*lit.* loaves) is not sufficient for them, that every one may take a little. (8) One of his disciples, Andrew, Simon Peter's brother, saith unto him, (9) There is a lad here, which hath five barley loaves, and two fishes: but what are these among so many?

Mk viii. 2 *b*—5 (R.V.)

they...have nothing to eat: (3) And if I send them away fasting to their home, they will faint in the way; and some of them are come from far. (4) And his disciples answered him, Whence shall one be able to fill these men with bread (*lit.* loaves) here in a desert place? (5) And he asked them, How many loaves have ye? And they said, Seven.

Mt. xv. 32 *b*—34 (R.V.)

they...have nothing to eat: and I would not send them away fasting, lest haply they faint in the way. (33) And the disciples say unto him, Whence should we have so many loaves in a desert place, as to fill so great a multitude? (34) And Jesus saith unto them, How many loaves have ye? And they said, Seven, and a few small fishes.

For the purpose of clearness, texts partially given above are repeated here. It will be noted that the six accounts all begin with some words of Jesus about the giving of food, or the need of food, any sense that seems in harmony with the narrative of a stupendous miracle. They seem to imply that Jesus was at some distance from the little store of food carried by the disciples. Finding them ignorant of its amount He sends them away to ascertain it. "Having ascertained it[1]"—for that is what the Greek means—they report "five, and two fishes." All this is very simple. But is it not too simple? Why record it? Matthew and Luke—possibly because it is too simple—do not record it. They represent the disciples as replying at once to Christ's "Give ye them to eat"—without any mention or indication of an interval—that they have only "five loaves and two fishes." In the miracle of the Four Thousand, there is the same absence of interval—"How many loaves have ye? And they said, Seven...."

John differs from all the Synoptists in that he does not represent Jesus as saying to the disciples "Give ye them to eat." On the contrary, Jesus says to Philip "Whence are we to buy loaves that these may eat?" It is added "This he said tempting (*or*, trying) him, for he himself knew what he would do." This seems to imply "He knew that, in truth, He did not purpose to buy loaves; He intended to prepare Philip to learn a lesson about *bread that could not be bought*." But on the other hand it might imply "He knew what Philip would say about denarii, and He purposed to teach Philip a lesson about *bread that could indeed be bought*—only for a very different price, the invisible 'denarius' of Redemption." In either case we are made to feel that we must look below the surface for some allusive meaning, indicating the doctrine of sacrifice, that is, of "buying," or "redeeming." Philip is to be taught this by being "*tried*" or "*tempted*." The Evangelist has probably some latent meaning in this mention of "tempting."

for the multitude to "*eat*." But John connects his mention of "loaves that these may eat" with "buying"—as a prospective act for Jesus and the disciples ("are we to buy?").

[1] Mk vi. 38 γνόντες, on which see *Proclam.* p. 268 n.

He never uses the word again. In N.T. it mostly implies the malignity of an adversary—and especially the Adversary called Satan—who tries us that we may fall. And though the Synoptists use it abundantly, and often of Jesus being tempted, they never describe Jesus as tempting others.

These considerations lead us to the story of God's "tempting" Abraham before the sacrifice of Isaac on Mount Moriah— the first Biblical instance of the word "tempt," and the only one in the whole of Genesis[1]. We have seen above, in the Johannine description of Jesus as "lifting up his eyes and beholding a great multitude coming to him," an allusion to Abraham seeing the vision of the Seed of the Promise. Here it should be added that the same phrase is applied to the Patriarch when he hospitably entertains the Three, who come to make the Promise[2]. In the Dialogue that follows the Feeding of the Five Thousand in the Fourth Gospel, Jews speak of the Giving of the Manna[3]; and Jewish Christians in the first century could not but connect the Manna with the Loaves and Fishes, both in comparison and in contrast. Now it was a

---

[1] Gen. xxii. 1 ἐπείραζεν. The Heb. is נסה, which also occurs in Syr. and Palest. of Jn vi. 6, and in Delitzsch's Hebrew. This must be distinguished from δοκιμάζω, "test," "prove," which mostly = בחן in LXX, but never נסה. There is perhaps a touch of irony when Paul tells the Corinthians—who "seek a *proof* (δοκιμὴν)" of the Christ that "speaks in" him—that they had better "*tempt, or make trial of*" themselves (2 Cor. xiii. 5) "*Make-trial-of* (πειράζετε) yourselves whether ye are in the faith, *prove* (δοκιμάζετε) yourselves." Πειράζω, applied to persons in N.T., almost always means trial proceeding from adversaries, and Rev. ii. 2 ἐπείρασας τοὺς λέγοντας ἑαυτοὺς ἀποστόλους is hardly an exception. But John perhaps felt that, if he had used δοκιμάζω, as in 1 Jn iv. 1 "*prove* (δοκιμάζετε) the spirits whether they be of God," he would have misled his readers. Jesus did not wish to "*prove*" Philip to see "whether" he would answer this or that; He wished to "tempt" him, as God "tempted" Abraham, as a preparation for a blessing that was to follow.

[2] Gen. xviii. 2 "He lifted up his eyes, and looked, and lo...."

[3] Jn vi. 31 foll.

recognised tradition among the Jews that whatever hospitality Abraham gave to the Three, God gave to the Israelites in the wilderness: "R. Jehudah said in the name of Rab: All that Abraham did for the angels by himself, the Holy One, blessed be He, did for his children by Himself; and what Abraham did for them through a messenger, the Holy One did the same for His children through a messenger[1]." What "messenger" is here meant? And is there anything in any of the Gospel narratives of Christ's miracles of feeding that includes something corresponding to Abraham's "messenger"? This will be considered in the next section, in the hope that it may throw some light on the Marcan tradition, at present unexplained, "Go [and] see."

§ 21. "There is a lad here," in John[2]

In the five Synoptic accounts of feeding it is stated by the disciples, or assumed by Jesus, that the loaves belong to the disciples ("we have no more than," "how many have ye?"). The Fourth Gospel alone, after Christ's question "How shall we buy bread?" and after Philip's reply about the insufficiency of two hundred pennyworth, represents Andrew as saying "There is a lad (paidarion) here that has five barley loaves and two fishes." About this Chrysostom says, "I think that he [i.e. Andrew] did not say this in simple ignorance, but because he had heard the wonders of the prophets and how Elisha worked the sign over the loaves[3]." The loaves brought to Elisha were an offering from a stranger; and Chrysostom seems

---

[1] B. Metzia 86 b. The context enters into detail, e.g. "Abraham's "butter" and "milk" are rewarded with "manna." Comp. Numb. r. on Numb. vii. 48 (Wü. p. 348) sect. 14, repeating the same doctrine of the reward of Abraham's hospitality.

[2] Jn vi. 9.

[3] Chrys. on Jn vi. 9, referring to 2 K. iv. 42 "And there came a man...and brought the man of God bread of the firstfruits, twenty loaves of barley...."

to assume that the loaves of the "lad" came also from some stranger, that is to say, they did not belong to the disciples or to any "lad" in their service. And this is the natural interpretation of the words in John.

It is not unlikely that John was influenced by the miracle of Elisha and the barley loaves, in conjunction with other causes. But the first cause might be Hebrew corruption. The first Biblical mention of "barley" in LXX arises from a misreading of a word meaning "measure" or "estimation[1]." "*Loaves estimated* at two hundred denarii" might be confused with "*loaves of barley* for two hundred denarii." Thus a tradition might arise about the loaves that they were "loaves of *barley*." This might naturally be added to the story, partly in view of Elisha's miraculous multiplication of barley loaves, and partly because "barley loaves" might seem to accord with the time of the year[2], and also with a symbolic application of Christ's act. But this hypothesis does not explain John's introduction of the word "*lad*," *paidarion*. For that is not used in the story of Elisha[3]. Moreover *paidarion* occurs nowhere else in N.T. and (with one exception) nowhere in Christian writers of the first century and a half[4]. We are therefore led to ask, outside Greek writings, for something corresponding to the Johannine *paidarion* in Hebrew Scripture, or in Jewish traditions about Scripture.

Now, *paidarion* in LXX regularly corresponds to a Hebrew word frequently rendered in Genesis "lad[5]." And the first Biblical mention of the Hebrew word corresponding to "*lad*"

---

[1] See *Son* 3420 *f—g*, quoting Gen. xxvi. 12.

[2] See § 11.

[3] 2 K. iv. 43 (A.V.) "his servitor" is explained (Gesen. 1058 *a*) as Elisha's "chief servant," LXX λειτουργός, superior to παιδάριον.

[4] Goodspeed gives it as occurring only in *Polyc. Mart.* §§ 6—7, where it refers to two servants of Polycarp, one of whom, under torture, betrays his master's hiding place.

[5] In A.V., "lad" sing. = נער 17 times in Genesis (but not again till Judg. xvi. 26) and 12 times in 1 Samuel.

is in the story of Abraham's hospitality to the Three Persons:
"And Abraham ran unto the herd and fetched a calf...and
gave it unto *the lad*, and he hasted to dress it[1]." Here A.V.
has "*a young man*," and R.V. "*the servant*." But the exact
rendering is "*the lad* [*in attendance*]," "*the young* [*servant*]."
It might be applied to "the youthful [son of the house]" if
the context suited such an application, and accordingly some
Jewish authorities interpret it here as Ishmael[2]. The LXX
does not here render the word by *paidarion*, but that is its
regular rendering of the word[3]. The "lad" mentioned in the
story about Abraham's hospitality appears to be the person
contemplated by R. Jehudah in the words above quoted
"What Abraham did [for the Three] through a *messenger*, the
Holy One did the same for His children through a *messenger*[4]."

The title of "messenger" or "apostle" would seem here to
apply to Moses. Through him God gave the manna to Israel;
and it has been shewn that Moses and Aaron are called God's
"*apostles*" or "*messengers*[5]." It is said about Moses in the
cradle, according to our English versions, that the daughter of
Pharaoh "saw *the child* and behold *the babe* wept[6]." But the
Hebrew text has, for "*babe*," the word regularly corresponding
to *paidarion*; and Rashi seems to render it by "*lad*," expressly
saying "His voice was deep (gravis) like that of a *lad* (pueri),
not like that of a very little infant (parvuli infantis)"—
apparently attaching a mystical or prophetic significance to

---

[1] Gen. xviii. 7 LXX τῷ παιδί.

[2] So *Gen. r.* and Rashi (on Gen. xviii. 7), and *Aboth R. Nathan*
(on *Aboth* i. 16).

[3] Heb. נער=(Tromm.) παιδάριον about 140 times, παιδίον (23), παῖς
(14), νεανίσκος (21), νεώτερος (10), νέος (7) etc.

[4] See p. 84.

[5] See *Proclam.* p. 392, quoting Jerem. ii. 2 (Targ.) "my two
apostles Moses and Aaron in the wilderness."

[6] Exod. ii. 6 (A.V. and R.V.) "child" = ילד, "babe" = נער,
LXX ὁρᾷ παιδίον κλαῖον, merging the two words in one.

the fact that the babe Moses in his cradle (like the babe Herakles in Greek story) was already more than an infant[1].

All this, however, though it may explain John's application of the tradition about the "lad" when it had arisen, does not explain how it arose. If such a "lad" existed, why was the fact omitted by the Synoptists? If there was not, how came John to suppose his existence[2]? To these questions there is at present no answer based on definite evidence. But there are reasonable (though conjectural) answers—derived from what we know about Mark and John in general, and about these Marcan and Johannine narratives in particular—namely, that John is attempting to explain Mark's "*Go, see.*"

One explanation may be conjecturally given to the following effect: "The disciples had no food of their own at hand. But, as Jesus bade them '*go*' and '*see*,' they '*went*' and '*saw*.' They found some one with five loaves and two fishes. These they brought to Jesus saying that they had no more. In reality, they had not even these. But as the owner was willing to give them, they brought them as their own. All this is obscurely suggested in the Marcan '*Go, see*,' and is altogether omitted by Matthew and Luke. But in fact this stranger with the 'five loaves and two fishes' whom the disciples '*went*' and '*saw*,' may have been a person not to be left out. He may have been

---

[1] See *Numb. r.* (on Numb. iii. 14, Wü. p. 42) quoting Exod. ii. 6 and *ib.* 23 and saying that the "sighing" of Israel and the "weeping" of Moses in the cradle were the preparation of the nation for fulfilling the purpose of God. On Zech. ii. 4 (8) "*this young man*," Kimchi, who assumes the prophet to be meant, says that he is so called, either as being literally "young" (like Jeremiah) or as being subordinate to a superior as Joshua was to Moses (Exod. xxxiii. 11 "Joshua the son of Nun *a young man*").

[2] To a third question, "If there was not, how came John to invent it?" my reply would be that repeated investigations in previous parts of *Diatessarica* have shewn that John does not "invent"—though he may have received visions that some would call "inventions." This tradition may have been one of "the sayings of Andrew" inquired into by Papias (s. above, p. 80, n. 3).

like the stranger in Genesis ('a certain man') who met Joseph
wandering in the field and said to him 'What seekest thou[1]?'
That 'man,' they say, was Gabriel. But Gabriel would not
be appropriate here. For in this action the Lord is recom-
pensing to Abraham's children the hospitality that He Himself
received from Abraham, in which Abraham was helped, not
by a 'man' but by a '*lad*.' Let us say, then, that this unknown
stranger was a '*lad*.' And as the '*lad*' assisted Abraham in
preparing food for the Lord, so let us now see a '*lad*' assisting
the Lord in preparing food for Abraham's descendants. The
'lad' then received 'a calf' from Abraham and 'prepared' it.
The 'lad' now gives 'five loaves and two fishes' to the Lord
Jesus, and He prepares them by letting them pass through
His hands as He distributes the food to all the people. This
'*lad*' was Moses, who wrote the five books of the Law, containing also songs and predictions[2]. As the five loaves are
symbolic of the Law, so the fishes might be symbolic of psalms
and prophecies, whether called 'a few,' or, as some might say,
'two fishes,' that is, 'the Psalms and the Prophets' considered
as two books. This was the food that Moses, the servant of
God, offered to the Messiah, the Son of God, who distributed
it to the people. And as Joshua, the first Jesus, is called a

---

[1] Gen. xxxvii. 15, on which see *Joh. Gr.* **2649** *b*.

[2] Jerome, on Mt. xiv. 17, says "In another Evangelist we read
(Jn vi. 9) *There is a lad here who has five loaves*—who seems to me to
signify Moses." The text continues: "Duos autem pisces vel
utrumque intelligimus Testamentum, vel quia par numerus refertur
ad legem." But one MS adds "*et prophetas*," which seems necessary
to the sense ("the even number refers to the Law and the Prophets").
Later on he says: "*The Law with the Prophets* is broken and divided
into fragments (in frusta discerpitur) and its mysteries are brought
forth to view, so that what did not nourish, as long as it was whole
and abiding in its pristine state, might, by being divided into parts,
nourish the multitude of the Gentiles (gentium)."

Origen, on Mt. xiv. 17, says that "perhaps" the five loaves
contained a veiled reference to "the sensible (αἰσθητοὺς) words of
the Scriptures corresponding in number on this account to the five
senses," and the two fishes to the λόγος προφορικός and the λόγος

'*lad*' when ministering to Moses[1], so is Moses himself called a '*lad*' when ministering to the second Jesus."

The second explanation, though similar to the first in detail, would differ in this respect, that it would base itself in part on apostolic tradition. It would go back to one of those "sayings of Andrew" about which Papias tells us that he used to make inquiry, something to this effect:—"Andrew, the Apostle, said (*or*, used to say) that *the Five Loaves and the Two Fishes did not appertain to the Twelve, but to a Servant* [meaning Moses]. Also Andrew said (*or*, used to say)—speaking of the Law and the Prophets in themselves and before they were broken up like bread and expounded by the Lord—'*What could they avail for the multitudes* [*seeking the Bread of Life*][2]?'"

The second of these explanations seems to me decidedly more probable than the first; but if either of them is even partially correct we find ourselves in an atmosphere of

---

ἐνδιάθετος ("which are a relish, so to speak, to the sensible things contained in the Scriptures") or, perhaps, to the word that had "already come (φθάσαντα)" to the disciples "about the Father and the Son"; but he adds that others may be able to give a fuller and better interpretation.

Clement of Alexandria 665—6, while implying that the "five pillars" of Exod. xxvi. 37 are less sacred than the "four pillars" of Exod. xxvi. 32, simply mentions "the five loaves" in connection with "the things of sense."

Thus, the further back we go, the less proof we find that "*five*" was regarded by Greek commentators as referring to the five books of the Law. They may be wrong. They may have failed to catch the poetic allusions of the Galilaean tradition. But still we have to keep our minds open to the possibility that "*five*" may have originally had some other reference (*e.g.* meaning "*a few*") and that the explanation of the "five loaves" as the five books of the Law came later. It certainly is not entirely satisfactory, because it is difficult to find a corresponding explanation of the "two fishes."

[1] Exod. xxxiii. 11 "His [*i.e.* Moses's] minister Joshua, the son of Nun, *a lad*," R.V. "*a young man*." Perhaps the Heb. word is intended to convey the double notion of youth and service.

[2] On the ambiguous "said" or "used to say"—ambiguous in Hebrew as well as in Greek (ἔλεγε), see *Joh. Gr.* **2470** *a*.

Jewish symbolism and mystical tradition through which we must look at the whole of the context. It is easy to realise this about the "two hundred denarii" discussed above. But the reader may feel it absurd that he should be asked to extend this hypothesis to the Marcan phrase *"Go, see!"* to which we now return. These words he may declare to be not only simple in themselves, but also in accord with another Marcan tradition about the disciples as having "forgotten" to bring "loaves with them[1]."

But the literal truth of that other tradition itself is very doubtful. It is omitted by Luke. And the Marcan context, saying "Save one loaf, they had not [any loaves] in the boat with them," is omitted by Matthew and is suggestive of metaphor literalised. We ought therefore to give a patient consideration to the suggestion that, in the present passage, *"Go, see!"* may be a Marcan misinterpretation of *"Come and see,"* a phrase used in Jewish tradition to call attention to weighty sayings, especially about the ways of God as superior to those of man. John uses a form of it thrice in passages where it is susceptible of a mystical meaning[2]. Also, in particular, *"See"* is applied to numbers when rabbinically interpreted. For example, *Horae Hebraicae* illustrates the "barley loaves" in John by quoting a fanciful exaggeration about the feeding of the sons of the prophets with "loaves of barley" by Elisha, in which *"See!"* occurs thrice; and the formula is sometimes repeated much more frequently[3]. Somewhat similarly,

---

[1] Mk viii. 14, parall. Mt. xvi. 5, om. Lk. xii. 1.

[2] See Schlatter, on Jn i. 39 "come and ye shall see," referring to *ib*. 46 and xi. 34 and quoting from *Mechilt.* (on Exod. xii. 1, xx. 12) *"Come and see* what God replies to him" and *"Come and see* their reward." See also Wetstein, *Hor. Heb.*, and Schöttgen, on Jn i. 39.

[3] *Hor. Heb.* on Jn vi. 9 quoting *Chetub.* 105. 2, 106. 9 on 2 K. iv. 42 "Twenty loaves, and the loaf of the firstfruits, *see*, one and twenty; the green ear, *see*, two and twenty...and so, *see*, there were two thousand and two hundred fed." I substitute "see" for "behold," as Wünsche habitually does, *e.g.* on Numb. vii. 66 foll. p. 372 *"siehe,*

in an early Galilaean tradition about the Feeding of the Five Thousand, attention may have been called to the number of the loaves: "*See* (or, *Go and see*) *there are five loaves*[1]." This was misunderstood by Gentile interpretation (adopted by Mark) as though the first half of the sentence came from Jesus, who said "*Go and see* [*how many loaves there are*]," and the second half from the disciples, who said "*There are five loaves.*"

It is perhaps worth noting that the phrase "five loaves" occurs in the narrative of an incident in the life of David to which Jesus Himself called attention—the eating of the sacred shewbread by laymen contrary to the Law. All the Gospels mention this. But they do not quote the exact words of David, which are "Give me *five loaves of bread* in mine hand or whatsoever is present[2]." No other passage in the Bible mentions "*five loaves.*" The meaning appears to be (as the Vulgate renders it) "*even* five [if you can give no more]." "Five" therefore may be regarded as typical of a small number[3]. In the Feeding of the Five Thousand, the Son of David restores and consecrates the "five loaves" that David might be said, in some sort, to have taken away and desecrated. It ought not to be surprising if, apart from other mystical views of the number "five," this allusion in itself caused a Jewish Christian Evangelist to call attention to the coincidence by means of the formula "*Come and see.*" It ought to be less surprising that the formula was misunderstood by Gentiles.

---

das sind zwei,...*siehe*, das sind vier..." where it occurs seven times. On p. 374 it occurs six times.

[1] The Heb. בוא, which regularly means "come," is frequently used for "go," *e.g.* Gen. xxxi. 18 R.V. "go," LXX ἀπελθεῖν.

[2] 1 S. xxi. 3 referred to in Mk ii. 26, Mt. xii. 4, Lk. vi. 4.

[3] See Lev. xxvi. 8 "*Five* of you shall chase an hundred," and Is. xxx. 17 "at the rebuke of *five*." The attempt to explain it otherwise (*J. Succa* vi. 8 (Schwab p. 50)) is unsatisfactory.

§ 22. *"Here," in all the Gospels*

The Johannine phrase discussed in the last section, *"there is a lad"* is followed by *"here."* *"Here"* is also inserted by Matthew as follows:—

Mk vi. 38	Mt. xiv. 17	Lk. ix. 13
They say (D and SS add "to him"), Five...	But they say to him, We have not *here* save five...	But they said (*lit.*) There are not to us more than five...

In *Corrections* it was suggested that *"here"* might be added by Matthew for emphasis, or that there might be some confusion between *"here"* and *"bread"* which are very similar in Hebrew[1]. The latter suggestion is favoured by a passage in the Psalms where Gesenius accepts an emendation based on this similarity[2]. But of course both causes might be at work. Matthew repeats the Greek *"here"* in the next verse after a verb of motion in words of Jesus that he alone records, "Bring them *here* to me[3]." Luke also, in a parallel to Mark-Matthew "the place is desert," has "We are *here* in a desert place[4]." Lastly, in the Feeding of the Four Thousand, "here" is inserted by Mark who has "Whence shall one be able *here* to satisfy these with loaves in a wilderness[5]?" but omitted by the parallel Matthew, "Whence [can come] to us in a wilderness so many loaves as to satisfy so great a multitude?" The recurrences of the same word meaning "here" or "hither" in the narratives of miraculous feeding suggest the examination of the Biblical use of the word above mentioned, meaning *"hither"* but confusable with "bread."

It occurs for the first time in the words of the fugitive Hagar whom "the angel of the Lord found by a fountain of

---

[1] See *Corrections* **403** (i), where it is also pointed out that "to him" and "not" are often confused in Hebrew (see Gesen. 520 *b*).

[2] See Gesen. pp. 240—1 on Ps. lxxiii. 10 adopting לחם "bread" for הלם "hither."

[3] Mt. xiv. 18 φέρετέ μοι ὧδε αὐτούς, not in parall. Mk-Lk.

[4] Lk. ix. 12.   [5] Mk viii. 4.

water in the wilderness of Shur." Hagar exclaims "Have I even *here* looked after him that seeth me[1]?" Rashi explains "*even here*" as meaning "*even here in the desert,*" and that makes good sense, recognising that God sees everywhere; but the Jerusalem Targums confused the word with an almost identical one meaning "dream" or "vision," and the LXX renders it "face to face[2]." As a rule, the word means "hither," not "here," and it will be observed that Matthew repeats it (in Greek) in the sense of "hither" on the second occasion.

In the sense of "*here,*" it would be appropriate to the disciples, ignorant of their Master's design and saying "*Here* [*in this lonely place*] we have no bread worth mentioning, or we can do nothing for the multitude." But, if "here" has this meaning, then "*in this lonely place*" is a desirable addition; for, without it, "*here*" might mean simply "*on the spot.*" Accordingly Mark (in the narrative of the Four Thousand) and Luke, who both use "*here,*" add "in a desert, or lonely place[3]." Matthew, in the narrative of the Four Thousand, does not follow Mark in inserting "*here*" along with "*in a desert*"; but, in the narrative of the Five Thousand, he inserts "*here*" twice, apparently taking it to mean, not "*here in a lonely place,*" but "*here on the spot*";—"We have no bread worth mentioning *here on the spot,*" to which Jesus replies "Bring it to me *here on the spot.*" Mark, in the Feeding of the Five Thousand, omits "*here,*" but apparently implies, like Matthew, that, if inserted, it would have meant "*on the*

---

[1] Gen. xvi. 13.

[2] In Daniel, חלם repeatedly means (Theod.) ἐνύπνιον, (LXX) ὅραμα. In Gen. xvi. 13 Onk. has "I have begun to see" (? confusing הלם with some form of חלל). LXX has ἐνώπιον (? corr. for ενυπνιον). In Gen. xvi. 14 LXX has ἐνώπιον again for לחי =viventis. Elsewhere LXX has ἐνταῦθα (4), ὧδε (4), etc. These facts indicate that ancient interpretation did not (as Gesen. does) limit the word to the sense of "*hither.*"

[3] Mk viii. 4 (the Four Thousand) πόθεν...ὧδε...ἐπ' ἐρημίας; Lk. ix. 12 (the Five Thousand) ὧδε ἐν ἐρήμῳ τόπῳ ἐσμέν.

spot"; although the disciples had no bread "*on the spot*," they had some a little way off, as to which Jesus sent to inquire how much it was.

Coming to John's phrase "There is a lad *here*" we have to confess at once that, but for all these variations and apparent allusions in the Synoptists, we should take it to mean simply "*on the spot*" or "*at hand*." But if the "*lad*" is to be regarded as the representative of Moses, and if John had before him various traditions likening the Five Thousand in the Desert to Israel in the Wilderness of Sinai, then we shall not reject as improbable the hypothesis that this saying of Andrew about "a lad here," besides having its literal meaning, might also mystically allude to "Moses *in the wilderness*[1]."

§ 23. "*By companies*[2]," "*by ranks*[3]," in Mark

The Greek for "company," *symposion*, means literally "drinking-party." The Greek for "rank," *prasia*, means perhaps literally "greenery," and in practice a rectangular "garden-bed[4]." Neither of these words is adopted by the

---

[1] In examining this hypothesis of allusion to the story of Hagar, or of confusion arising from Hebrew corruption, we must not ignore the fact that elsewhere Matthew and Luke appear to insert "hither" simply for emphasis. (See *Corrections* **425** on Mk ix. 19, Mt. xvii. 17, Lk. ix. 41.) And the LXX does sometimes insert it for this reason where it is not in the Hebrew, besides omitting it sometimes where it is in the Hebrew. (See *Corrections* **425** (i) *a* and *b*.) But the recurrence of "here" in these narratives of feeding is rather too frequent to be explained thus.

[2] Mk vi. 39 συμπόσια συμπόσια.   [3] Mk vi. 40 πρασιαὶ πρασιαί.

[4] Hesych. says that πράσα=τὰ βρύα κ. τὰ φυκία, and πρασιαί=αἱ ἐν τοῖς κήποις τετράγωνοι λαχανιαί. The facts suggest that the word originally denoted "*green*" and was then applied to any very common green vegetable, *e.g.* the leek (comp. in English, "*greens*"). L.S. gives πράσιον="horehound," and πράσον=(1) leek, (2) a leek-like sea-weed. Hesych. suggests πέρας "boundary" as the origin of the word :—οἷον περασιοὶ διὰ τὸ ἐπὶ πέρασι τῶν κήπων. The word πρασιά is frequent in Homer. Field (on Mk vi. 40) shews that the word was *not* (as has been maintained) associated with the thought of "flower-beds" or "parterres" implying variety of colour.

parallel Matthew, Luke, or John[1]. The question therefore arises whether John has, or has not, in his context, something that expresses the thought underlying Mark's peculiar expressions. If he has not, this passage will have to be recognised as an instance of the failure of the Rule of Johannine Intervention.

Symposion occurs only once in canonical LXX. There it represents the Hebrew phrase *"drinking-party of wine[2]."* Philo, it is true, repeatedly uses it in describing the sacred meals of the Therapeutae. But he expressly uses it as a paradox, *"contrasting their symposia with the symposia of other*

---

[1]

Mk vi. 39—40 (R.V.)	Mt. xiv. 19 a (R.V.)	Lk. ix. 14—15 (R.V.)	Jn vi. 10 (R.V.)
(39) And he commanded them that all should sit down (*lit.* recline) by companies upon the green grass. (40) And they sat down in ranks, by hundreds, and by fifties.	And he commanded the multitudes to sit down (*lit.* recline) on the grass.	(14) For they were about five thousand men. And he said unto his disciples, Make them sit down (*lit.* recline) in companies (κλισίας), about fifty each. (15) And they did so, and made them all sit down (*lit.* recline).	Jesus said, Make the people sit down. Now there was much grass in the place. So the men sat down, in number about five thousand.

In the Feeding of the Four Thousand the reclining is mentioned merely as a command thus :—

Mk viii. 6 a (R.V.)	Mt. xv. 35 (R.V.)
And he commandeth the multitude to sit down on the ground.	And he commanded the multitude to sit down on the ground.

R.V. in these six columns does not represent several differences in the Greek. For example, R.V. "command"=ἐπιτάσσω, κελεύω, and παραγγέλλω.

[2] Esth. vii. 7 συμπόσιον="*drinking-party* (משתה) *of wine* (היין)." Συμπόσιον οἴνου=the same Heb. in Sir. xxxv. (xxxii.) 5, xlix. 1. In Is. i. 22 (Aq.) and Hos. iv. 18 (Sym. and Quint.) συμπόσιον represents Heb. סבא (Gesen. 685 a) "drink," "liquor," (?) "drunken-revelling." The parallel Lk. ix. 14 has κλισίας. Κλισία, in literary Greek (Steph. *Thes.*) means a "booth" (comp. 3 Macc. vi. 31, the single instance in LXX). But Luke appears to mean "sitting-place" as in Joseph. *Ant.* xii. 2. 12.

folk," for the Therapeutae, he says, drink nothing but "running water[1]." In Mark there is no such contrast. Mark's choice of the word therefore requires explanation. It seems singularly unsuitable in a narrative about feeding with bread and fish where there appears no suggestion, and certainly no mention, of wine, or of anything to drink.

But in fact there *is* such a suggestion, though a most obscure one, in the Marcan word *prasiai*. For this, though literally meaning only "garden-beds," can be shewn to have practically meant *garden-beds that need irrigation,* that is to say, meta-phorically "*drinking.*" Aquila assumes this in his rendering of the words "As the hart *thirsteth* (R.V. *panteth*) after the water brooks, so *thirsteth* (R.V. *panteth*) my soul after thee, O God[2]." Here Aquila uses a verb formed from *prasia,* "garden-bed," to signify "thirsting [like a garden-bed that thirsts for water from heaven]." Ben Sira, too, after repre-senting Wisdom as saying "They that eat me shall yet be hungry and they that drink me shall yet be thirsty," *i.e.* athirst for heavenly knowledge, uses the word *prasia* as follows: "I will water my best garden, and will water abundantly my *garden-bed*[3]." The thought is of the irrigating trenches of a garden or vineyard, opening their mouths like panting animals, and crying to heaven for water to feed the rows of vegetation. The word occurs in a papyrus of the first century in such a

---

[1] Philo ii. 477 ἀντιτάξας τὰ τῶν ἄλλων συμπόσια (the word is mentioned about a dozen times in the context). The Therapeutae drink (*ib.* 477) ὕδωρ ναματιαῖον.

[2] Ps. xlii. 1, see Gesen. 788, עָרַג, "long for," עֲרוּגָה "garden terrace or bed." Rashi gives various explanations, and says that "Menachem" illustrates from Cant. v. 12 (R.V. 13) where Aq. has πρασιαί. Aq. also has πρασιοῦσθαι in Joel i. 20 "the beasts of the field *pant* (A.V. *cry*) unto thee," where Jerome says "*like a garden-bed thirsting for rain. For this is what Aquila means, in one word,* saying ἐπρασιώθη."

[3] Sir. xxiv. 21, 31 ποτιῶ μου τὸν κῆπον, καὶ μεθύσω μου τὴν πρασιάν, where μεθύσω, "I will *satisfy as if with wine,*" harmonizes with a hypothesis connecting πρασιαί with συμπόσια.

context as to shew that it would be naturally connected with irrigation[1].

The Targum on a passage in Ezekiel mentioning what Aquila calls "*garden-beds*" has a slightly different form of the word, meaning "*trenches*," and especially trenches for the irrigation of vines[2]. And the metaphorical name "the vineyard in Jabneh" (some indeed call it no metaphor but a name based on fact) was applied to "the university in that place," the reason being that "the scholars sat *rows* [*and*] *rows* like a vineyard that is planted *rows* [*and*] *rows*[3]."

These facts, taken together, explain Mark's two peculiar traditions. The original appeared to him to describe the multitude as placed "[*in*] *rows* [*and*] *rows*," meaning either "like vines," or "like vineyard trenches," waiting for water, the living water of the Word[4]. This was at first expressed by *prasiai*. But as this did not convey clearly to Greeks the notion of thirst, Mark prefaced it by *symposia*[5]. Matthew and Luke omitted both these terms:—*symposia*, "drinking-parties," because it might convey the notion of carousing, and *prasiai*, "garden-beds," because it did not convey to them the

---

[1] *Berlin Urkunde* 530. 27 "The water scarcely gives drink enough for one *row*" μόλις γὰρ μίαν πρασεὰν (*sic*) ποτίζει τὸ ὕδωρ. Comp. I Cor. xii. 13 ἐν πνεῦμα ἐποτίσθημεν and iii. 2 γάλα ὑμᾶς ἐπότισα, also iii. 6 Ἀπολλὼς ἐπότισεν, "watered" (after "I planted").

[2] Ezek. xvii. 7, 10 Heb. עֲרֻגוֹת, A.V. "furrows," R.V. "beds," Aq. πρασιαί, Targ. עֻנְיָת, which="trenches," see Levy iii. 625 *b* and Levy *Ch*. ii. 205 *b*.

[3] *Hor. Heb.* on Mk vi. 40 quoting *Jevamoth* cap. 8. For a similar explanation see *Jer. Berach.* iv. 1 fol. 7 *d*, and elsewhere (Levy ii. 408 *b*). The word for "*rows*" is rare in O.T. (Gesen. 1004 *b*, quite diff. from the one meaning "garden-bed") but freq. in later Heb. (Levy iv. 525—6).

[4] This is the aspect of "rows" that commended itself to Mark. But there is also the military aspect in which the "rows" would be regarded as "files," see below, § 25.

[5] See *Clue* 31 shewing that "the correct rendering in a conflation mostly follows the incorrect one."

suggestion of spiritual thirst, and they did not see any reason for such an out-of-the-way metaphor.

What course does John adopt? In the narrative of the actual miracle, it must be admitted, he says nothing that in the remotest degree implies a *symposium*. But in Christ's comment we are taught that the "loaves" with which the Five Thousand have been "filled" are but types of a "bread from heaven"; then we learn that this "bread" is Christ Himself; then we are told that He—not the bread but Christ Himself—satisfies *"thirst" at the same time as hunger*: "He that cometh unto me shall never hunger, and he that believeth on me shall never *thirst*[1]." Subsequently the epithet "living"— familiar to the Jews as an epithet of running water—is applied to this "bread" as being a source of spiritual life[2]. And thus we are finally led to a new and astonishing revelation of the nature of this new "food" that is to be "bought" by Jesus— namely that it is to be His own "flesh." The literalising Jews ask "How can this man give us his flesh to eat?" Jesus, in His answer, increases (for literalisers) the impossibility. He abruptly implies that the "flesh" will not be separated from "blood." Thus at last we are brought to the actual mention of the word "*drink*," for which we have been gradually prepared: "Except ye eat the flesh of the Son of man and *drink* his blood, ye have no life in yourselves[3]." This, once mentioned, is reiterated: "He that eateth my flesh and *drinketh* my blood," "My blood is *drink* indeed," "He that eateth my flesh and *drinketh* my blood abideth in me and I in him[4]." Such is the Johannine expansion of the Marcan *symposia*.

It has not been maintained above that *symposia* was a part of Mark's original, or that Matthew and Luke were wrong in omitting it. The question for us has been, not as to Mark's

---

[1] Jn vi. 35. This is in response to the prayer "Lord, evermore give us this bread."
[2] Jn vi. 51.   [3] Jn vi. 52—3.   [4] Jn vi. 54—6.

correctness, but as to whether John intervenes in order to bring out some spiritual doctrine latent under Mark's text, even when Mark is incorrect or (as in this case) inappropriate in expression. The result has been to reveal, apparently, not a failure but an instance, of Johannine Intervention. And it is a peculiarly interesting one. For here Mark's error appears to have been a Greek husk, so to speak, containing a kernel of Jewish doctrine. This kernel John has extracted, amplifying the exposition of its doctrine so that it illuminates the whole of his conception of Christ's character and action.

As regards *prasiai*, or "garden-beds," it cannot be conclusively shewn that John has similarly intervened. If he regarded the *prasiai* as the Jewish equivalent of the Gentile *symposia*, he may have decided that he had done enough when he had expounded the doctrine implied for Greeks in the Greek word *symposia*[1].

---

[1] The thought of πρασιαί as "rows of vines," thirsting for water, would be very distinct from John's conception of the one Vine. The latter (not "vine-rows" but "vine") may have been in his mind when he writes, as words of Jesus, (vi. 56) "He that...drinketh my blood abideth in me and I in him."

If we drink His blood, it follows that, in some sense, He is in us; but how does it follow that we "abide" in Him? An explanation is not given in the doctrine that follows the Feeding, but one is suggested later on, when it is said (Jn xv. 4) that we abide in Christ as branches in the Vine. This means that we are in the Christ-Nature or Vine-Nature, in the Nature that produces the sap and the fruit and that juice of the Vine which is called in Scripture (Gen. xlix. 11) "the blood of grapes." It is *in us*, but we are also *in it* because it is *in us*. This metaphor of the single Vine is more accordant with the ancient Hebrew imagery than is the later Jewish tradition about "vine-rows [and] vine-rows" describing the array of disciples in "the vineyard" of "the university of Jabneh."

§ 24. "*On the green grass*[1]," *in Mark*

Barely stated, the facts bearing on this Marcan phrase might be summed up as a case of Johannine Intervention thus: "Mark has 'on the *green grass*,' Matthew 'on the *grass*,' Luke no mention of '*grass*' at all, John '*There was much grass in the place*'; John obviously intervenes. The Greek *chortos*, '*grass*,' mostly means 'hay' in literary Greek, and may have that meaning here. But that does not affect either the fact that Luke omits and John inserts the Marcan *chortos*, or the inference—that it is a case of Johannine Intervention."

All this is true. But if we passed on, content with this, we should pass over a great deal that will be found interesting and illuminative for those who are prepared to recognise truth under metaphor, and to accept guidance toward some parts of the truth from ancient Christian commentaries that must be admitted to be, as to other parts, fanciful and extravagant. Such a comment is that of Jerome (on Matthew): "They are commanded to '*lie down on grass* (or, *hay*) (foenum)' and, according to another (alium) Evangelist, '*on the earth*[2],' in fifties or hundreds, in order that, after they have trampled (calcaverint)[3] on their '*flesh*' and all its '*flowers*,' and placed

---

[1] Mk vi. 39—40 ἐπέταξεν αὐτοῖς ἀνακλιθῆναι πάντας...ἐπὶ τῷ χλωρῷ χόρτῳ, καὶ ἀνέπεσαν..., Mt. xiv. 19 κελεύσας τοὺς ὄχλους ἀνακλιθῆναι ἐπὶ τοῦ χόρτου, Lk. ix. 14—15 Κατακλίνατε αὐτοὺς κλισίας..., καὶ κατέκλιναν ἅπαντας, Jn vi. 10 Ποιήσατε τοὺς ἀνθρώπους ἀναπεσεῖν. ἦν δὲ χόρτος πολὺς ἐν τῷ τόπῳ. ἀνέπεσαν οὖν οἱ ἄνδρες....

[2] "*On the earth*" is not said by any Evangelist here. Did Jerome suppose it to be implied by Luke ("make them lie down")? Luke omits "*on the grass*." On the Feeding of the Four Thousand Jerome (on Matthew) remarks "Ibi *super foenum* discumbunt, hic *super terram*." If Jerome is referring to that we must read here "another [place of the] Evangelist (Mt. xv. 35)."

[3] "Trampled," comp. the expostulation in Ezekiel (xxxiv. 18) to the "rams" and "he-goats," which not only eat up the pasture of the weaker cattle but also "*tread down*" the "residue." What they do in a bad sense, Jerome here supposes to be done in a good sense.

under [their feet] the pleasures of the world as being merely *drying grass* (or, *hay*) (arens foenum)[1], they may then ascend through the penitence denoted by '*fifty*' to the perfect height denoted by '*a hundred*[2].'"

In his interpretation of "grass," Jerome is here following Origen, who says "I think He bade the multitude *lie down in the grass* by reason of that which is said in Isaiah 'All flesh is grass'—that is to say, place beneath [their feet] '*the flesh*' and subjugate the disposition of '*the flesh*[3].'"

This passage of Isaiah is quoted also in the Petrine Epistle as contrasting "*flesh*," which is "*as grass*," with the utterance of the everlasting God; and it is alluded to in the Epistle of James[4]. Jesus Himself did not command His disciples to "trample" on "the flowers"; but He bade them "consider the lilies" and ask themselves whether they might not trust their heavenly Father to clothe them, since He "so clothed the *grass* (*chortos*) of the field[5]."

It is important to recognise that this word *chortos*, when connected with a mention of men and not cattle or agriculture, is likely to have a depreciative meaning. Paul uses it to describe a false and flimsy structure (of "*hay*") built by some

---

[1] Comp. Is. xl. 6—8 "All flesh is grass ($\chi\acute{o}\rho\tau os$), and all the goodliness thereof is as the *flower* of the field.... Surely the people is *grass*. The *grass* withereth ($\dot{\epsilon}\xi\eta\rho\acute{a}\nu\theta\eta$ = *arens*), the *flower* fadeth: but the word of our God shall stand for ever."

[2] "Fifty" is mentioned by Mark and Luke, but not by Matthew; "a hundred" is mentioned by Mark alone.

[3] Origen (on Mt. xiv. 19) $\tau o\grave{v}s$ $\ddot{o}\chi\lambda ous$ $\dot{\epsilon}\kappa\acute{\epsilon}\lambda\epsilon v\sigma\epsilon\nu$ $\dot{a}\nu a\kappa\lambda\iota\theta\hat{\eta}\nu a\iota$ $\dot{\epsilon}\nu$ (*sic*) $\tau\hat{\wp}$ $\chi\acute{o}\rho\tau\wp$...$\tau o v\tau\acute{\epsilon}\sigma\tau\iota\nu$ $\dot{v}\pi o\kappa\acute{a}\tau\omega$ $\pi o\iota\hat{\eta}\sigma a\iota$ $\tau\grave{\eta}\nu$ $\sigma\acute{a}\rho\kappa a$ $\kappa a\grave{\iota}$ $\dot{v}\pi o\tau\acute{a}\xi a\iota$ $\tau\grave{o}$ $\phi\rho\acute{o}\nu\eta\mu a$ $\tau\hat{\eta}s$ $\sigma a\rho\kappa\acute{o}s$.

[4] 1 Pet. i. 24, Jas. i. 10, 11.

[5] Mt. vi. 30 $\epsilon\grave{\iota}$ $\delta\grave{\epsilon}$ $\tau\grave{o}\nu$ $\chi\acute{o}\rho\tau o\nu$ $\tau o\hat{v}$ $\dot{a}\gamma\rho o\hat{v}$... Note the difference in Lk. xii. 28 $\epsilon\grave{\iota}$ $\delta\grave{\epsilon}$ $\dot{\epsilon}\nu$ $\dot{a}\gamma\rho\hat{\wp}$ $\tau\grave{o}\nu$ $\chi\acute{o}\rho\tau o\nu$... Luke rejects the phrase "grass of the field" used by Matthew and frequent in LXX. He substitutes: "*But if [while it is still] in the field* [or, *in a field*] the grass—living (*lit.* existing) to-day and [to be] thrown into the oven to-morrow—is so clothed by God." His object is to shew Greek readers that $\chi\acute{o}\rho\tau os$, in this passage, does *not* have its ordinary meaning "*hay*."

Christians who profess to accept Christ as their "foundation[1]." Also in literary Greek the noun *chortos* is regularly used to mean food for beasts, as distinct from corn or wheat that is food for men; and hence the verb *chortazein* is used to mean, not only when applied to cattle "fill with hay (*or*, with fodder)," but also when applied to men, "cram, or stuff, oneself with food," after the manner of swine[2].

In LXX, *chortos* is represented mainly by two Hebrew words. Both of these signify "herbage," but one signifies more definitely "green grass" and is once rendered by LXX "green[3]." It seldom has any such opprobrious sense as in literary Greek[4]. In O.T., where A.V. has "*hay*" R.V. has "*grass*" in text or margin[5]; and it is said that people in Palestine do not dry grass as we do for winter fodder, and that there is no evidence that the Hebrews had such a custom[6].

---

[1] I Cor. iii. 12.

[2] See Steph. *Thes.* χόρτος, and add Epictet. ii. 14. 24 "most men value nothing more than *fodder*—for wealth is *fodder*" (comp. *ib.* 29). Epictetus uses χορτάζω similarly (ii. 16. 43) and once in a passage that resembles a bitter version of a saying of Christ's (i. 9. 19) "You are [as good as] dead. When you are *crammed* (χορτασθῆτε) for the day, you sit weeping about the [fodder of the] morrow." Ast's two instances in Plato are *Pol.* II. 372 D, IX. 586 A in which men are likened to "swine," or to creatures "stooping down to dinner-tables," εἰς τραπέζας [κεκυφότες] βόσκονται χορταζόμενοι καὶ ὀχεύοντες.

[3] See Gesen. 348 חָצִיר "green grass, herbage," 793 עֵשֶׂב "herb, herbage." Χόρτος = the former about 12 times, the latter about 25 times (besides other Heb. words much more rarely). In Prov. xxvii. 25, חָצִיר = LXX "green [things]" χλωρῶν, R.V. "*the hay* (marg. *grass*) is carried and the tender grass sheweth itself."

[4] The Hebrew "grass" denotes transience but not degradation except in special contexts such as Ps. cvi. 20 "the similitude of an ox that eateth *grass*," on which see *Tehill.* and Rashi *ad loc.*, also *Mechilt.* (on Exod. xiv. 29, Wü. p. 108) and Dan. iv. 25—33 (of Nebuchadnezzar).

[5] Prov. xxvii. 25, Is. xv. 6, the only instances of "hay" in A.V. (O.T.).

[6] See Hastings' *Dict.* "Hay," which says "The winter is the season

Mark has previously used *chortos* in a sense unprecedented (so far as is known at present) to mean the shooting blade of corn (perhaps taking it to mean the early green shoot of corn which the eye cannot distinguish from grass)[1]. Here Mark goes further and inserts "green." Perhaps he wishes to make it clear to his readers that he means, not "hay," but "grass[2]."

Are we then to infer that in the present passage Mark is simply stating a literal fact in the language of the LXX without any allusion to Hebrew Scripture or Jewish tradition? It would be safer to say that he stated what he believed to be a literal fact and to leave it an open question whether his original had an allusive character. For we are dealing with a Gospel narrative about a miraculous giving of "bread," or literally "loaves"; and it is certainly a coincidence to be noted that, in the LXX, the first mention of *"bread"* (or *"loaf,"* artos)— "In the sweat of thy face wilt thou eat *bread"*—immediately follows the words, pronounced as a curse, "Thou shalt eat the *grass* (chortos) of the field[3]."

The question was asked by ancient Jewish teachers "Was there really a change in the doom pronounced by God on Adam? If so, how explain it?" The Jerusalem Targums say it was changed because of Adam's piteous expostulation, and Talmudic tradition supports them: "Lord of the world," cried Adam, "shall I and my ass eat out of one crib[4]?" These

---

of green grass here." The ignorance of this fact might lead to early misunderstandings.

[1] Mk iv. 28.

[2] Wetstein, on Mt. vi. 30, says that χόρτος is "hay (foenum)," but that here and elsewhere in the Gospels it is used of grass still green, and he quotes Plutarch *Q. N.* p. 25 c χόρτος ὑόμενος, κόπτεται γὰρ οὐ ξηρὸς ἀλλὰ χλωρός.

[3] Gen. iii. 18—19.

[4] *Pesach.* 118 a, and sim. *Aboth R. Nathan* on *Aboth* i. 1 "Said the Holy One, Blessed be He: 'As thou hast trembled, therefore in the sweat of thy face thou shalt eat *bread*'" (where Rodkinson italicises *"bread"*). See *Son* 3422 a, which quotes the fuller dialogue

traditions are not of the first century. But even in the first century we find Philo making a distinction between the symbolism of "grass" and "green [grass][1]." This, though perhaps derived from Greek influences, indicates that discussions about "grass," and "fodder," and also about the relation of these to that "bread" which is "the word of God," were likely to be current in the first century, among Jews as well as among Christians[2]. On the whole we may say that there is nothing so absurd as there appears to be at first sight in the hypothesis that *"on the green grass"* in the Marcan narrative had, from the first, a poetic and allusive as well as a literal meaning.

Before passing to the Johannine equivalent (in the phrase "now there was much grass in the place") we must note, as a part of John's consistent treatment of the whole subject, his way of dealing with the verb *chortazein* derived from *chortos* "grass," and meaning *"to fill with grass."* It is applied by all the Synoptists to the multitudes, meaning "they were filled" in the sense of "satisfied[3]." For this, they have some authority in the LXX, but hardly any except in the Psalms[4].

---

in the Targums, where God is regarded not as altering, but as interpreting, "the herb," עֵשֶׂב. This = χόρτος seven times in Genesis, beginning with i. 11 βοτάνην (דֶּשֶׁא) χόρτου (עֵשֶׂב).

[1] Philo i. 48 (on Gen. ii. 4 foll.). "Grass"=χόρτος, "green [grass]"=χλωρόν.

[2] Χόρτος occurs in early Christian writers (s. Goodspeed) only in Justin's *Dialogue* § 20 *passim* (apart from quotations in *ib.* §§ 34 and 50). There Justin, after saying that God (Gen. ix. 3) gave Noah the right to eat of every animal, represents the Jew as on the point of interrupting him: "And as he was ready to say '*as the herbs of green-vegetation* (λάχανα χόρτου)' I anticipated him." This shews that *chortos* was a recognised topic of discussion.

[3] Mk vi. 42, Mt. xiv. 20, Lk. ix. 17. Comp. Mk viii. 4—8, Mt. xv. 33—7 (about the Four Thousand).

[4] The Heb. שָׂבַע meaning "satisfy" or "sate" = (Tromm.) ἐμπλήθω or ἐμπίμπλημι 50 times, and πλήθω 19 times, but χορτάζω only 13 times (Tromm., by error, 12), and, of these 13 instances, 9 are in the Psalms.

It must be admitted that Paul once uses it about himself. And his language might be rendered (somewhat tamely) "I have been initiated into the secret both of *having-my-fill* (*chortazein*) and hungering[1]." But it is better to regard it as Pauline hyperbole (almost equivalent to "stuffing and starving"). And to most Greeks, unacquainted with the LXX, the Synoptic statement would certainly sound like a reproach—as if it meant that the Five Thousand were "filled like swine" without thanks to the giver and without sense of the nature of the gift[2]. By John the word is thus reproachfully used, not in his own words but (which is more weighty) in the words of Jesus to condemn their unintelligent greediness: "Ye seek me, not because ye saw signs, but because ye ate of the loaves and *were filled [like cattle with fodder]*[3]." The words that follow enjoin "*labour*"— and labour like that of the husbandman, which distinguishes

---

[1] Philipp. iv. 12 μεμύημαι καὶ χορτάζεσθαι καὶ πεινᾶν. On this, Lightfoot, while admitting that it was originally not applied to men except in a depreciatory sense, adds that "in the later language it has lost this sense...being applied commonly to men and directly opposed to πεινᾶν, e.g. Matth. v. 6. On χορτάζειν see Sturz *de Dial. Mac.* p. 200."

But Sturz *does not give a single instance where a serious writer of literary Greek, uninfluenced by the Gospels, applies it to men without depreciation.* The Synoptic Gospels prove nothing except that they were influenced by the usage of the Psalms. Epictetus always uses it of men in a bad sense and so does Plutarch (ii. 616 A) in the single instance given in the Index. The first ten volumes of the *Oxyrhynchan Papyri* and the first four volumes of the *Berlin Urkunde* do not contain the word in any sense.

[2] Goodspeed shews that the only Christian instance of χορτάζω up to A.D. 150 is Clem. Rom. § 59 τοὺς πλανωμένους τοῦ λαοῦ σου ἐπίστρεψον, χόρτασον τοὺς πεινῶντας. But this (like Polyc. *Phil.* § 6) alludes to Ezek. xxxiv. 16 πεπλανημένον ἐπιστρέψω...καὶ βοσκήσω, which follows *ib.* 15 "I myself will feed my sheep." This indicates that Clement uses the word metaphorically in a prayer to God to "satisfy" His hungering "sheep."

[3] Jn vi. 26. This is Jn's only instance of χορτάζω.

man from cattle: "Labour not for the food that perisheth, but for the food that abideth unto eternal life[1]."

In conclusion, the apparent attitude of the other Evangelists to Mark's peculiar tradition "on the green grass," may be roughly described as follows. Matthew omits "green," possibly regarding it as a mere picturesque epithet. Luke omits the whole phrase, perhaps as being of doubtful meaning, and perhaps because, looking at Mark's picture from a western point of view as an expanse of long grass not yet cut, he thought that five thousand men, lying down on it, would do mischief such as Jesus would not have sanctioned. John, omitting "green," suggests that it may have been "hay," not "grass." Also he suggests the same thing by slightly altering the context. For he does not speak of "*the* grass" as a natural element in the scene (like "*the* trees," "*the* forest," etc.). He suggests that there *happened to be a great quantity of hay lying about in swaths in that district*[2]. If that was, or was supposed to be, the case, it would be an occasion on which Jesus might naturally be supposed to say to the multitude, somewhat as in the Sermon on the Mount, "*consider the grass of the field* how God provideth it with clothing." This, in Hebrew or Aramaic, might be expressed by "*set [your minds] on the grass of the field.*" But this is liable to be confused with "*set yourselves on*, i.e. *lie down on*, the grass of the field[3]."

---

[1] Jn vi. 27, on which (and on ἐργάζεσθε, meaning agricultural labour) see *Son* **3017, 3421** *f.* The words accord with the above-mentioned prayer of Adam to God that he might be allowed to work for bread instead of browsing on grass.

[2] If the Passover was (Jn vi. 4) "at hand," hay-making might naturally be supposed to be going on. Nonnus seems to imply "happened to be" by τις in his paraphrase of Jn vi. 10 ἦν δέ τις αὐτόθι χόρτος ἀπείριτος. The multitude (he says) took their meal "*on the top of the hay*," ὑψόθι χόρτου. "Each man was leaning as it were against a party-wall all of them reclining in rows," ἕκαστος ἐρείδετο γείτονι τοίχῳ κεκλιμένοι στοιχηδόν. That is, they leaned against the "swaths" covering a widely extended space.

[3] See Gesen. p. 963 on Judg. xix. 30 where the Heb. has "*Set ye for yourselves* (לכם) *upon it*"=R.V. "*consider of it*," LXX (Swete) θέσθε

This would give, as the original, a tradition somewhat resembling the spiritual interpretation of Origen and Jerome, but with an important difference. It would be, not "Set yourselves *above*, or *against*, the grass of the field, as if it were an enemy to be conquered," but "*Set yourselves [to think] over it* in order to learn the lesson that it teaches[1]."

§ 25. "*By hundreds and by fifties*," in *Mark*[2]

Mark is the only one of the Evangelists that mentions "hundreds" in this connection. What he has in view is five thousand men in a hundred parallel rows, each row containing fifty men[3]. If he had previously mentioned five thousand as

ὑμῖν αὐτοὶ ἐπ᾽ αὐτήν..., Targ. "set your hearts upon it." The Gk varies greatly. Field reads αὐτοῖς. And θέσθε ὑμῖν αὐτοῖς ἐπ᾽ αὐτήν might be supposed to be an error for θέσθε ὑμᾶς αὐτοὺς ἐπὶ αὐτήν.

[1] Comp. 4 Esdr. ix. 24—27 "'Ibis in campum florum, ubi domus non est aedificata, et manduces (*sic*) solummodo de floribus campi....' Et sedi ibi in floribus et de herbis agri manducavi...in saturitatem... et *ego discumbebam supra foenum*." The meaning is obscure, but it is probable that "*reclining on the hay*" has a metaphorical meaning. The thought in the context (ix. 29—37) does not appear to be Christian. It speaks of the "sowing" of "the Law" in "the wilderness." A receptacle (it says) remains as a rule when its contents perish. But Israel, the receptacle of the Law, perishes while the Law abides. This is (in word at all events) opposed to Jn xii. 24 "except a grain of wheat...die, it abideth by itself alone."

[2] Mk vi. 40   Mt. om.   Lk. ix. 15   Jn vi. 10

καὶ ἀνέπεσαν πρασιαὶ πρασιαί, κατὰ ἑκατὸν καὶ κατὰ πεντήκοντα.   καὶ ἐποίησαν οὕτως καὶ κατέκλιναν ἅπαντας.   ἀνέπεσαν οὖν οἱ ἄνδρες (or, ἀνέπεσαν οὖν, ἄνδρες) τὸν ἀριθμὸν ὡς πεντακισχίλιοι.

In the preceding verse, Luke (ix. 14), after stating the total number himself, has represented Jesus as dictating to His disciples the number *in each group*, κατακλίνατε αὐτοὺς κλισίας ὡσεὶ ἀνὰ πεντήκοντα. The total number is not specified by Mark and Matthew till the conclusion of the narrative (Mk vi. 44, Mt. xiv. 21).

[3] "Rows." This is the word suggested by Mark's "garden-borders." But the reader must be prepared to substitute "files" for "rows," if it appears later on that the original contemplated a military arrangement in which each "row" or "file" was composed

---

the total (as Luke has done) he need not have mentioned "hundreds," for "five thousand [arranged] *by fifties*" (which, in effect, is what Luke says) implies "fifty *hundreds*." But Mark has not yet mentioned "five thousand." Moreover he desires his readers to see the multitude in regular array—geometrically, so to speak—in oblong "garden-borders," as has been pointed out above. Hence his peculiar tradition—in effect, "a hundred by fifty."

It is not surprising that Matthew omits the Marcan phrase, for it would interfere with Matthew's addition of "women and children[1]." But it is, if not surprising, at least worth considering, that Luke, desiring perhaps to condense Mark, chooses to omit "hundred" rather than "*fifty*." Is there any indication that he may have been influenced by Jewish traditions about companies of "*fifty*," in connection with Israel—either Israel in the wilderness receiving the Law of God, or Israel as God's army marshalled for war?

For poetic or prophetic Jewish traditions about companies of fifty we naturally turn to comments on the words of Isaiah about "the judge and the prophet...*the captain of fifty*[2]." Jerome dilates on the mystical significance of "*fifty*," in connection with "repentance," "Pentecost," etc. He does this (he says) because the "captain (princeps)" of repentance is Christ, and he quotes the words of the Jews to Jesus "thou

---

of 50 men. See L. and S. on στοῖχος, "esp. of persons standing one behind another," and "of soldiers, *a file*."

[1] Also it might mean "a hundred at a time and fifty at a time." Comp. 1 K. xviii. 4 "a hundred...and hid them *fifty* [*at a time*] (κατὰ πεντήκοντα)," or "*fifty in one place and fifty in another*." See *Sanhedr.* 39 *b*. Rashi says that there were "two caves." Origen (*Comm. Matth.* xi. 3) says that the ranks were hundreds and fifties "since there are *different ranks* (τάγματα) *of those who need the nourishment* [*that comes*] *from Jesus*, because not all are nourished by equal *logoi* (τοῖς ἴσοις λόγοις)"—an explanation of which the chief value is that it proves that he considered some explanation of Mark's twofold numbering to be necessary.

[2] Is. iii. 2—3.

art not yet *fifty years old*," as indicating their refusal to accept
Him as their "*captain of fifty*[1]." Whence did Jerome receive
this explanation of "*captain of fifty*"? Rashi and Ibn Ezra
say nothing about it. One of the most poetic treatises of the
Talmud says "Do not read '*captain of fifty*,' but '*captain of
fifths*[2].' This is he who knows how to handle matters in the
five sections of the Law." But it adds another explanation
"An interpreter is not appointed over the congregation who
is less than *fifty years old*[3]." This accords with Jerome's above-
quoted application of "*captain of fifty*."

Another Jewish tradition, also highly poetic and mystical,
after quoting Zechariah and Jeremiah on "The Branch" and
adding "This is the Messiah," represents God as saying "I will
set up a '*captain over fifty*,'" implying that this "*captain*,"
too, is the Messiah. Then it numbers the books of the Bible,
and the divisions of some of the books, and makes out the total
to be "*fifty*." Thus "*captain of fifty*," without any change
of "*fifty*" to "*fifths*," is made to mean the same thing as
"captain of *fifths*" above, that is, "Master of Scripture[4]."

These Jewish variations of interpretation are partly caused
by the fact that, in Hebrew, "*fifty*" is the plural of "*five*"
and easily confused with "*five*," and partly by the fact that
the word, when used as the plural participle of a verb, means
"*arranged in battle array*[5]." A notorious instance of such

---

[1] In some of these remarks Jerome resembles Origen (on
Numb. iv. 3, 47, Lomm. x. 35, 41), but Origen does not there quote
Is. iii. 3 (nor Jn viii. 57, perhaps, anywhere).

[2] "*Fifths*" (Levy ii. 78 *b*) a name given to the five books of the
Pentateuch, and the five books of the Psalms.

[3] *Chag.* 14 *a*.

[4] *Numb. r.* on Numb. xvi. 35 (Wü. p. 451).

[5] See Gesen. 332 *b*. An explanation suggests itself from "quincunx," *e.g.* Caes. *Bell. Gall.* vii. 73 "obliquis ordinibus *in quin-
cuncem dispositis*." Gesen., however, does not offer this explanation,
but suggests doubtfully (1) "Ar. *army*," and (2) "army as composed
of *five parts*" (not explaining what the "*five parts*" are). The

confusion occurs in the description of the going forth of Israel from Egypt, "And the children of Israel went up *arranged-in-battle-array* out of the land of Egypt[1]." Here R.V. has "*armed*"; A.V. "*harnessed*" (i.e. "*in armour*") in text, but "*by five in a rank*" in margin; LXX "*in the fifth generation*"; Aquila "*in armour*"; Symmachus "*hoplites*," i.e. "*heavy-armed soldiers*"; Theodotion "*on the fifth day*[2]." Besides these variations, there are others in Jewish tradition. Onkelos adopts "*armed*," and the second Jerusalem Targum "*armed with good works.*" But the first Targum has "*every one with five children.*" Rashi, who accepts "*armed*," adds "Others say '*the fifth part*,' because four-fifths died in the darkness of Egypt." There are other interpretations of all kinds, some of which take the word as meaning "*fifty*," or even "*five hundred*[3]."

---

quincunx is so called from its resemblance to the arrangement of the five spots on dice $\overset{* \; *}{\underset{* \; *}{*}}$. The Heb. occurs only in Exod. xiii. 18, Josh. i. 14, iv. 12, Judg. vii. 11 (but perhaps it should be read also in Numb. xxxii. 17).

[1] Exod. xiii. 18.

[2] Exod. xiii. 18, Field agmine instructo, LXX πέμπτῃ γενεᾷ, Aq. ἐνωπλισμένοι, Symm. ὁπλῖται, Theod. πεμπταίζοντες—which Field illustrates from the medical use of τριταιαΐζω and τεταρταΐζω, to suffer from a "tertian" or a "quartan" fever. Does Theod. regard the Israelites as being delivered from disease (comp. Deut. xxviii. 60 "the diseases of Egypt")?

Jerome, quoted by Field, defends Aquila's rendering, but says "Licet pro eo quod nos *armati* diximus...*instructi*, sive *muniti*, propter supellectilem qua Ægyptios spoliaverunt, possit intelligi." He seems to see the difficulty of supposing that the Israelites had "armour" before they took it from the Egyptians who were drowned in the Red Sea (as Josephus says *Ant.* ii. 16. 6).

[3] *J. Sabb.* vi. 4 has "*with five kinds of arms*," *Mechilt.* ad loc. also has this, but adds (2) "*ready*" or "*alert*," (3) "*one out of five*," (4) "*one out of fifty*," (5) "*one out of five hundred.*" *Pesikt.* (Piska x. Wü. p. 110) gives, as the last of five explanations, "R. Jose said that they went forth '*to five generations* (*zu fünf Geschlechtern*)'"— apparently including great-great-grandparents with the babes descended from them (not, as LXX, "in the fifth generation [from the Coming of Israel into Egypt]").

It is reasonable to suppose that poetic Jewish Christian traditions describing one of Christ's Eucharists, or Common Meals of Thanksgiving, accompanying the Giving of the Word of God, might lay stress (as Philo repeatedly does in describing the meals of the *Therapeutae*) on the order and harmonious regularity pervading the assembly[1], and that this might be expressed in language that alluded to the Going Forth of Israel from Egypt to receive the Bread of the Law, as well as to narratives about the actual giving of bread by Elisha, or about the giving of manna. The language of Paul—like the language of Exodus—often takes a military aspect. Mostly he connects it with the single Christian warrior. But he appears to be thinking of Christians "in the ranks," when he tells the Colossians that, though he is absent from them, he rejoices to call to view the "[soldier-like] order and solid-formation" that characterize them as believers in Christ[2].

If at one or more of what we may call Christ's camp-meetings He commanded the people to be arranged in groups for the purpose of order, it would be natural that the group should be "fifty" (rather than the Latin military unit of a hundred). This would of course not imply military intention or anything except Jewish custom. But when the story afterwards came to be told in Christian traditions, Greeks would not be able to see any reason for grouping "according to fifty." It might be explained to them that it meant "in military order"—for example, "*according to the pattern of the quincunx*"—and that, as there were five thousand men, and fifty centuries, the division might be indifferently described as into a hundred fifties or fifty centuries. Mark thus inserts both numbers. But to some it might occur that vines also

---

[1] See Philo ii. 481 "before the lying down (κατακλίσεως), standing *consecutively*, [*row by row*], *in order* (ἑξῆς κατὰ στοῖχον ἐν κόσμῳ)," *ib.* 483 ἐν αἷς ἐδήλωσα τάξεσι...ἐν κόσμῳ, *ib.* 484 κατὰ τάξεις ἐν κόσμῳ.

[2] Coloss. ii. 5 τάξιν καὶ στερέωμα, comp. Philo on τάξεις above quoted.

were habitually planted "*according to the quincunx*," and that groups of that kind (*prasiai* or *symposia*) were better suited to the scene of a Christian love-feast than companies of soldiers. Hence might spring the other details in Mark's version. To Matthew all these detailed illustrations, especially those based on the military meaning of "fifty," would naturally seem doubtful in view of the presence of "women and children" whom he (alone of the Evangelists) adds to the five thousand[1]. Luke follows Mark as to the traditional "*fifty*," but appears to regard all the rest of Mark's context as superfluous.

Since Luke does not reject the Marcan "*fifty*" and can hardly be said to reject the Marcan "hundred"—because he virtually implies it by his context—there is no ground for expecting, as to these numerical details, any Johannine Intervention. But it has been pointed out above that John does appear to intervene as to the Marcan *symposia*, so as to emphasize an interpretation of these "companies" alien from military thought. Consistently with this non-military aspect, John also rejects the Mark-Luke numbers of the "companies." We cannot say that he does it for Matthew's reason—because "women and children" are to be added. For John does not mention them. Perhaps he does it because this division of the five thousand into small companies of men—as a Roman army might be divided into centuries under centurions, or a Jewish army into fifties under "captains of fifty"—introduces a kind of intermediate agency between each of the five thousand and the One Lord. This intermediation John dislikes. In his Gospel, Jesus alone distributes the bread to each—as we shall see later on—not through the instrumentality of His disciples, but with His own hands.

---

[1] Mt. xiv. 21, also xv. 38.

§ 26. *"Taking," "blessing," and "looking up to heaven*[1]*"*

(1) "Taking" occurs in all the six narratives, with the same Greek verb, and mostly as a participle[2]. Its meaning will depend on the place or person whence the loaves are "taken." If they are on the spot, "taking" would appear to mean a solemn and emblematic taking up in the hands, such as might denote a "taking up," or "offering," to God, or an appropriation of the food to God, as though the breaker of bread said to God in the name of the company "We bless thee for *this*, which we lift up[3]."

---

[1] Mk vi. 41 (R.V.)	Mt. xiv. 19 (R.V.)	Lk. ix. 16 (R.V.)	Jn vi. 11 (R.V.)
And he took (λαβών) the five loaves and the two fishes, and looking up to heaven, he blessed, and brake the loaves; and he gave to the disciples to set before them; and the two fishes divided he among them all.	...And he took (λαβών) the five loaves, and the two fishes, and looking up to heaven, he blessed, and brake and gave the loaves to the disciples, and the disciples to the multitudes.	And he took (λαβών) the five loaves and the two fishes, and looking up to heaven, he blessed them, and brake; and gave to the disciples to set before the multitude.	Jesus therefore took the loaves; and having given thanks, he distributed to them that were set down; likewise also of the fishes as much as they would.

"Brake" in Mk vi. 41, Lk. ix. 16 is κατέκλασεν, see § 27.

In the Four Thousand, as in the Johannine Five Thousand, "give thanks" is substituted for "bless."

Mk viii. 6—7 (R.V.)	Mt. xv. 36 (R.V.)
(6) ...And he took (λαβών) the seven loaves, and having given thanks, he brake, and gave to his disciples, to set before them; and they set them before the multitude. (7) And they had a few small fishes: and having blessed them, he commanded to set these also before them.	And he took the seven loaves and the fishes; and he gave thanks and brake, and gave to the disciples, and the disciples to the multitudes.

[2] John in the Five Thousand, and Matthew in the Four Thousand, have ἔλαβεν, not λαβών.

[3] Schöttgen on Mt. xiv. 19 says "*Sumptio* ista, quae hic et alibi memoratur, actus est peculiaris patris familias," and quotes *Sabb.* 117 *b* נקט (Goldschmidt "hielt"). But Schlatter on Jn vi. 11

The first Biblical instance of "take," in connection with sacrifice, is where God says to Abraham "*Take for me* a heifer," and other creatures, and it is added that Abraham "*took for him* all these...¹." Philo comments on the pregnancy of "*Take for me,*" which implies, he says, first, that we have nothing good of our own except that which we "*take*" from God; secondly, that we are to "*take*" it *for Him*, as being the loan or deposit that He has placed with us, for which we must give account². He also comments on the paradox implied in human "giving," since, "strictly speaking, we merely *take* (or, *receive*) but are only popularly said to give³."

In doctrine of this kind there is sometimes difficulty in passing from a Greek translation back to a Hebrew original because the same Hebrew word, as a rule, represents both "take" and "receive⁴." But we find Paul, as well as Philo,

---

quotes *Siphri* נטל on Numb. vii. 6 "Mose nimmt sie (נוטלם)."
Hor. Heb. (on Mt. xxvi. 26) quotes, from the Passover Service, "He *takes up* the unleavened bread in his hand, and saith, 'We eat this unleavened bread...'...then...*taking* two loaves, he breaks one," and (p. 352, from *Berach.* 51 *a*) "he *takes up* (נוטלו) the cup in both hands, but puts it into his right hand; he *lifts it* from the table a hand's breadth and...fixes his eyes upon it, etc."

Λαβών, or ἔλαβεν, also occurs in the Synoptic and Pauline accounts of the Lord's Supper. Lk. xxii. 17 δεξάμενος ποτήριον εὐχαριστήσας εἶπεν is exceptional. Λαμβάνει occurs in Jn xxi. 13 "Jesus cometh and *taketh* the loaf and giveth to them...."

¹ Gen. xv. 9—10. Λάβε μοι (A.V. and R.V. "take me")....ἔλαβεν δὲ αὐτῷ (A.V. "took unto him," R.V. "took him"). Onkelos has "offer *coram me*," Jer. Targ. "accipe *mihi* oblationes et offer *coram me*."

² Philo i. 487 λάβε, μὴ σεαυτῷ, δανεῖον δὲ ἢ παρακαταθήκην νομίσας τὸ δοθέν.

³ Philo i. 490 κυρίως μὲν λαμβάνομεν, καταχρηστικῶς δὲ διδόναι λεγόμεθα. In *Quaest. ad Genes.* it is said, *ad loc.* "Pro illo *Ferto mihi*, optime dictum est *Accipe mihi*."

⁴ Heb. לקח = λαμβάνω more than 800 times, δέχομαι 26 times. The total number of instances of δέχομαι in *Oxf. Conc.* correctly representing a Heb. original is only 42. The LXX throws too great a burden on λαμβάνω and too little on δέχομαι. Luke alone

inculcating that we have nothing that we did not "*take*," that is, "*receive*," and, in the Acts, reminding the Ephesians of "the words of the Lord Jesus, how he said that it was more blessed to give than to *take*[1]." The testimony of these two early writers, when combined with the use of the Greek "*take*" in the Pentateuch and in the Synoptic and Pauline accounts of the Eucharist, makes it probable that "take" has a ritual meaning also in the Gospel miracles of feeding, and that the Evangelists regarded its meaning there as akin to its meaning later on in the Last Supper.

Passing to the Fourth Gospel we find that the "taking" is the one point—out of the three mentioned at the beginning of this section—in which it verbally agrees with the Synoptists. But, by introducing "a lad" on the spot as "having" the loaves and fishes, it introduces a possible difference as to the nature of the "taking"—leaving us in doubt whether Jesus receives them as an offering from the "lad," or takes them from the "lad" as the property of the disciples. There is an indefiniteness here like that in the Feeding of the Seven Disciples who "when they got out upon the land, see a fire of coals there and a fish laid thereon and a loaf[2]." The "loaf" that they "see" reminds us of what Elijah "looked" at when he "looked, and behold, there was at his head a cake baken on the coals." Elijah is bidden by "an angel" to "arise and eat[3]." In the Feeding of the Seven, no "angel" is mentioned, but a supernatural origin of the food is clearly indicated; and then the "taking" of it

---

uses δέχομαι in Eucharistic narrative (xxii. 17) δεξάμενος ποτήριον (Mk-Mt. λαβών). Delitzsch renders it by the same word (לקח) as he uses to represent the Eucharistic λαμβάνω.

[1] 1 Cor. iv. 7, Acts xx. 35.

[2] Jn xxi. 9.

[3] 1 K. xix. 5 (Heb.) "Behold an angel (LXX 'some one (τις)') touched him, and said unto him, Arise and eat." This Hebrew word "coals" occurs only in 1 K. xix. 6 and Is. vi. 6 of Isaiah's preparation for the work of prophecy (Gesen. 954 a).

by Jesus is described thus: "Jesus *cometh* and *taketh* the loaf and giveth to them—and the fish likewise[1]."

It has been shewn above that the "lad" might well correspond to Moses. Now the Prologue of the Fourth Gospel, after saying that the Word, or Only Begotten, was full of grace and truth, and that "from his *fulness* we all received," explains the reception thus: "For the Law was given through Moses; the grace and the truth" [of God, whether latent and included in the Law of Israel, or latent and included in the laws of conscience and human nature] "came into being through Jesus Christ[2]." "The Law" is expressed by the five loaves and the fishes. "Moses" is expressed by "the lad." The "fulness" that brings forth "the grace and the truth" is expressed by that multiplying power of the Saviour which results in food for five thousand souls with a superabundance of what Mark calls "the fulnesses of twelve baskets."

(2) "Blessing" is not used by John, who substitutes "giving thanks," expressed by the Greek *eucharistein*, familiar to us in "Eucharist." One reason for this is indicated by the variations in the versions of Mark and Luke where "blessed *them*" is altered to "blesses *over them*[3]." Jews regarded food as God's gift, *over* which, or *for* which, men were bound to bless the Giver; but they did not bless the food[4]. On the other

---

[1] Jn xxi. 13 ἔρχεται Ἰησοῦς καὶ λαμβάνει τὸν ἄρτον καὶ δίδωσιν αὐτοῖς. The impression left on the reader is that Jesus "comes" to each disciple separately, and "takes" and "gives" the loaf to each separately, and that there is no "breaking." The whole loaf is perhaps regarded as given to each, being miraculously reproduced. *Acts of John* § 8 uses "distributed" or "divided" of a single loaf, thus, τὸν δὲ αὐτοῦ [ἄρτον] εὐλογῶν διεμέριζεν ἡμῖν.

[2] Jn i. 14—17, on which see *Joh. Gr.* Index.

[3] In Mk viii. 7 εὐλογήσας αὐτὰ εἶπεν καὶ ταῦτα παρατιθέναι, Delitzsch omits "*them*," SS has "and *upon* them also *having blessed*," D has εὐχαριστήσας εἶπεν καὶ αὐτοὺς ἐκέλευσεν παρατειθέναι (sic). In Lk. ix. 16 εὐλόγησεν αὐτούς, Delitzsch, D, *a*, and *b* have "*blessed upon them*," and SS has "*blessed upon them* (or, *upon it*)."

[4] Gesen. 139 gives only 1 S. ix. 13 as instance of a priest "blessing"

hand, when God Himself is said for the first time in Scripture to "bless," He blesses the fishes and the birds and bids them "multiply." Also when He blesses "bread," or "fruit," or other articles of food, it signifies that He gives increase as well as wholesomeness[1]. Hence in Christ's Feeding of the Multitudes, where loaves and fishes were assumed to be multiplied, it is readily intelligible that some Evangelists would regard the word "blessing" as being used in a special and divine sense, so that it implied multiplying, while others would regard it as meaning the usual "blessing" before a meal in the ordinary way.

One way of avoiding ambiguity would be to substitute "give thanks" for "bless." In the Feeding of the Four Thousand Matthew does this, while Mark has, first, *"gave thanks and brake"* about the loaves, and secondly, *"blessed them* [i.e. *the fishes*]." It is not surprising that John almost entirely avoids the word "bless," as being a technical Jewish term[2]. Origen says that "when men '*bless*' God it stands for '*praising*' or '*thanking*' God[3]." In Leviticus and elsewhere, where LXX has "*praise*," Aquila has *eucharistia*, or "*thanksgiving*[4]." The latter includes a sense of gratefulness and

a sacrificial meal, and here Rashi says that the Targum has "*over* the food." But Breithaupt points out that in the extant text of the Targum, "*over*" is omitted. See Levy *Ch.* ii. 293, taking פרס as "spread out [the hands]," but Breithaupt takes it as "break."

[1] Gen. i. 22, Exod. xxiii. 25, Deut. vii. 13.

[2] John uses no form of εὐλογέω except in xii. 13 εὐλογημένος—the cry of the multitude, perhaps regarded as the fickle multitude. Philo (i. 453), quoting Gen. xii. 2 (on which see Rashi), says that εὐλογημένος "is reckoned along with (παραριθμεῖται) *the* [*vain*] *opinions and reports of the multitude* (ταῖς τῶν πολλῶν δόξαις τε καὶ φήμαις)," but that εὐλογητός is reckoned "along with *that which is in truth praiseworthy* (τῷ πρὸς ἀλήθειαν εὐλογητῷ)."

[3] Origen (Lat.) *Comm. Rom.* ix. 14 (on Rom. xii. 14).

[4] Lev. vii. 12 "If he offer it for (עַל) a *thanksgiving* (תודה)," περὶ αἰνέσεως, Aq. ἐπὶ εὐχαριστίας. Εὐχαριστία recurs several times in Aquila, especially in the Psalms. But neither Aquila nor canon. LXX uses εὐχαριστέω.

spontaneousness, not so manifest in "praise"; and the latter, *eucharistein*, is the term adopted by John in the Feeding of the Five Thousand as a substitute for the Synoptic "bless[1]."

(3) "Looking up to heaven" is expressed in the Synoptists by a word that often means "*recovering sight*[2]." John substitutes "lifting up his eyes[3]"; but places it, not where the Synoptists do, before the breaking and distribution, but at the outset of the narrative, where Jesus "seeth that a great multitude is coming to him," that is, sees the vision of the coming of the spiritual seed of Abraham which was to constitute the Church. The action, both here and in the two other Johannine instances of it, seems to imply a looking up to heaven, not so much to bring down a blessing as rather to behold, and to exult in, and to fulfil, the glory of God. At the grave of Lazarus, when Jesus "lifted his eyes above," He utters, not prayer but thanks, "Father, I give thanks to thee

---

[1] "*Bless*" might be substituted for "*give thanks*" in translating from Hebrew. The Heb. ידה, "*acknowledge* [*God's greatness, glory, kindness,* etc.]" is rendered εὐλογέω in Isaiah xii. 1 (LXX) εὐλογῶ σε, κύριε, xxxviii. 19 οἱ ζῶντες εὐλογήσουσίν σε (and in effect a third instance occurs in Is. xxv. 3 εὐλογήσουσίν σε (ירא mistaken for ידה)). The Heb. ידה is given by Delitzsch in Mt. xi. 25, Lk. x. 21 ἐξομολογοῦμαί σοι, πάτερ, R.V. "I *thank* (marg. or, *praise*) thee, O Father," where John would probably have written, as in the words uttered at the grave of Lazarus, (xi. 41) εὐχαριστῶ σοι. In wrestling with death for the sake of Lazarus there was an act of sacrifice which some would have called the subject of prayer rather than of a thankoffering. But Jesus "thanks" God for the power to perform it. In the Johannine Feeding of the Five Thousand, Jesus is regarded not merely as breaking bread and blessing God over it as at a meal, but also as offering up a thankoffering to the Father for giving power to the Son to offer Himself to, and for, the multitude. They do not accept Him; nevertheless Jesus, looking into the future, might see cause for *eucharistia* as in Mt.-Lk. referred to above, "I thank thee, O Father... that thou didst hide these things from the wise and understanding and didst reveal them unto babes."

[2] Ἀναβλέπω, used in no other sense by John (ix. 11, 15, 18, comp. Mk viii. 24, x. 51, etc.).

[3] Jn vi. 5 ἐπάρας οὖν τοὺς ὀφθαλμοὺς....

that thou hast heard me[1]." Before the Last Discourse, though there is prayer, there is also a vision of "the hour" of glory: "Lifting up his eyes to heaven he said, Father, the hour is come. Glorify thy Son that the Son may glorify thee[2]."

§ 27. *"Breaking in pieces" or "breaking"*

We now approach a subject of unusual difficulty and complexity—complicated partly by verbal ambiguities, partly by early Christian custom arising out of Jewish custom, and partly by Christian doctrinal considerations and applications of Hebrew prophecy—the "breaking" of bread in the miracles of Feeding.

In the Feeding of the Five Thousand (but not in that of the Four Thousand) Mark emphasizes this act by using a compound verb that means literally "break down," "snap off," or (metaphorically) "break down in spirit[3]." But it is apparently used by him to mean "break in pieces." It occurs but once in LXX and is non-existent in Christian writers of the first century and a half. Yet Luke follows Mark in using it here, though it occurs nowhere else in N.T., and though the uncompounded verb is quite frequent (as also is the noun) to denote Christian "breaking of bread." Mark may have desired to shew that this was *not* an ordinary "breaking of bread," but that Jesus broke a loaf into minute parts each one of which was magnified. Luke may have followed Mark for the same reason.

At all events Luke does follow Mark, and this is one of

---

[1] Jn xi. 41.   [2] Jn xvii. 1.

[3] Mk vi. 41, Lk. ix. 16 κατέκλασεν. The word is not in Goodspeed's Concordances. In LXX, it occurs only in Ezek. xix. 12 (Heb.) "she was *plucked up* in fury," κατεκλάσθη ἐν θυμῷ. It occurs also in Job v. 4 (Symm.) Heb. *"they are crushed* in the gate." Steph. *Thes.* does not give any instance where the word must necessarily be interpreted "break in pieces," but a great number where it has a different meaning.

several cases where, when Luke agrees with Mark, John appears to disagree, or at all events tacitly dissents. For John omits all mention of any kind of "breaking." By this course he avoids such a question as "Were the fishes broken as well as the loaves?" Mark implies that they were not. For he (and he alone) specially inserts "*the loaves*" after the mention of "*breaking*," and then he (alone) adds "he divided the two fishes to all," apparently implying that, although they were "divided" in the sense of "distributed," the fishes were *not* "broken[1]."

It may be suggested that John had also another reason, based on the axiom that the Bread, or the Fish, is to be regarded as One and as diffusing unity among those who partake of it. In accordance with this thought, he (and he alone of the Evangelists) quotes, as a prophecy about the Crucifixion, the precept concerning the Paschal Lamb, "A bone of him shall not be broken[2]." Later on, in the presence of the Seven Disciples, Jesus "cometh, and taketh the loaf and giveth to them, and the fish likewise"; but no mention is made of "*breaking*[3]." The hypothesis that John was influenced by a mystical view of the unity of the Eucharistic food is confirmed by what Philo says concerning the dividing, and the reuniting, of the parts of the whole burnt offering which "from one, becomes many, and from many becomes one[4]." It is also favoured by the fact that John

---

[1] See the next section, where it will appear that Matthew obscures this difference, and Luke omits it altogether. The distinction is also clear in Mk viii. 6—7 καὶ λαβὼν τοὺς ἑπτὰ ἄρτους εὐχαριστήσας ἔκλασεν...καὶ εἶχαν ἰχθύδια ὀλίγα· καὶ εὐλογήσας αὐτά (without any mention of breaking in the case of the fishes)....

[2] Jn xix. 36 quoting Exod. xii. 46, Numb. ix. 12, comp. 1 Cor. v. 7.

[3] Jn xxi. 13. Contrast with this Lk. xxiv. 30—35 "Having taken the loaf he blessed [God] (εὐλόγησεν) and having broken [it] he offered [freely] (ἐπεδίδου) to them...how he was known by them in the breaking (τῇ κλάσει) of the loaf."

[4] Philo ii. 241. This is preceded (*ib.* 240), and followed, by

(alone) tells us that in the parting of Christ's garments by the soldiers, His "coat"—a type of the Church—escaped "rending," and that in the miraculous draught of fishes, the "net"—another type of the Church—"was not rent[1]."

That John would have been influenced by motives of this kind is very probable. But it is not probable (according to our experience of his Gospel hitherto) that he would have omitted this ancient tradition of "breaking" if he had not believed it to be either erroneous or, at all events, likely to give a wrong spiritual impression. There are reasons for thinking that confusion arose in early times from various interpretations of Isaiah's precept rendered by our Versions "*Deal* (Heb. *pâras*) thy bread to the hungry[2]." *Pâras* is nowhere rendered "deal" except in this passage. It means "*break in half*," and here, "*break in half* thy loaf for the hungry[3]." Ibn Ezra takes it thus. But the Talmud records a tradition that the word ought to be written as *pâras(h)*[4]. Then it might mean "separate"

---

mentions of εὐχαριστία, *e.g.* ib. 243 ὅταν βουληθῇς σῇ διανοίᾳ εὐχαριστῆσαι θεῷ περὶ γενέσεως κόσμου τὴν εὐχαριστίαν....

[1] Jn xix. 24, xxi. 11 using σχίζω in both cases. Luke in his narrative of the Draught of Fishes says (v. 6) "the nets began to be torn asunder (διερήσσετο)."

[2] Is. lviii. 7 פרס (but Targ. פרנס "*sustentabis* pane tuo"). Ibn Ezra says "it means here to break a loaf of bread" (and he compares Lam. iv. 4 "no man *breaketh* (פרש not פרס) to them"). Jerome *ad loc.* says "frange...non plures panes sed unum panem." "*Deal*" means "distribute"—but does not give the full Hebrew sense. Modern emendations and modern suggestions as to what the text of Isaiah originally was, however interesting and valuable they may be, do not concern us when we are endeavouring to approximate to Jewish interpretations of the passage in the first century.

[3] Gesen. 828 *a* "break in two," "divide" (of the divided hoof) (Lev. xi. 3 etc.). On Jerem. xvi. 7 "neither shall men *break* [bread] for them (להם)," Gesen. suggests להם "bread," instead of להם.

[4] *Baba Bathra* 9 *a*, Goldschmidt renders this "forsche nach und dann gib ihm." He adds in a note that many MSS have פרש, but that the Masora on Numb. iv. 7 expressly says that פרס is the right reading. Gesen. 831 gives פרש = "spread out, spread," but פרש

or "spread out." In this form it might be applied to the "spreading out" of the hands in blessing, or to the "separation" of Scripture into sections, or to its "explanation" in plain words, or to any technical "separation" in Jewish ritual[1].

The Hebrew *pâras* (used by Delitzsch in Christ's Miracles of Feeding) is particularly appropriate to meals given willingly

---

"make distinct, declare, New Heb. separate oneself, separate, explain."

[1] The authorities, and even the texts, so differ as to the terms פרם, פרשׂ, and פרשׁ that it is impossible here to do more than refer to what is said about them by Levy, Levy *Ch. sub voc.*, by *Hor. Heb.* on κλάσας in the Gospels, and by Schöttgen (in the Gospels and on 2 Tim. ii. 15). Wetstein says practically nothing. The Targumists avoid פרם in Is. lviii. 7, and פרשׁ in Lam. iv. 4, but they retain פרם in Jerem. xvi. 7 "Neither shall men *break* [*bread*] for them in mourning," A.V. "*tear* [*themselves*] for them in mourning."

On this last passage Rashi has a note obscure, but most instructive, indicating the possibility of confusing פרם in Heb. "breaking a loaf in half" with some technical use of פרם in Aramaic, perhaps "spreading out the hands," referring to a benediction. He says that *pâras*, in Jeremiah, "significat fractionem" as in Dan. v. 25, 28 "*u-pharsin*," i.e. "*and divided*" (*pharsin* being a form of *pâras*). Then he adds "For with food did they refresh the mourners in the street, and they did *spread out for them that Benediction* [which is called] 'He that bringeth forth' (eisque explicabant benedictionem illam, המוציא)." This refers to the words of the Benediction pronounced by the father of the family, or the principal Rabbi, over the breaking of bread at a meal: "Blessed art thou, O Lord our God, Lord of the world, '*Thou that bringest forth* [*food from the earth*].'"

Rashi proceeds, "Jonathan istud: 'nam ipse יברך,' id est, 'benedicet convivio,' Chaldaice vertit 'nam ipse פרים,' id est, 'frangit cibum.'" This mention of "Jonathan" refers to the Targum of "Jonathan" on 1 S. ix. 13 "he [*i.e.* Samuel] *doth bless* (יברך) the sacrifice," where the Targum has (lit.) "*doth break* (פרים) the food," which Rashi renders freely "benedicit super cibum, id est, benedictionem facit super cibo." "Bless [God] *over* (or break [? bread] *over*) the sacrifice," would be more regular; but Breithaupt rejects the insertion of "over" as erroneous. These passages establish the conclusion that the Hebrew "*bless*," in connection with food, might be expressed in Aramaic by a word that in Hebrew means "*break*."

out of a small store to the hungry. There is another word mostly used in New Hebrew for the literal breaking of bread; but that, in the Bible, has a bad sense[1]. The Talmud uses *pâras* to remind a master of a house that, at a meal in his house, he must not "pronounce the benediction" (*lit.* "divide the dividing") for "travellers," his guests, unless he eats with them, but he may do it for his family in order to accustom them to the fulfilment of the precept[2]. Another passage— but one of doubtful meaning—uses the word *pâras* concerning a distribution of fishes to the citizens of Jerusalem[3].

There is no clear indication in the Gospels that the "breaking (*pâras*)" of bread by Jesus was connected with the thought of the "explanation (*pârash*)" of the Law[4]. It is true that the Lucan narrative of the manifestation of Jesus "in the *breaking of the bread*," at Emmaus, at all events prepares the way for that manifestation by a mention of His "*interpretation*" of the sayings in the Scriptures concerning the Messiah, which is

---

[1] See Levy i. 251 *b* on בצע which, as a Heb. verb, means (Gesen. 130) "cut off, break off, *gain by violence*," and, as a noun, "*gain made by violence*." That is the word used by Delitzsch about breaking bread in the narratives of the Eucharist, though he uses פרס in the miracles of feeding.

[2] See Levy *Ch.* ii. 294 *a* quoting *R. haschana* 29 *b*, and adding, as a common phrase, "the time needed to eat a פרס, i.e. *half [of a loaf]*."

[3] *Sanhedr.* 49 *a*, on 1 Chr. xi. 8, Joab "merely tasted" them and then "*distributed* (פרים) to them." This suggests that, in the Feeding of the Five Thousand, "*breaking*," which John omits, might have been regarded by him as an error for "*distributing*," which he inserts. The food is called by Goldschmidt "Fischtunke (*sic*) (מונינו) und kleine Fische (צחנתא)." But the latter (Gesen. 850 *a*, and Levy *Ch.* ii. 320 *a*) would seem to mean stinking fish. Hence the interpretation is doubtful. "Joab" is the distributer, and there may be irony in the description of him as attempting to feed Jerusalem with "fishes" not only "stinking," but also broken in pieces.

[4] Onkelos uses פריש in Deut. i. 5 (R.V.) "Moses began to *declare* this law," where Heb. באר (Gesen. 91) = "make plain," "explain."

subsequently called His "*opening* of the Scriptures," and the
result is that "their eyes were opened and they knew him[1]."
But such a scriptural "opening" is connected with a word
that means the opening of a door, rather than the opening or
spreading out of the hand. It is frequently called "opening
[with] an opening," and in that form occurs repeatedly in the
Talmud where a Rabbi "*opens*" his discussion of some passage
of Scripture by quoting another[2]. Nevertheless Luke helps us
to perceive a very real sense in which it may be maintained
that beneath the narratives of miraculous feeding, and of
Christ's meals with disciples before and after the Resurrection,
there was originally and historically (whether we easily perceive it or not) a connection between the "breaking" of the
bread of the Law, and the "opening," or "spreading out," of

---

[1] Lk. xxiv. 27 διερμήνευσεν, comp. *ib.* 32 διήνοιγεν ἡμῖν τὰς
γραφάς. In LXX, פרשׂ = ἀνοίγω in Is. xxxvii. 14, describing a
literal "spreading out" of a letter before the Lord, and = διανοίγω
in Prov. xxxi. 20 "she *spreadeth out* (A.V. stretcheth out) her hand
(*lit.* palm) to the poor." The contextual repetition of διανοίγω in
Lk. xxiv. 31 διηνοίχθησαν οἱ ὀφθαλμοί suggests a kind of play on
the thought of "*opening.*" It is repeated again, after Jesus has
partaken of the broiled fish, in Lk. xxiv. 45 "then he *opened* (διή-
νοιξεν) their mind." Διανοίγω occurs elsewhere in N.T. only in
Mk vii. 34 "Be thou *opened,*" Lk. ii. 23 (quoting Exod. xiii. 2
"that *openeth* the womb"), Acts vii. 56 "the heavens *opened,*"
xvi. 14 "whose heart the Lord *opened,*" xvii. 3 "reasoned with
them from the scriptures, *opening* and alleging that it behoved the
Christ to suffer."

[2] Comp. *Megill.* 10 *b* "R. Jonathan *opened the opening* (פתח לה
פתחא) for this section (פרשתא, from פרשׂ, *separate*) from the following [text]"—a phrase repeated about a dozen times in 10 *b*—11.
Delitzsch uses פתח in Lk. xxiv. 32 and Acts xvii. 3 "Paul...reasoned
with them from the scriptures, *opening* and alleging that it behoved
the Christ to suffer, and to rise again from the dead...." *Hor. Heb.*,
Wetstein, and Schöttgen are silent as to any Hebrew authority for
this use of "opening," and no satisfactory Greek authority is alleged.
It might mean "opening" the discussion of, for example, the
"section" in Isaiah about the Suffering Servant by quoting such
passages as Hos. vi. 2 "After two days he will revive us."

the meaning of the Law, and the "opening" of the minds of the disciples to that meaning, and, at the same time, the "opening" of their hearts to the divine character of their Master and Saviour, the Bread of Life. We may illustrate this connection from a Talmudic passage that speaks of the material "breaking" of bread (*bâtsa* as distinguished from Isaiah's *pâras*) and defines its spiritual object: "The Master of the House *breaks* [*the bread*] that he may *break it* with *a good eye*[1]."

Now it was one of Christ's fundamental doctrines that the "*eye*" of His disciples must not be "*evil*," but must be "*single*," *i.e.* straightforwardly and lovingly fixed on God, and on Man regarded as in God, being made in God's image. It was to be an "eye" of kindness and goodness, recognising as the two great commandments of the Law, the love of God and the love of the neighbour. These two precepts, taken up and expressed in the Psalms and the Prophets, might be regarded as the relish, or flavour, of the Law, which, without them, was what we should call "dry bread." In the Sermon on the Mount Jesus might be described as taking and breaking the dry bread of the five loaves of the Law, and flavouring it, so to speak, with the *opson* of these two fishes, and distributing it to the multitudes[2].

It would be a fanciful but brief and not inaccurate summary of many of the charges brought by Jesus against the formalists who in His days constituted the majority of

---

[1] *Berach.* 46 *a*, a tradition of R. Jochanan in the name of Simeon ben Jochai.

[2] Some "breaking," or "spreading out," or "interpretation," of the Law in this sense would be included in Mark's (vi. 34) statement that Jesus "taught" the Five Thousand "many things" before feeding them with the five loaves and the two fishes. Not much importance can be attached to the traditions in *Sabb.* 116 *a* and *Gen. r.* (on Gen. xxvi. 17, Wü. p. 307) where it is said by Samuel Bar Nachman and by Ben Kaphra that there are seven books of the Law (see contexts).

the Pharisees, to take as our text Isaiah's ancient word, in its ancient Hebrew meaning, and to say that they modernised it by their Jewish traditions. They thought of it as inculcating the religious duty of *"spreading out"* the hands in prayer to God in heaven; but Jesus thought of it as inculcating the duty—moral and spiritual rather than religious—of *"breaking one's loaf in half,"* even our single loaf, in order to give it to the spiritually, as well as the materially, "hungry."

Returning to the Fourth Gospel we may say that a great deal of evidence converges to the conclusion that John's omission of the "breaking" was due in part to various and perplexing inferences as to the nature and results of the act, though in part also to a Johannine motive, namely, the desire to avoid everything that could give rise to the notion that Christ was so "divided" as not to be always One[1].

§ 28. *"And the two fishes he divided among [them] all,"*
in Mark[2]

Mark, in both his narratives, makes a distinction, not made by Matthew or Luke, between the loaves and the fishes.

---

[1] Comp. 1 Cor. i. 13 "Is Christ divided ($\mu\epsilon\mu\epsilon\rho\iota\sigma\tau\alpha\iota$)?"

[2] In the accounts of the Distribution, Mark (four times) and Luke use $\pi\alpha\rho\alpha\tau\iota\theta\eta\mu\iota$ of the food "set before" the multitude, Matthew never uses it except previously about (xiii. 24, 31) *"parables"* which Jesus *"set before"* the disciples. John here uses $\dot{o}\psi\dot{\alpha}\rho\iota o\nu$ instead of $\dot{\iota}\chi\theta\dot{\upsilon}s$ for "fish."

The R.V. does not express all the shades of difference which will be found in the Greek text printed below:

(The Five Thousand)

Mk vi. 41	Mt. xiv. 19	Lk. ix. 16	Jn vi. 11
καὶ λαβὼν τοὺς πέντε ἄρτους καὶ τοὺς δύο ἰχθύας ἀναβλέψας εἰς τὸν οὐρανὸν εὐλόγησεν καὶ κατέκλασεν τοὺς ἄρτους καὶ ἐδίδου τοῖς μαθηταῖς ἵνα παρατιθῶσιν αὐτοῖς, καὶ τοὺς δύο ἰχθύας ἐμέρισεν πᾶσιν.	καὶ...λαβὼν τοὺς πέντε ἄρτους καὶ τοὺς δύο ἰχθύας, ἀναβλέψας εἰς τὸν οὐρανὸν εὐλόγησεν καὶ κλάσας ἔδωκεν τοῖς μαθηταῖς τοὺς ἄρτους οἱ δὲ μαθηταὶ τοῖς ὄχλοις.	λαβὼν δὲ τοὺς πέντε ἄρτους καὶ τοὺς δύο ἰχθύας ἀναβλέψας εἰς τὸν οὐρανὸν εὐλόγησεν αὐτοὺς καὶ κατέκλασεν καὶ ἐδίδου τοῖς μαθηταῖς παραθεῖναι τῷ ὄχλῳ.	ἔλαβεν οὖν τοὺς ἄρτους ὁ Ἰησοῦς καὶ εὐχαριστήσας διέδωκεν τοῖς ἀνακειμένοις, ὁμοίως καὶ ἐκ τῶν ὀψαρίων ὅσον ἤθελον.

In the Five Thousand, he says that Jesus (not the disciples) "divided" the fishes. In the Four Thousand, he seems to introduce the fishes as a kind of after-thought or addition ("that they were to set *these, too,* before [the multitude]").

Moreover Mark distinguishes between "setting-before" and "dividing." "Set-before" he uses four times, and always of the action of the disciples. Jesus Himself is described by Mark as (1) "giving" to the disciples, and as (2) ordering the disciples to "set before" the people. These clauses contain no difficulty. But there is difficulty in "he divided the two fishes to all." Perhaps we may explain it from the precedent of David, who

---

(The Four Thousand)

Mk viii. 6—7	Mt. xv. 36
καὶ λαβὼν τοὺς ἑπτὰ ἄρτους εὐχαριστήσας ἔκλασεν καὶ ἐδίδου τοῖς μαθηταῖς αὐτοῦ ἵνα παρατιθῶσιν καὶ παρέθηκαν τῷ ὄχλῳ. καὶ εἶχαν ἰχθύδια ὀλίγα· καὶ εὐλογήσας αὐτὰ εἶπεν καὶ ταῦτα παρατιθέναι.	ἔλαβεν τοὺς ἑπτὰ ἄρτους καὶ τοὺς ἰχθύας καὶ εὐχαριστήσας ἔκλασεν καὶ ἐδίδου τοῖς μαθηταῖς οἱ δὲ μαθηταὶ τοῖς ὄχλοις.

In Mk vi. 41, SS and Walton Syr. have *"they divided"* (for *"he divided"*), and in Mk viii. 7, codex ℵ has *prima manu* παρέθηκεν, corrected into εἶπεν καὶ ταῦτα παρατιθέναι. These variations do not appear in Swete (ed. 1898).

The Diatessaron, in the Four Thousand, omits the whole of Mk viii. 7 *"and they had a few little fishes; and having blessed them he said [to them] that they should set these also before [the multitude]"*—except "a few little fishes," which it places earlier (as Matthew does). Thus it omits one of the Marcan mentions of παρατίθημι. On the other hand, in the Five Thousand, it mentions παρατίθημι twice (where Mark has it only once) thus: "Then Jesus said unto them, 'Bring hither those five loaves and the two fishes.' And when they brought him that, Jesus took the bread and the fish, and looked to heaven, and blessed and divided"—substituting "dividing" for "breaking-in-pieces" (κατέκλασεν) or "breaking" (κλάσας)—"and gave to the disciples to *set before them*; and the disciples *set for the multitudes* the bread and the fish." This last clause ("set...fish") appears to come from Mk viii. 6 *b* "and they *set [them] before* the multitude," and to be a substitute for Mk vi. 41 *b* "and the two fishes he divided unto all."

"*divided* to every man of Israel" food specified in the context[1]. It is not meant that David himself "set the food before" Israel, but that he specified the portion to be "divided" to each and caused it to be set before each.   In Mark, the meaning may be that, whereas the loaves were broken and set before the people, "*the two fishes*" were *not* "broken," but "*divided to all,*" that is, "*distributed to all, the two fishes being given to each person.*" This miraculous reproduction of the two fishes for each person Mark may intend to describe as a separate act of Jesus.

In the Four Thousand, the fishes are called "little" and "few"—terms that might easily be interchanged[2]. Also the number "two" is dropped, so that any suggestion of "two for each person" is avoided, and we may suppose them to have been multiplied not in pairs but indefinitely by Jesus who commanded that the disciples should set an indefinite number of them before the people. This hypothesis would help us to see why Mark here calls them "little-fishes"—a word not elsewhere used in N.T. or LXX.   It might also explain John's peculiar addition "and of the fishes *as much as they desired*"— that is, they were not restricted to "*the two*[3]."

But there is another way of explaining this Greek diminutive, as well as the use of "two." We find corresponding peculiarities in the LXX where the widow in Zarephath says to Elijah "I have...but an handful of meal...and, behold, I am gathering *two sticks*...that I may...dress it and die[4]." "*Two*"

---

[1] 2 S. vi. 19 καὶ διεμέρισεν παντὶ τῷ λαῷ εἰς πᾶσαν τὴν δύναμιν τοῦ Ἰσραὴλ..., 1 Chr. xvi. 3 καὶ διεμέρισεν παντὶ ἀνδρὶ Ἰσραὴλ....

[2] In Mt. xv. 34, SS and Curet. have different words for "few" (Burk. "a few fishes," Walton "aliquot pisces minutos"), and in Mk viii. 7, Burk. and Walton have "a few fishes."

[3] Some reasons for John's preference of ὀψάριον to ἰχθύς here are given in *Proclam.* p. 86. Also, if John had used ἰχθύς, he would have seemed to prefer it to ἰχθύδιον. As it is, he puts both the Synoptic terms aside, introducing one of his own.

[4] 1 K. xvii. 12 "two (שְׁנַיִם) sticks (עֵצִים)," δύο ξυλάρια. This is

is here uniquely used in O.T. for "*a very few*[1]." The Greek translators, feeling in a confused way that scantiness—not small number—is implied by "*two*," and yet not liking to suppress the literal meaning, compromise by rendering the Hebrew "*sticks*" into a Greek diminutive ("two little-sticks") nowhere else found in LXX.

Mark seems to have done something of the same kind but not so accurately as the LXX. In the Five Thousand he takes "two" literally, and explains it as the literal answer to a question of Jesus "How many loaves have ye?" They answer "five, and two fishes," though nothing was asked about the fishes[2]. In the Four Thousand, writing in his own person, Mark does not venture to say "*They had two fishes*." This would have been as inappropriate as it would have been for the narrator of the story of the Widow to write in his own person that "*she was gathering two sticks*." Such hyperbole, allowable in a complainant, is not allowable in a historian. So Mark paraphrases "two" by "a few." Yet he might well feel that this was unsatisfactory. "A few fish" might naturally mean more, not less, than "two fish," and thus the wonder of the miracle would be impaired. So Mark compromises by changing "fishes" into "little fishes."

John shews us dramatically how the "two" and the "five" might have originated in the expostulation of a single disciple like Andrew, who exclaims "There is a lad here with five

---

the only instance of ξυλάριον in LXX, but ץע = ξύλον nearly 250 times. The translators felt that "*two*," like "*handful*," implied some kind of minuteness, and this they expressed by the diminutive ξυλάρια while retaining "*two*."

[1] Gesen. 1041 *a* gives no other instance but this where "*two*" is thus used (without the juxtaposition of "three" (or "one") as in "two or three").

[2] Matthew and Luke go back more closely to the original by representing the "five" and the "two" to be part of a remonstrance on the part of the disciples, somewhat like that of the widow of Zarephath.

barley loaves and *two opsaria*; but what are these among so many?" It should be noted that John never mentions the fishes as "two" when writing in his own person, as the Synoptists do. He mentions "the five barley loaves" thus[1], but not "the two fishes."

As to the Synoptic distinction—expressed in various ways—between the giving by Christ to the disciples, and the giving by the disciples to the multitudes, John puts this aside. He represents Jesus as Himself "distributing"—like David, who in an instance above mentioned[2], is said to have "distributed" to all Israel[3]. John rejects the Synoptic word "*set-before* [*the people*]" although it is associated in LXX with the thought of Abraham "setting before" the Three his hospitable food[4], a hospitality for which (according to Jewish tradition) requital was made by God, in every detail, to Abraham's descendants.

Lastly—when describing Jesus as "distributing"—John does not use Mark's word "divide." Perhaps he felt that, for Greeks, it might suggest the thought of "divided in dissension," as when Paul says to the Corinthians "Is Christ *divided*[5]?" At

---

[1] Jn vi. 13.   [2] See above, pp. 127–8.

[3] Mk vi. 41, Lk. ix. 16 ἐδίδου (Mt. xiv. 19 ἔδωκεν) τοῖς μαθηταῖς followed by Mk *ib.* ἐμέρισεν πᾶσιν, compared with Jn vi. 11 διέδωκεν τοῖς ἀνακειμένοις, may be illustrated by Gen. xlix. 27 יחלק (Field) "dividet, LXX δίδωσι (potior scriptura διαδώσει), Aq. μερίσει." This exhibits the same three variations that we find in N.T. (1) "*give* (δίδωμι)," (2) "*give separately* (διαδίδωμι)," (3) "*divide* (μερίζω)."

[4] Gen. xviii. 8 παρέθηκεν. There it = Heb. "*gave before their faces.*" In Exod. xix. 7 παρέθηκεν αὐτοῖς πάντας τοὺς λόγους (and *ib.* xxi. 1), it=Heb. "*set before their faces.*" See Gesen. 817 *b* which says that both "give" and "set" are thus used of food, but that "give before the face" usually means "propound," and is applied to laws. Matthew (see above, p. 126, n. 2) uses παρατίθημι only about parables.

Comp. 2 K. iv. 43 "Am I to *set this before* an hundred men?"—which is the exclamation of Elisha's servant—and *ib.* 44 "so he *set it before them.*" John passes over this intermediate act of service.

[5] 1 Cor. i. 13 μεμέρισται ὁ Χριστός; Μερίζω denotes "divided by conflict" in Mk iii. 24 etc.

all events he chooses an ambiguous word that may mean either
(1) "give in turn what one has received" or (2) "give to
separate persons[1]." The word is hardly used in LXX, but
may very well represent the Hebrew "*apportion*," while at the
same time the Greek reader receives from it the suggestion that
the Son is here giving in turn to men something that He has
Himself received from the Father. This is confirmed by
Christ's subsequent words "My Father *giveth you* the true
bread out of heaven" and "*I am the bread of life*"—when taken
with a previous utterance "As the Father hath life in himself,
even so *gave he to the Son* also to have life in himself[2]." The
Son, giving Himself utterly to the Giver of eternal life, the
Father in heaven, receives from Him power to become the
Bread of Life for the Father's children on earth.

In connection with the multiplication of the fishes, the
following facts indicate that it might have a Messianic allusiveness in the Galilaean Church. The New Hebrew and Aramaic
for "fish," *nun*, though non-existent in the Bible as a noun,
occurs once as a verb (*yinnon* or *jinnon*), meaning literally
"*shall abound with offspring*," thus, "His name *shall-abound-
with-offspring* (Field *sobolescet*, Walton *filiabitur*) before the
sun[3]." On the Hebrew "*shall abound*," *Jinnon*, Schöttgen
says "It means 'shall be multiplied like fishes.' But the

---

[1] Διαδίδωμι (= Heb. word) occurs only in Gen. xlix. 20, 27
(A), and Josh. xiii. 6 (LXX). In Genesis it = נתן and חלק, and
B has (*bis*) δίδωμι. For διαδίδωμι = "give in succession" see Steph.
Thes. ii. 1139. Goodspeed gives διαδίδωμι only in Hermas *Sim.* v.
2. 9 where the faithful servant, having received ἐδέσματα from his
Master, "distributes" some of them to his fellow-servants.

[2] Jn vi. 32, 35, v. 26.

[3] Ps. lxxii. 17 R.V. txt "*shall be continued*," marg. "*shall have
issue.*" The Biblical Heb. for "fish" is דג (Aram. נון). The
verb דגה occurs but once (Gesen. 185 *b*), Gen. xlviii. 16 R.V.
"*grow-into-a-multitude*," where A.V. marg. says "(Heb.) *as fishes do
increase*," and Onkelos has "increase like *the fishes* (נוני) of the sea."

Jews *took it as a proper name*[1]." This, though over-stated, is confirmed by several passages in Midrash and Talmud, which indicate that in poetic traditions the Jews regarded *Jinnon*, in this Psalm, as one of the names of the Messiah existent before the Creation[2]. Now the preceding verse says "There shall be *abundance* (marg. *an handful*) of corn in the earth on the top of the mountains[3]"; and on the word rendered "abundance" Rashi says "Our rabbis expound it as meaning *cakes in the days of the Messiah, and the whole of this Psalm they explain as being about the King Messiah*[4]."

The Jewish Commentary on the Psalms quotes a tradition of this kind as going back to R. Jochanan: "The land of Israel will *bring forth little round cakes*[5]." The commentary does not quote any corresponding tradition about "*Jinnon*," that the waters of Israel "will bring forth a multitude of little fishes," or that the Messiah "will multiply fishes." But it is not difficult to see that such a tradition would be likely to find favour in the first century among the Jews and especially among the fishermen and others who dwelt round the sea of Galilee. The commentary on Numbers called *Siphri* says "There went with Israel in the wilderness a well, and supplied fat fishes more than their need required[6]." The "well" was believed to flow from a "rock" that "followed" Israel; and

---

[1] Schöttgen ii. 20. This is not universally true, for the Targum has "*was prepared* before the sun," perhaps (like the LXX) having a different reading; and Rashi takes it as meaning "kingdom" and "empire." Gesen. 630 *b* suggests that the original may have been יכון "be established," "endure," LXX has διαμενεῖ.

[2] See Levy ii. 246 *a* quoting three passages, and Schöttg. ii. 240 quoting others.

[3] Ps. lxxii. 16, see Gesen. 821 *a*.

[4] Rashi himself explains the word as meaning either "additionem et multitudinem" or "beneplacitum."

[5] *Tehill.* ad loc. mentions R. Chija bar Asi as uttering it "in the name of R. Jochanan" (who lived in the time of Vespasian).

[6] *Siphri* on Numb. xi. 22.

according to Paul, "the rock was Christ[1]." In proportion as
Christianity advanced, such traditions about "fishes," or
"loaves," or "round cakes" of the Messiah, would fall into
disrepute among the Jews, as having a Christian sound. I have
not found Jochanan's tradition quoted elsewhere, although
many passages in Midrash and Talmud refer to the verse in
the Psalms. But, if it was avoided because of its resemblance
to Christian traditions, the same motive may explain the
silence of Jewish tradition about multiplication of fishes in
Messianic times[2].

---

[1] I Cor. x. 4.

[2] In view of the very early use of the Greek *ichthus*, "fish," to
denote by means of the letters *i, ch, th, u, s*, "Jesus Christ, Son of
God, Saviour (or, Crucified)"—see *Orac. Sibyll.* viii. 217 foll.—it may
be of interest to note the very different use made by the Jews of *n*,
the initial letter of "*nun*," "fish." They called attention to the fact
that *n* and the two next letters of the alphabet (נ, ס, ע) were initial
letters of (1) נון "fish," (2) סממא "remedy," (3) עין "eye," thus
indicating that "fish" was a "remedy" for the "eye" (as it is in
Tobit xi. 4—11).

Also the Jewish dependence on fish for a sumptuous meal in
which they were to "*honour*" the [Friday] evening preceding the
Great Sabbath is illustrated by a story (Levy iii. 360, *Gen. r.*, Wü.
p. 47) about a Jewish tailor, who ventured to outbid the servant of
"a ruler" in Rome by buying a fish, the only one in the shop, for
twelve denarii. The ruler called the tailor before him to explain
his conduct. "My lord," said the tailor, "it is a day on which all
our sins, which we have committed during the whole year, are to
be forgiven. When such a day comes *ought we not to honour it?*"

It is worth noting that in the Double Tradition of Matthew
(vii. 9—11) and Luke (xi. 11—13) where Jesus wishes to describe
the willingness of the Father in heaven to give (Mt.) "good [things]"
or (Lk.) "the Holy Spirit," to those that ask Him, the one metaphor
in which Matthew and Luke agree (according to the text of W. H.)
is that in which the good gift is represented by "a fish" (as the
opposite of "a serpent"). For the rest (Mt. "bread...stone," Lk.
"egg...scorpion") they disagree.

§ 29. *"Twelve basketfuls"* (R.V.), *in Mark*[1]

Of the differences between the parallel columns printed below, one has been discussed incidentally above, namely, the Synoptic use of the verb "satisfied" (literally "foddered") where John has "filled[2]." Mark's phrase "and *of* [Gk *from*] the fishes" may either be taken with "broken pieces" so as to mean "and [*broken pieces*] of the fishes," or with "some," understood, so as to mean "and [some] of the fishes[3]." The frequent use of the Hebrew *"from"* to mean *"some of"* decidedly favours the latter interpretation here; and so does the Johannine use of "from" in the saying of Jesus to the

[1] Mk vi. 42—3 (R.V.)	Mt. xiv. 20 (R.V.)	Lk. ix. 17 (R.V.)	Jn vi. 12—13 (R.V.)
(42) And they did all eat, and were filled (ἐχορτάσθησαν). (43) And they took up broken pieces, twelve basketfuls (κοφίνων πληρώματα), and also of the fishes.	(20) And they did all eat, and were filled (ἐχορτάσθησαν): and they took up that which remained over of the broken pieces, twelve baskets full (κοφίνους πλήρεις).	(17) And they did eat, and were all filled (ἐχορτάσθησαν): and there was taken up that which remained over to them of broken pieces, twelve baskets (κόφινοι).	(12) And when they were filled (ἐνεπλήσθησαν), he saith unto his disciples, Gather up the broken pieces which remain over, that nothing be lost. (13) So they gathered them up, and filled twelve baskets (κοφίνους) with broken pieces from the five barley loaves, which remained over unto them that had eaten.

Mk viii. 8 (R.V.)	Mt. xv. 37 (R.V.)
And they did eat, and were filled (ἐχορτάσθησαν); and they took up, of broken pieces that remained over, seven baskets (σφυρίδας).	And they did all eat, and were filled (ἐχορτάσθησαν): and they took up that which remained over of the broken pieces, seven baskets full (σφυρίδας πλήρεις).

[2] See above, p. 104 foll.

[3] Gesen. 580 *b*, *inter alia*, quotes Exod. xvi. 27 "there went out [some] *from the people*" (where LXX inserts τινὲς), Lev. xxv. 49 "[*some one*] *from the kinsfolk* may redeem it," LXX ἢ ἀπὸ τῶν οἰκείων ... λυτρώσεται, which would naturally be rendered "redeem *from the kinsfolk*."

seven fishermen after Christ's resurrection "Bring [some] of (lit. *from*) *the fish* that ye have now caught[1]."

A more important point is the ambiguity of the Marcan "they took up," referring to the broken pieces. Grammatically, "*they*" would mean the previously mentioned "*all*," that is to say, the multitude. Luke—in accordance with Mark's vague use of "they" in such phrases as "*they say*" to mean a passive ("*it is said*")—substitutes a passive "*there was taken up.*" John defines the agents with remarkable distinctness, not only assigning the act to the disciples but adding that Jesus gave express commandment to them to perform it: "Gather ye the broken-pieces that have superabounded that nothing may be lost[2]."

Here, if "crumbs" falling from the food had been meant, the Greek word for "crumbs" used in Christ's Dialogue with the Syrophoenician woman might have been employed[3]. Nor would any form of the word "superabundant" (in Greek, *perissos*) have been needed[4]. On the other hand, to suppose that the meaning is "portions deliberately broken off," and that Jesus broke them off, raises the question, "Is it likely that John would represent Jesus as breaking off 'superabundant' pieces, so as to cause waste?" The difficulty might lead us to con-

---

[1] Jn xxi. 10 Ἐνέγκατε ἀπὸ τῶν ὀψαρίων ὧν ἐπιάσατε νῦν. Chrys. retains "from," κελεύει ἐκ τῶν ὀ. ἐνεγκεῖν, but Nonnus (ἄξατε...νεπόδων...ἄγρην) drops it. The context does not shew why "*the fishes*" might not have been mentioned instead of "*some of the fishes*," nor why the latter is expressed in an idiom unusual except in Hebraic Greek. After Christ's command, Peter "went on board and drew the net to land full of great fishes." It may be implied, but it is not stated, that he "brought [*some*] *of them*" to Jesus as specimens and proofs of success.

[2] Jn vi. 12 Συναγάγετε τὰ περισσεύσαντα κλάσματα.

[3] Mk vii. 28, Mt. xv. 27 ψιχία, on which see Levy iv. 140 *a* and *Pes.* 10 *b* describing a "child" as "crumbling his bread."

[4] Some form of περισσεύειν is used by Mt., Lk., and Jn in the Five Thousand, and by Mt. in the Four Thousand, but περισσεύματα by Mk in the Four Thousand.

clude—especially as John has not described Jesus as "breaking" the bread—that the multitude are to be regarded as wastefully breaking off from their portions large "pieces" too big to be called "crumbs," and that John meant such "pieces" as these. This would accord with Origen's view that it is the unworthiness of the multitude that prevents them from consuming all the nourishment provided for them[1].

But these arguments may be misleading unless supplemented by the probability (we may almost say the certainty) that John is influenced by the words of Elisha over the barley loaves, "Thus saith the Lord, They shall eat and *they shall cause to superabound* or *leave thereof*," that is to say, "*They shall be satisfied and shall have a superfluity*[2]." This saying about the barley loaves of Elisha, if applied to the Johannine barley loaves of Jesus, might meet the objection "The Lord could not have broken more pieces than were needed." The mystical answer might be, in John's words, "He knew what he would do," that is to say, "He knew that what was apparent waste would not be waste, because it would come back as in a future 'gathering together,' so that 'nothing should be lost[3].'" In this sense, the pieces that were broken were *not* "more than were needed," if the lesson of the sign was to be fully taught. It was intended that some of the food should be "*left*," or that there should be a "*superabundance*."

These remarks may explain why Mark (alone of the Evangelists) omits, in his Feeding of the Five Thousand, all mention

---

[1] Origen *Comm. Matt.* xi. 19 (Lomm. iii. 125). The four thousand are superior to the five thousand, and "more receptive ($\chi\omega\rho\eta\tau\iota\kappa\dot{\omega}\tau\epsilon\rho o\iota$)" (comp. Jn viii. 37 $o\dot{\upsilon}$ $\chi\omega\rho\epsilon\hat{\iota}$) so that they leave less unconsumed.

[2] 2 K. iv. 43—44. The verb יתר, "leave," may mean "leave as a remnant saved from destruction," but it may also mean "leave as superfluous"; and forms of יתר $=\pi\epsilon\rho\iota\sigma\sigma\epsilon\acute{\iota}a$ about 13 times, and $\pi\epsilon\rho\iota\sigma\sigma\acute{o}s$ more than 20 times.

[3] Jn vi. 12. What the Jews rejected might be regarded as coming back to the Apostles in the form of a "gathering" of the Gentiles (see Rom. xi. 15—32).

of "*superabundance*," and substitutes, literally, "*fillings*," in a curious phrase rendered by R.V. "*basketfuls*," but by A.V. "*baskets full*[1]"; Matthew has the latter, "*baskets full*," but retains "*superabundant*[2]"; Luke makes no mention of "*full*" in any form, but has "*superabundant*[3]." The explanation suggested is, that the Hebrew "*left*," or "*superabounding*," twice repeated in the miracle of Elisha, was taken by Mark in the Feeding of the Five Thousand as meaning "*running over*" or "*quite full*[4]." By taking it thus, the charge of imputing to Jesus a superfluous multiplication of food would be somewhat softened[5].

Luke inserts the dative "*to them*" after "superabounded." John inserts a similar dative, but one of a much more special kind—"*to those who had consumed* [*the food*]." This Greek word "*consume* [*food*]"—meaning in literary Greek "*gnaw*," "*eat up*," and often applied to eating raw flesh, etc.— occurs in LXX fairly often to represent the ordinary Hebrew

---

[1] Mk vi. 43 κλάσματα δώδεκα κοφίνων πληρώματα καὶ ἀπὸ τῶν ἰχθύων, A.V. "twelve baskets full of the fragments, and of the fishes." "*The* fragments" suggests "*the* fragments that would naturally fall from such a meal." But there is no "*the*." The literal rendering is "broken pieces, fillings of twelve baskets, and of (*lit.* from) the fishes."

[2] Mt. xiv. 20 τὸ περισσεῦον τῶν κλασμάτων δώδεκα κοφίνους πλήρεις, "that which was [found] superabounding of the broken pieces, twelve baskets [quite] full," where "full" is emphasized by its position.

[3] Lk. ix. 17 τὸ περισσεῦσαν αὐτοῖς κλασμάτων κόφινοι δώδεκα, "that which was [found] superabounding by them (*or*, for them) of broken pieces, baskets [precisely] twelve," where "twelve" is emphasized by its position.

[4] Πλήρωμα occurs rather rarely (15 times) in LXX. It corresponds to Heb. "full." Cant. v. 12 "*channels* of waters" is paraphrased as "*fillings* (πληρώματα) of waters" to express full-flowing streams. Much more defensibly might the Heb. "*left*," יתר, be thus paraphrased.

[5] Note however that Mark does not avoid περισσεύματα in Mk viii. 8 (the Four Thousand).

"eat," but mostly in a bad sense. In the Prophets it refers to the devouring effect of fire, rust, or blight, or the eating of food defiled or offered to idols. In Genesis it does not occur once. But in Exodus and Leviticus it is frequent, occurring about ten times in prohibitions ("this shall not be eaten") (as well as positively). For our purposes, however, the two points of special importance are that (1) it occurs for the first time in connection with the Paschal Lamb, of which it is said "It shall be *consumed* in one house," and that (2) this follows the precept "Ye shall cause none of it to *superabound* (lit. *be left over and above*) till the morning[1]."

Do not these facts go some way toward justifying what at first sight seems the wild imagination of Origen—namely, that a fault of non-receptiveness is implied in those who "leave broken pieces"? May it not be that John had in view both *dicta*:—(1) that of the Law "Ye *shall cause none of it to superabound*," and (2) that of Elisha "They *shall cause to superabound*"? At all events John would probably regard the "superabounding" as divinely ordained in order that remnants from the Bread of the Gospel, rejected by the unbelievers among the Jews, might pass to the Gentiles; and yet, as in the Epistle to the Romans, the rejection would be regarded as a fault in the Jews, who did not discern, and receive in its entirety, the Living Bread, which was also the Paschal Lamb.

Jerome calls Christ's distribution of bread "a sowing of food," and implies, somewhat obscurely, that the food was "divided into (*or* with a view to) a manifold harvest[2]." About the distribution, the following comment has been preserved as coming from Ammonius: "He [*i.e.* Jesus] did not give

---

[1] Exod. xii. 10 "ye shall let none of it remain," Exod. xii. 46 "it shall be eaten ($\beta\rho\omega\theta\eta\sigma\epsilon\tau\alpha\iota$)." The word for "superabound" is יתר, the same as that in 2 K. iv. 43—44.

[2] Jerome, on Mt. xiv. 19, "Frangente Domino, *seminarium fit ciborum*. Si enim fuissent integri...nec divisi in *multiplicem segetem*...."

[the food] to the multitudes to carry (?), but to the disciples, since He above all things desired to train these—the destined teachers of the world. For the multitude was not destined to receive any great fruit from the miracle (*lit.* wonder). For they straightway forgot it and began to ask for another miracle (*lit.* wonder). But these [*i.e.* the disciples] were destined to receive no common gain[1]." This appears to express at all events an important part of John's meaning. The first harvest was, so to speak, a failure—the harvest for the multitude, the Five Thousand, that is, for Israel after the flesh. The second harvest—the gathering of the fragments by the Apostles, regarded as their harvest by Ammonius—was not a failure. It was the harvest of souls to be subsequently gathered by the Twelve, who (in spite of Judas) were typical of the Twelve Tribes of Israel after the Spirit. The key to the Johannine meaning lies in the words of Jesus "that nothing may be lost"—a phrase peculiar (with slight variations) to the Fourth

---

[1] Cramer p. 243 on Jn vi. 13. The words οὐκ ἔδωκε δὲ τοῖς ὄχλοις βαστάζειν ἀλλὰ τοῖς μαθηταῖς somewhat resemble a passage from Origen's commentary on Mt. xiv. 16 (quoted below, see § 33) where Origen applies φέρειν to the disciples. And Origen there, like Ammonius here, uses παιδεύω to describe Jesus as "training" the disciples through the miracle of the Five Thousand. But Origen represents Jesus as saying, in effect, to the disciples, "I *have trained* you to give the Bread. Now give it." Ammonius—much more accordantly with Johannine doctrine—regards *the "training" as now going on* in the course of this miracle ("since He especially desired to train these (ἐπειδὴ μάλιστα τούτους παιδεῦσαι ἐβούλετο)"). And Ammonius speaks of the disciples, not as "teaching" but as "*destined* to be teachers (τοὺς μέλλοντας ἔσεσθαι διδασκάλους)." Ammonius meets the objection that Judas received a basketful by saying that, as the rest of the Twelve received "no ordinary *gain*," so Judas received "no ordinary *condemnation* when he carried the basket (ἦν δὲ καὶ τῷ Ἰούδα κατάκριμα τὸ γινόμενον οὐ τὸ τυχὸν, βαστάζοντι τὸν κόφινον)." Does Ammonius mean, in his first sentence, "He did not give to the multitudes [the right] to *carry* (βαστάζειν) [*the baskets of fragments*] but to the disciples," and does he, in the last, allude to Jn xii. 6 "[Judas] (R.V. marg.) *carried* (ἐβάσταζεν)..."?

Gospel, and used to describe something corresponding to what the Prophets call the "remnant" of Israel[1].

As regards Mark's ambiguous words "and from the fishes" John intervenes, at least negatively, so far as to indicate that there were no fishes or fragments of fishes in the twelve baskets. The baskets were "filled [to the top] from the five barley-loaves[2]." According to his view, the fishes that Mark described as being "taken up" were not placed in the twelve baskets. They must have been brought to Jesus, if at all, separately.

As to the difference between the "twelve *cophinoi*" filled in the earlier miracle, and the "seven *sphurides*" filled in the later one, we have seen above[3] that a distinction between kinds of "baskets" is recognised by Jewish Tradition in connection with the "basket" of firstfruits which is made the subject of a kind of votive hymn in Deuteronomy[4]. Philo paraphrases this hymn in a fragment of a treatise on the Feast of Baskets in which he says that it was celebrated "*on two seasons*" of the year[5]. But Rashi says expressly "*once in the year, not twice*[6]." In this, he is following the Talmud, which says "Firstfruits

---

[1] Comp. Jn iii. 16 ἵνα...μὴ ἀπόληται, vi. 12 ἵνα μή τι ἀπόληται, vi. 39 ἵνα...μὴ ἀπολέσω, x. 28 οὐ μὴ ἀπόλωνται, xvii. 12 οὐδεὶς...ἀπώλετο εἰ μή..., xviii. 9 οὐκ ἀπώλεσα.

[2] John expresses Mark's πληρώματα, Mt. πλήρεις, Lk. om., by (vi. 13) ἐγέμισαν, using the same word that he used before (ii. 7 *bis*) in the miracle of Cana, to describe the waterpots as "filled to the top."

[3] See § 2.

[4] Deut. xxvi. 2—4 "Thou shalt put it in a basket...the priest shall take the basket," LXX κάρταλλον, Aq. ἀγγεῖον. The Heb. occurs (Gesen. 380 *b*) only there and *ib*. xxviii. 5, 17 LXX ἀποθῆκαι.

[5] See Philo *post* ii. 298 ἔστι δέ τις παρὰ ταῦτα ἑορτὴ μὲν θεοῦ, ἑορτῆς δὲ πανήγυρις ἦν καλοῦσι Κάρταλλον... § 3 τὸ ᾆσμα τοῦτο (*i.e.* Deut. xxvi. 5—15) ᾄδεται δυσὶ καιροῖς.

[6] On Deut. xxvi. 3 Rashi says "una vice in anno, non vero bis," and (on *ib*. 10) "non...nisi a fine septem septimanarum," *i.e.* from the end of the week of weeks which introduced the Feast of Pentecost.

are *not to be offered before Pentecost*[1]." The Targum on Deuteronomy paraphrases "basket" by three words, and the LXX renders "basket" in a later passage of Deuteronomy by "receptacles[2]." Also a Jewish distinction is made between these "*baskets*" when made of metal and when made of twigs or similar material[3].

Pseudo-Jerome says "The seven *sportae* (i.e. *sphurides*) are the first seven Churches. The broken pieces of bread are the mystical perceptions belonging to *the first Pentecost*[4]." This mention of "Pentecost" connects the Christian narrative with the "baskets" in Deuteronomy, according to the Rabbinical view adopted by Rashi ("*not before Pentecost*"), and with the Symposion of the Therapeutae described by Philo as honouring not only the seventh day but also the square of seven, *i.e.* the Pentecost[5]. On the other hand, Philo's mention of "*two seasons*" indicates another view in accordance with which there might be "*two*" Symposia, one of a rudimentary character. Such a rudimentariness would be symbolized by "barley," which, as we have seen, John alone mentions in connection with the Feeding of the Five Thousand.

---

[1] *Biccurim* (Mishna) i. 3 quoted by Wagenseil (*Sota* p. 661).

[2] On Deut. xxvi. 3 the three words of Targ. Jer. I are rendered by Walton (1) "canistra," (2) "sportulas," (3) "cophinos papyraceos." In Deut. xxviii. 5, 17, LXX has ἀποθῆκαι.

[3] So *Tosephoth* quoted by Wagenseil (*Sota* p. 662). *J. Biccurim* (Mishna) iii. 8 says "The rich offered their firstfruits in κάλαθοι plated with gold and silver." Levy ii. 168 *a* gives טְנֵי (the Deuteronomic "basket") as "ein grosses, metallenes Gefäss" and quotes *j. Sota* ix. 24 *b* "a leaden *receptacle* full of barley bran."

[4] On Mk viii. 1 foll. "Septem panes dona sunt septem Spiritus Sancti. Quatuor millia annus est Novi Testamenti cum quatuor temporibus. Septem sportae primae septem Ecclesiae. Fragmenta panum *mystici intellectus primae septimanae sunt*," i.e. they are the outpourings of "*mystical understanding* (or, *perception*)," with the gift of tongues, recorded in Acts ii. 1 foll.

[5] Philo ii. 481 οὐ μόνον τὴν ἁπλῆν ἑβδομάδα ἀλλὰ καὶ τὴν δύναμιν [*i.e.* the power or square of the hebdomad] τεθηπότες...ἔστι δὲ προεόρτιος μεγίστης ἑορτῆς, ἣν πεντηκοντὰς ἔλαχεν.

At this stage, the following objection may be raised: "John is supposed to regard the Feeding of the Five Thousand as rudimentary. Mark is supposed to relate the Feeding of the Four Thousand as a miracle of an advanced character. Luke omits the latter. According to the rule of Johannine Intervention, John ought to insert it. But he does not. Is not the rule broken?"

We reply that the rule is not broken because John does insert a second miracle of feeding, and that, too, "of an advanced character." Only John, as often, does not repeat what is in Mark but adds something corresponding to what is in Mark. This John places after the Resurrection. Whereas Mark symbolizes the advance by a change from the Jewish *cophinos*[1] to the Gentile *sphuris* or *sporta*, John symbolizes it in a different way by representing Jesus as feeding seven disciples from one loaf (*artos*) and one fish after they have caught and presented to Him an offering of "a hundred and fifty-three" fishes. Through that mystic number, representing the Law merged in the Spirit[2], and through the context as a whole, John leads us to see, in that final meal after the Resurrection, a type of divine Unity working through human multitudinousness, so as to lift mankind above Jewish and Gentile distinctions, bringing about for all alike the fulfilment of Christ's promise about the one "bread" or "loaf": "The *bread* (*artos*) that I will give is my flesh, for the life of the world[3]."

§ 30. *"They that ate the loaves," in Mark*[4]

Instead of the past participle Matthew has the present participle of a different verb (*esthiein*) never used by John,

---

[1] The connection of *cophinus* with *Judaeus* twice by Juvenal iii. 14, vi. 542, justifies our regarding it as being thus connected in the minds of Gentile readers of the Gospels in the first century.

[2] See *Joh. Gr.* **2283** *c*.

[3] Jn vi. 51.

[4] Mk vi. 44 οἱ φαγόντες τοὺς ἄρτους, Mt. xiv. 21 οἱ δὲ ἐσθίοντες.

but used by the Synoptists in discussions about eating and in the narratives of the Eucharist where a past tense is not required[1]. We have seen above that John here uses about the eaters a word ("*consume*") that seemed to allude to the eating of the Paschal Lamb[2]. This hypothesis of allusion will be confirmed if we can shew that John had some reason, or at all events some consistent method, in his avoidance of *esthiein*.

This is shewn by a passage where John represents Jesus as quoting from the Psalms "He that *eateth* my bread lifted up his heel against me[3]." Here the LXX uses *esthiein*. But John uses a word signifying "*chew* (*trōgein*)," which occurs nowhere in the LXX and only once in N.T. outside the Fourth Gospel[4]. In that single instance—which occurs in Matthew's description of the luxurious feeding (lit. "*chewing* and drinking") in the days of Noah—the parallel Luke has the ordinary *esthiein*[5]. This is easily intelligible, but why should John—

The latter might be rendered "the eaters," the former "those that had eaten the loaves." For the parallels, see below, p. 146, n. 3.

[1] See *Joh. Voc.* 1680 *b*. Φαγεῖν is freq. in the Synoptists and fairly freq. in Jn, but Jn never uses ἐσθίειν. The difference between ἐσθίειν and φαγεῖν is often simply a difference of tense, *i.e.* of time, ἐσθίειν having no aorist, and φαγεῖν no present or imperfect.

[2] See pp. 137–8.

[3] Jn xiii. 18 ὁ τρώγων μου τὸν ἄρτον. Nonnus has ἔρεπτων, a word applied to horses, geese, fishes, feeding in multitudes, but applicable to men with a notion of greediness.

[4] Τρώγω is mostly used with an object. But it is frequently used without an object where the juxtaposition of "drinking" makes the meaning clear. Steph. *Thes.* quotes πίνειν καὶ τρώγειν from Demosth. p. 402, 21, and Plutarch *Mor.* 716 E, and τρώγειν καὶ πίνειν from *ib.* 613 B.

[5] Mt. xxiv. 38 τρώγοντες καὶ πίνοντες (Lk. xvii. 27 ἤσθιον, ἔπινον) describing the revels of those on whom the deluge came. Τρώγω, "chew," is applied in various contexts to feeding on uncooked food. In Mt., it means "chewing" delicacies that might be called "dessert," where "eat for pleasure" would express the meaning, as in Hermas *Sim.* v. 3 "Take only bread and water, and give in alms from your *delicacies* that you were intending (lit.) *to chew* (τρώγειν)"

without any justification derivable from the Hebrew text of Scripture—represent Jesus as quoting from the Psalms the words "He that *cheweth* my bread"?

The following explanation is obscurely suggested by Jerome's commentary on the Psalm, and (more clearly) by Origen's commentary on earlier passages in the Gospel where John represents Jesus as using the word "chew[1]." Jerome says that Judas "was receiving celestial food...and distributing it to others[2]." Origen, when commenting on what he calls the "paraphrase" of the Psalm as quoted by Jesus, says that the bread referred to was "most nourishing[3]." Elsewhere, in his treatise on the daily bread in the Lord's Prayer, he takes in order the passages in which Jesus speaks of the need of His disciples to "*chew*" His flesh and "*drink*" His blood, and not only repeats the epithet "nourishing" again, but adds to it others such as "solid," and "athletic[4]." Taken together, Origen's references indicate that the Greek word had, for him, in one aspect, its usual sense, but in another aspect, a sense so new as to be startling—"gnawing" raw flesh[5].

---

i.e. to eat for pleasure. In other contexts it might mean "*chew (a crust)*" and be applied to a beggar. See Steph. *Thes.* τρώγω, which shews that the grammarians expressly distinguish τρώγω, as having a more particular meaning than ἐσθίω, and as being applied to the eating of τραγήματα, "sweetmeats."

[1] Jn vi. 54, 56, 57, 58. In all these, Jesus is speaking. John never uses τρώγω in his own person.

[2] Jerome on Ps. xli. 9.

[3] Origen on Jn xiii. 18 (Lomm. ii. 419) παραπέφρασται, (*ib.* 420) τροφιμωτάτων.

[4] Origen *De Orat.* § 27 (Lomm. xvii. 205 foll.) leads us from ὁ τρόφιμος λόγος to the thought of its στερρότης and εὐτονία, as being ἀθλητικὴ τροφή distinguishing it from "manna" and "milk."

[5] The food is not subjected to the action of fire, so that the Greek τρώγω may be used in speaking about it. It is also "flesh" with the "blood" in it, so that "chewing" and "drinking" go together.

A close examination of the Greek justifies Origen. Neither the Latin, nor the Syriac, nor the English Versions represent the abruptness with which the word "*chewing*" is as it were thrown in the faces of the Jews by the Fourth Gospel after they have said "How can this [man] give us his flesh to *eat* (*phagein*)?" It is true that Jesus is made to reply at first with a repetition of their word ("Except ye *eat* (*phagein*) the flesh of the Son of man and drink his blood, ye have not life in yourselves"). But He immediately adds "He that *cheweth* (*trōgein*) my flesh and drinketh my blood hath life eternal....He that *cheweth* (*trōgein*) my flesh and drinketh my blood abideth in me, and I in him. As the living Father sent me and I live because of the Father, [so] also he that *cheweth* (*trōgein*) me— he too shall live because of me. This is the bread that came down from Heaven. Not as the fathers *ate* (*phagein*) [manna] and died[1]—[not so is it now]; he that *cheweth* (*trōgein*) this bread shall live for ever[2]."

These last words, contrasting the death that came after Israel "*ate*" the manna with the life that will belong to him that "*cheweth*" the "bread" that "came down from heaven," should be illustrated from Israel's complaint about the manna that it had no sustaining moisture for them. "Our soul is *dried away*," they cried, and "who shall give us *flesh* to eat[3]?" The Fourth Gospel represents Jesus as affording to the spiritual Israel a food of spiritual nature that should satisfy both hunger and thirst. It was to be the "*flesh*" of the living Son, which

---

[1] "Died." See Numb. xiv. 30 "save Caleb...and Joshua."

[2] Jn vi. 52—8. Our English Versions have "*eat*" throughout, and so have the Syriac. The Latin Versions vary somewhat strangely; *d* renders φαγεῖν by "manducare" in 52 and 58 (where *d* has "non sicut manducaverunt (ἔφαγον)...qui manducat (ὁ τρώγων)." Chrysostom, commenting on this passage, makes no comment on the transition in Jn from φαγεῖν to τρώγειν.

[3] Numb. xi. 4—6 בשר. Comp. Ps. lxxviii. 20 "Will he provide flesh (שאר)," LXX τράπεζαν, where Rashi says that שאר (which rather suggests flesh with blood in it, Gesen. 984—5) stands for בשר.

could not possibly be received apart from the reception of His blood. Isaiah invites the soul to "eat" the food of heaven as being "wine" and "milk," not mentioning, but assuming, that it included "bread[1]." So John connects the life and being of the Son with "bread" and with "flesh," and even with "blood," not mentioning, but assuming, that this included "wine[2]."

§ 31. *"Five thousand men" or "about five thousand [men][3]"*

The following questions arise out of the Marcan phrases. Why does Mark insert "men (*viri*, not *homines*[4])" in one narrative and omit it in the other? Why does Mark insert *"about"* in one narrative and omit it in the other? Why does John insert *"in number"* before "about five thousand"? Why does Matthew in both narratives insert "apart from women and

---

[1] Is. lv. 1 "buy and *eat*," where Ibn Ezra remarks of "wine" and "milk" that each serves for food as well as for drink.

[2] John's above-noted application of τρώγειν to Judas in an altered quotation from LXX is perhaps part of a consistent tradition (not mentioned by the Synoptists) concerning the bread dipped in wine and given to Judas alone.

[3]

Mk vi. 44 (R.V.)	Mt. xiv. 21 (R.V.)	Lk. ix. 14 (R.V.)	Jn vi. 10 (R.V.)
And they that ate the loaves were five thousand men.	And they that did eat were about five thousand men, beside women and children.	For they were about five thousand men.	So the men sat down, in number about five thousand.

Mk viii. 9 (R.V.)	Mt. xv. 38 (R.V.)
And they were about four thousand.	And they that did eat were four thousand men, beside women and children.

Note that ἄνδρες is inserted except in Mk viii. 9. The Greek phrases are as follows. In the Five Thousand, Mk vi. 44 πεντακισχίλιοι ἄνδρες, Mt. xiv. 21 ἄνδρες ὡσεὶ π., χωρὶς γυναικῶν καὶ παιδίων, Lk. ix. 14 ὡσεὶ ἄνδρες π., Jn vi. 10 οἱ ἄνδρες (or, ἄνδρες) τὸν ἀριθμὸν ὡς π. In the Four Thousand, Mk viii. 9 ὡς τετρακισχίλιοι, Mt. xv. 38 τετρακισχίλιοι (marg. ὡς τετρακισχίλιοι) ἄνδρες, χωρὶς γυναικῶν καὶ παιδίων (marg. παιδίων καὶ γυναικῶν).

[4] "Men," ἄνδρες. Ἀνήρ occurs in Mk elsewhere, only in the sing. vi. 20 "a righteous *man*," x. 2, 12 "*husband*."

146

children"? And why do Luke and John omit Matthew's clause?

If we look for illustrations from Scripture to answer these questions, we find that the first Hebrew instance of *"about"* *with numbers of men* occurs in the description of Israel going forth from Egypt[1]. The same passage contains almost the first instance of the plural of "man of military age[2]," as distinguished from women and children: "And the children of Israel departed... *about* six hundred thousand *on-foot* (or, *footmen*)—*the men* [*of military age*], apart from children[3]." This looks back to the first Biblical use of the plural of the word, uttered by Pharaoh, who refuses to let the *"children"* go, but will let the *"men"* (Heb. *geber*) go. In the LXX, these two passages are the first where we find Mark's Greek word for "men" representing the Hebrew *geber*[4]. Later on, the Pentateuch omits both *"about"* and "men of military age" in the passionate exclamation of Moses "*Six hundred thousand footmen* (or, *travellers on foot*) *are the people amid whom I am*[5]." Jewish tradition notes the apparent discrepancy between this and the preceding mention of the same number; for, during

---

[1] Exod. xii. 37 Heb. כ "like," *i.e.* about. LXX εἰς "amounting to." This is the first instance mentioned in Gesen. 453 *a*. Strong's Concordance, which is generally very accurate, omits it.

[2] Heb. גבר, *geber*. See Gesen. 149—50.

[3] Exod. xii. 37 "apart from *children* (טף)," LXX πλὴν τῆς ἀποσκευῆς. 'Αποσκευή, outside LXX, would mean "baggage," the Latin "impedimenta," but in LXX it freq. represents טף, "*children*." Here Aq. has χωρὶς ἀπὸ νηπίου, Sym. ...τοῦ ὄχλου. Comp. Exod. x. 10—11, where Pharaoh says to Moses that he will not let go the "children (טף)" (LXX, Aq. and Sym. as here) but "Go ye, now, *the men* [*of military age*]," Aq. πορεύεσθε δή, οἱ ἄνδρες, LXX πορευέσθωσαν δὲ οἱ ἄνδρες (a variation that somewhat resembles the variation in the punctuation of Jn vi. 10). Steph. *Thes.* does not mention this meaning of ἀποσκευή, but see Gen. xxxiv. 29, xliii. 8, etc.

[4] 'Ανήρ in Pentateuch occurs about 180 times, but not as representing *geber* except in these two passages and Deut. xxii. 5 (forbidding an adult male to put on woman's clothing, and *vice versa*).

[5] Numb. xi. 21.

the interval, the number is stated elsewhere to have increased. Accordingly Rashi says "Moses was not solicitous" about including additions[1]. Many passages in Midrash comment on the numbering of Israel on or before the night of the Exodus as one of ten occasions on which Israel was numbered[2].

Passing to the Gospels we see that some of their variations correspond to variations in Hebrew Scripture or Jewish tradition. Mark's omission in one narrative, and insertion in another, of "*about*" and "*men [of military age]*," corresponds to the omission of these words in Numbers and the insertion of them in Exodus. Matthew's insertion of "*men*" in both narratives indicates that he regarded "*men*" as emphatic, meaning "*men, not to speak of women and children.*" This followed the precedent of Exodus, where "apart from *children*" was interpreted by R. Ishmael as "apart from *the women and the little ones*," and by R. Jonathan as "apart from *the women, the children, and the aged*[3]."

---

[1] See Exod. xxxviii. 26, Numb. i. 45—6 "all that were able to go forth to war...603,550" (comp. Numb. ii. 32). Rashi, on Numb. xi. 21, says "Non solicitus fuit [Moses] ut singulatim numeraret," and tells us of a Rabbi who suggested that the additional 3550 (called by him 3000) were not included because they did not murmur—so that they did not belong to the sixty myriads destined to die in the wilderness.

This view is confirmed by Sir. xvi. 8 "So were 600,000 רגלי, edd. *footmen, that were taken away in the arrogancy of their heart*," Sir. xlvi. 8 "two alone were reserved, *out of* 600,000 רגלי, edd. *men on foot.*" Clem. Rom. § 43 calls them "*the* 600,000," although at the time mentioned (Numb. xvii. 1 foll.) the number would have been increased, συνεκάλεσεν πάντα τὸν Ἰσραήλ, τὰς ἑξακοσίας χιλιάδας τῶν ἀνδρῶν.

Sota 12 *b* gives a quaint interpretation of רגלי, "footmen," in the utterance of Moses. It meant "*on my account*," and implied a presumption for which Moses was punished!

[2] Ten occasions are mentioned in *Numb. r.* on Numb. ii. 32, and *Pesikta* sect. 2, Wü. p. 18 etc. In *Numb. r.* on Numb. xxvi. 2 it is said that whenever Israel went wrong it needed to be numbered.

[3] See *Mechilt.* on Exod. xii. 37.

It is more difficult to say why John inserts *"in number,"* before "about five thousand." It is apparently superfluous. Yet in his subtle, mystical, and allusive Gospel cautious critics will very seldom confidently commit themselves to a statement that they have found superfluities. Can it be that John is affected by Jewish traditions above referred to concerning the "numbering" of Israel as being connected with imperfection or evil?

That, perhaps, is the Johannine view. When Luke in the Acts mentions "number" in passage after passage describing the growth of the Church, he does it with obvious satisfaction[1]. But it is doubtful whether John has any such satisfaction in the numbering of the Five Thousand. Regarded mystically, the number "five" is of the flesh, like the "five husbands" of the woman of Samaria; and "the five barley loaves" are typical of rudimentary revelation. Regarded historically (according to John's view), the Five Thousand so completely fail to understand the nature of Christ's sign that they are described as purposing "to snatch him away that they may make him a king[2]." We can at least say that this explanation is more probable than the hypothesis that John inserted *"in number"*—and this in a narrative so familiar to the Church in various forms and so obviously typical—without attaching to the insertion some meaning, or at all events some allusive significance.

---

[1] Ἀριθμός occurs in the Acts (iv. 4, etc.), four times out of five, about the growth of the Church. But in the Epistles it occurs only in Rom. ix. 27 "If the *number* of the children of Israel be as the sand of the sea *it shall be the remnant that shall be saved.*" This appears to depreciate the value of "numbering." The other N.T. instances of ἀριθμός (except Lk. xxii. 3 "Judas...of the number of the twelve") are all (10) in Revelation. This book also (vii. 9) speaks of "a great multitude which no one could number, standing before the throne." The first mention of "counting" and "numbering" in the Bible is in Gen. xiii. 16 (comp. xvi. 10) and declares that the seed of Abraham *cannot* be numbered.

[2] Jn vi. 15.

§ 32. *Irenaeus and Origen on the "five thousand" in the Acts, and Clement of Alexandria on the "five loaves"*

The narratives of the Feeding of the Five Thousand are likely to have been influenced not only by allusions to the events in the history of Israel, and particularly the giving of the manna, but also by prospective allusions to the growth of the Christian Church, more particularly during the period when thousands at a time were converted, according to the Acts, by the preaching of Peter. This influence is not likely to have been so great as that of Eucharistic allusion, but still it is not to be passed by.

Irenaeus says that the convincing effect of prophecy in bringing souls into the Church explains the success of the apostolic preaching, whereby "on one day there were baptized *three thousand men, and four, and five*[1]." The Acts mentions the "baptizing" of "three thousand," and subsequently speaks of "five thousand," but nowhere "*four thousand*"; and such language, however it may be explained, shews that early variations might arise about the details of the growth of the Church, some of which might bear on the Gospel narratives of miraculous Feeding[2]. Origen, if his text is not corrupt,

---

[1] Iren. iv. 23. 2 "et una die baptizati sunt hominum tria millia, et quatuor, et quinque."

[2] Acts ii. 41 οἱ μὲν οὖν...ἐβαπτίσθησαν, καὶ προσετέθησαν ἐν τῇ ἡμέρᾳ ἐκείνῃ ψυχαὶ ὡσεὶ τρισχίλιαι, iv. 4 πολλοὶ δὲ τῶν ἀκουσάντων τὸν λόγον ἐπίστευσαν καὶ ἐγενήθη ἀριθμὸς τῶν ἀνδρῶν ὡς χιλιάδες πέντε. Grabe on Irenaeus points to Acts ii. 47 ὁ δὲ κύριος προσετίθει τοὺς σωζομένους καθ᾽ ἡμέραν as a possible explanation. The tradition from which Irenaeus borrowed may have stated that the number of the baptized "*became* on one day 3000, and then 4000, and then 5000." "The [total] number *became*" might easily be confused with "the number [added on this or that occasion] *was*." Comp. Acts iv. 4 ἐγενήθη, A.V. "*was*," R.V. "*came to be*." This may be illustrated by a difference between Lk. ix. 13—14 Curet. "'But let us go ourselves [and] buy food for all this multitude,' *for they were become five thousand men*," and SS "'Except we go and buy ourselves food for all this multitude, *for*

appears to combine the Feeding of the Five Thousand by our Lord with the conversion of the Three Thousand in the Acts, and to regard both as fulfilments of the exclamation of Isaiah, "Shall a nation be brought forth at once[1]?" Jerome, commenting fully on the same prophecy, says "It also refers to that time when, on one day, there believed three thousand, and five thousand, of the Jewish people[2]." But Origen's text, as it stands, by inserting a mention of *the Saviour's " Incarnation,"* and also by placing the Five Thousand before the Three Thousand, makes it difficult to suppose that he is referring merely to the Acts. Possibly "three," in Origen's text, is an error for "four." His view certainly was that the miracle of the Four Thousand typified the inclusion of the Gentiles. This "including," if Origen wrote "four thousand," he may have described (in the language of the Acts) as "adding," just as he describes the miracle of the Five Thousand (in the language of the Acts) as "believing":—"When the Saviour

---

they are five thousand men.'" Possibly Acts iv. 4 ἐγενήθη ἀριθμὸς τῶν ἀνδρῶν is a corruption of some tradition that "there was made a numbering (ἀρίθμησις) of the men." Something is needed (but Hebrew origination might suffice) to explain the omission of ὁ before ἀριθμός (comp. Acts vi. 7 ὁ ἀριθμὸς τῶν μαθητῶν).

[1] Origen *Jerem. Hom.* ix. 3 (on Is. lxvi. 8) "But 'a nation was brought forth (ἐτέχθη) at once' *when the Saviour* (?) *had been with us on earth* (ὅτε ἐπιδεδήμηκεν ὁ Σωτήρ) and in one day five thousand believed (ἐπίστευσαν) and on another day there were added (προσετέθησαν) three thousand." I do not understand the force of the perfect ἐπιδεδήμηκεν contrasted with the aorists. Is it possible that we should read the pluperf. ἐπεδεδημήκει, i.e. "when the Saviour *had [recently] been incarnate"*? Comp. the earliest instance of ἐπιδημέω quoted in Euseb. *H.E.* iv. 3. 2 (from Quadratus) οὐδὲ ἐπιδημοῦντος μόνον τοῦ Σωτῆρος ἀλλὰ καὶ ἀπαλλαγέντος. In that case we must suppose that Origen is quoting from the Acts but reverses the order of the Acts in order to put the larger number first: "There 'believed,' as the Acts says, five thousand men, and on another [and earlier] day there were added [to the Church], as the Acts says, three thousand."

[2] "Et ad illud tempus referre quando una die tria millia et quinque millia de Judaico populo crediderunt."

was on earth and there '*believed*' (Acts iv. 4) in one day Five
Thousand, and in another day there were '*added*' (Acts ii. 41)
Four Thousand[1]."

Other early Christian literature throws little light on
distinctions between the Synoptic "five thousand" and "four
thousand," or the "five loaves" and the "seven loaves."
The plural "loaves" is not used by the Apostolic Fathers and
Apologists[2]. The only mention of the "five loaves" by
Irenaeus is in an attempt to shew that the number "five" is
of frequent occurrence in Scripture and need not have the
mystical meaning attributed to it by heretics. In doing this,
he asserts that "*five*" is the number of the pillars that support
the veil of the Holy of Holies. But in fact there were "*four*[3]."
His error is the less excusable because Philo had taught that
the "*four*" pillars before the Holy of Holies were spiritually
superior to the "*five*" pillars before the screen of the Taber-
nacle[4]. Clement of Alexandria adopts Philo's interpretation of
the "*five* pillars" as referring to the things of the senses and
applies it depreciatively to "the *five* loaves," which, he says,
"are most mystically broken by the Saviour, and supply
fulness (?) to the crowd of those hearing Him; for great [indeed
is] *the [crowd] that gives heed to the things of sense as being alone
realities*[5]." Clement then mentions "the four pillars" that

---

[1] That is to say, the *order* of the two miracles is that of the
Gospels, but the *language* is that of the Acts, because Origen regards
the miracle placed second in the Gospels as being of the nature of
an "addition" such as the Acts connects with "three thousand."
If Origen wrote thus, it would be very natural for scribes to alter
his "four" into "three" (Δ into Γ).

[2] Goodspeed gives it, however, as a v. r. of Cod. A in Justin
Martyr *Apol.* lxvii. 3 ὡς προέφημεν...ἄρτος προσφέρεται, where προέφημεν
refers to ch. lxv. and ch. lxvi. mentioning the sing. ἄρτος.

[3] Iren. ii. 24. 4.

[4] Philo on Exod. xxvi. 32—37. Irenaeus (see Grabe's note
which should have been added in Clark's translation) has confused
the two verses.

[5] Clem. Alex. 665 ταύτῃ τοὶ μυστικώτατα πέντε ἄρτοι πρὸς τοῦ Σωτῆρος

stand at the entrance of the Holy of Holies, as being typical of a more inward and spiritual knowledge. Then he passes to the number "seven," as being that of the planets and of the branches of the sacred lamp, and of "the seven eyes of the Lord" which ("they say") are "the seven spirits resting on the rod that flowers from the root of Jesse[1]." Although Clement does not, in this connection, make mention of the "seven loaves" that were broken for the "four thousand," the transition suggests that he had that thought in his mind. If he had, it would be consistent with Origen's view that the miracle of the Four Thousand was higher in the spiritual scale than the earlier miracle of the Five Thousand.

§ 33. *"Give ye them to eat," why omitted by John*

This omission has not been commented on above because our first business has been to discuss Marcan passages omitted or altered by Luke, and this is not one of them. All the Synoptists have the words "Give ye them to eat," and all of them, especially Luke, emphasize the pronoun "*ye*[2]." Origen explains the emphasis, allegorizing the "eating," as if Jesus meant "*Ye*, my disciples, *ye* whom I have trained to give the Bread of Life to others, give *ye* them to eat, and do not think of sending away the hungry multitude unfed[3]." Origen also, in his own person, declares that Jesus "said *Give ye them to*

κατακλῶνται καὶ πληθύνουσι τῷ ὄχλῳ τῶν ἀκροωμένων, πολὺς γὰρ ὁ τοῖς αἰσθητοῖς ὡς μόνοις οὖσι προσανέχων. Πληθύνω is perhaps used as a mild paraphrase of χορτάζω.

[1] Rev. v. 6, Is. xi. 1.

[2] In Mk vi. 37, Mt. xiv. 16 δότε αὐτοῖς ὑμεῖς φαγεῖν, the addition of ὑμεῖς to δότε shews that the pronoun in "give *ye*" is emphasized; but in Lk. ix. 13 (W.H. txt) δότε αὐτοῖς φαγεῖν ὑμεῖς, "*ye*" is extraordinarily emphatic, coming at the end of the sentence.

[3] Origen on Mt. xiv. 16 (Lomm. iii. 68) Ἐπεὶ οὖν παιδεύσας ὑμᾶς ἱκανοὺς ἐποίησα πρὸς τὸ διδόναι τοῖς δεομένοις λογικὴν τροφήν, ὑμεῖς δότε....

eat because of that power to feed others besides themselves which He had bestowed on the disciples[1]."

It may be taken as certain that John did not believe that the disciples had received at this time the "power to feed others" in the full spiritual sense. Origen adds "So long as these five loaves and two fishes were not *borne* (or, *brought*) by the disciples of Jesus, they did not increase[2]." But John represents Jesus as Himself distributing the bread to the multitude[3], and excludes the disciples from any part in the miracle except the collecting of the broken pieces. The Johannine view of the miracle is quite different from that of the Synoptists. In John, Jesus cannot say to the disciples "Give *ye* them to eat," for they have nothing to give. The loaves do not belong to them. Origen himself points out this, though he quaintly connects it with the inferior nature of the "barley" loaves: "John alone says that the loaves were 'barley loaves.' Wherefore, perhaps, in the Gospel of John, the disciples *do not acknowledge that the loaves are with them,* but say, in John, 'There is a lad here who has five barley loaves and two fishes[4].'"

It must be admitted that John, by omitting Christ's precept to the Twelve, not only greatly lowers the spiritual character of the Feeding of the Five Thousand, but also departs from what appears to be the earliest and most faithful traditions about it. In the Synoptists, the miracle is a kind of firstfruits of the Eucharist, illustrating the Christian Law of Giving. In the Fourth Gospel, it is a kind of last repetition of the old

---

[1] Origen (Lomm. iii. 69) δι' ἣν ἔδωκε δύναμιν καὶ ἑτέρων θρεπτικὴν τοῖς μαθηταῖς.

[2] Origen (Lomm. iii. 70) ὅσον μὲν...οὐκ ἐφέροντο. Is it possible that he is referring to Mt. xiv. 18 φέρετέ μοι ὧδε αὐτούς, "bring them hither to me," so that the meaning is "Until they were *brought by the disciples of Jesus [to their Master]*"? Ἐφέροντο does not seem a suitable word to mean "*distributed*" by the disciples to the multitudes.

[3] Jn vi. 11, omitted in the Arabic Diatessaron.

[4] Origen (Lomm. iii. 70).

gift of Manna, and the old gift of the Law, exemplifying the failure of both to satisfy and redeem mankind, and demonstrating the need of a new source of spiritual life[1].

§ 34. *"Eating" in the presence of the Lord*

We have spoken above of the meal provided by Elisha for a hundred of the sons of the prophets; but some mention should also be made of an earlier Scriptural precedent, when Aaron and two of Aaron's sons and seventy of the elders of Israel went up with Moses, "and they saw the God of Israel...and they beheld God *and did eat and drink.*" The latter part of this is paraphrased by Onkelos, "They saw the Glory of the Lord, and *rejoiced in their sacrifices, which were accepted with favour, as though they had eaten and drunk,*" but by the Jerusalem Targum, "They saw the glory of the Shekinah of the Lord, and *rejoiced that their oblations were received with favour, and so did eat and drink[2].*" The passage is frequently referred to in Midrash, where it is mostly implied that Aaron's sons were led into error, perhaps an error of familiarity, in eating and drinking, and were punished for it[3]. But other passages

---

[1] If many versions or MSS followed Lk. ix. 13 (codex *a*) "date eis manducare" (omitting "*vos*") we might suppose that textual variations induced John to omit a phrase that meant no more than "give them something to eat." But the omission in codex *a* is so exceptional that nothing can be based on it. And the conclusion seems necessary that John's omission was dictated almost entirely by the feeling that the real Eucharistic "giving" was not understood and indeed was not instituted till after the Resurrection when Jesus gave the command "Feed my sheep."

[2] Exod. xxiv. 9—11. The Targums are quoted from Etheridge.

[3] See *Exod. r.* (Wü. pp. 38, 317), *Lev. r.* (Wü. p. 136), *Numb. r.* (Wü. p. 411), *Pesikt.* (Wü. p. 252). Rashi says *ad loc.* "contemplati erant illum curiose (*or*, animo elato) etiam inter edendum ac bibendum, sic interpretatio Tanchumae habet; sed Onkelos non ita interpretatus est." Comp. Lev. x. 8 (Jer. Targ.) "Drink neither wine nor anything that maketh drunk,...as thy sons did, who have died by the burning of fire."

connect the "eating and drinking" with a "banquet" on "the glory of the Shechinah," quoting from Proverbs "In the light of the King's countenance is life[1]." This "banquet," and the "sitting down" with Abraham and Isaac and Jacob in the aeon that is to come, are referred to in the tradition of Matthew and Luke[2]. Luke also once connects "table" and "covenant" and "thrones" in such a way as to constitute a parallelism between his words and those of the Pentateuch describing the "eating and drinking" of the "nobles" of Israel[3]; but the parallel Matthew has nothing that suggests a banquet. Nor has Matthew any mention of eating in his parallel to an earlier passage where Luke has "We ate before thee and drank; and in our streets didst thou teach[4]."

In the passage last quoted from Luke, Cyril paraphrases "*ate*" as the imperfect "*used to eat*," supposing that the words were uttered as an appeal to the Father (not to the Son) and that the words "*ate before thee*" referred to sacrifices eaten in the Temple. But if that had been the meaning, the imperfect

---

[1] See Taylor's note on *Aboth* iii. 25 "Everything is prepared for the banquet," quoting *Berach.* 17 *a*, and *Numb. r.* xxi., which says that the ministering angels "are fed on the splendour of the Shechinah, for it is said (Prov. xvi. 15) '*In the light* etc.'" On Prov. xvi. 15 see *Pesikt.* Wü. pp. 70, 140, 252, etc.

[2] Mt. viii. 11, Lk. xiii. 29.

[3] Lk. xxii. 29—30. Comp. Exod. xxiv. 11 "nobles," a noticeable word, LXX ἐπιλέκτων (one of 13 deviations of LXX discussed in the Talmud, see Levy i. 508 *a*). The parall. Mt. xix. 28 mentions "thrones" and "judging," but has nothing that suggests a banquet.

[4] Lk. xiii. 26 ἐφάγομεν ἐνώπιόν σου καὶ ἐπίομεν. The parall. Mt. vii. 22 οὐ τῷ σῷ ὀνόματι ἐπροφητεύσαμεν is blended by Origen repeatedly with Lk. so as to drop the difficult phrase ἐνώπιόν σου. Cyril (see Cramer *ad loc.*) explains "*thee*" as "*God*," thus: "How then used they to eat and to drink (ἤσθιον καὶ ἔπινον) in the presence of *God*? By performing the sacrificial-service (λατρείαν) of the Law." And he explains "thou didst teach" as referring to the Scriptures, the word of God, heard by the Jews in the synagogues.

might have been used by Luke here as elsewhere[1]. Nevertheless Cyril is right in supposing that *"ate before thee"* is not the same as *"ate with thee,"* and that it suggests some act of a disciple of Christ corresponding to the eating of a sacrifice by an Israelite "in the presence of" Jehovah to whom it is offered. But what act, what "eating," could be meant? The least unsatisfactory explanation, perhaps, is that Luke has placed the words in such a position that they may refer to the "eating" of the Five Thousand, which, according to Mark and Luke, was preceded by "teaching" or something corresponding to teaching (so as to fulfil the saying *"thou hast taught* in our streets[2]"). That would bring the Lucan tradition into harmony with the Johannine view, that the Five Thousand, for the most part, though they *"ate in the presence of"* Jesus, never truly knew Him or believed in Him. He "taught" in their "streets," but they did not accept the teaching.

We are not, however, on safe ground in attempting to build positive conclusions as to fact on this Lucan passage[3]. For there may have been other occasions to which "we ate" might definitely refer, *e.g.* the Feeding of the Four Thousand. That Luke does not mention this miraculous act does not exclude the possibility that he collected traditions referring to it although he did not know the reference. And if there were two such miraculous acts why should there not have been three or more—believed to have occurred before the Resurrection? It does not follow that there were only two because Mark has recorded only two, any more than it follows that there was only

---

[1] Lk. xvii. 27, 28 ἤσθιον, ἔπινον, followed by ἐγάμουν and ἠγόραζον. Ἐσθίω is freq. used for habitual or uncompleted eating.

[2] Mk vi. 34 διδάσκειν, Lk. ix. 11 ἐλάλει περὶ τῆς βασιλείας τοῦ θεοῦ.

[3] The fact that Matthew deviates from Luke, and the nature of Matthew's deviation, indicate that we have not here actual words of Christ, but early evangelistic explanations, indicating how extremists, on either side, whether anti-judaizers or judaizers, would be rejected by Jesus if they rejected His Spirit.

one because Luke and John have recorded only one—that is to say, only one before the Resurrection. The Acts of John boldly declares that every meal of the disciples with Jesus, even at a Pharisee's table, was miraculous: "Now if ever, having been invited by one of the Pharisees, He went in compliance with such an invitation, we used to go with Him. And one loaf used to be set by the inviter for each [of the guests], among whom He also used to receive one [and no more]. But He, blessing His [own] loaf, would distribute [it] to us. And from the little [thus distributed] each [of us] used to be filled-to-repletion, and our loaves were kept whole and sound, so that amazement fell on those who invited Him[1]."

§ 35. *"That he should give something to the poor,"*
in John

John tells us that after the Last Supper, when Jesus said, "That thou doest, do (R.V.) quickly," some supposed that Jesus meant "Buy what things we have need of for the feast, or, that he should give something to the poor[2]." Either supposition implies that Judas had been tardy about performing one of two duties that ought seemingly to have been performed before the Supper. We can understand this about the things needed "for the feast"; but how does it apply to the words "that he should give something to the poor"? Was that a duty calling for immediate performance? Only if the duty was connected in the minds of the disciples with the meal at

---

[1] *Acts of John* § 8. "One loaf (ἄρτος εἷς)" appears to be meant to be more emphatic than ἄρτος would have been (without εἷς). "One" is emphasized by its position in "among whom He also used to receive *one* [*and no more*] (ἐν οἷς καὶ αὐτὸς ἐλάμβανεν ἕνα)." "Filled to repletion," ἐχορτάζετο is here used as in the Synoptists, and not in a bad sense (as in Jn vi. 26). Incidentally the mention of "one loaf" is important as shewing the smallness of such "loaves" as we read of in the Bible.

[2] Jn xiii. 29.

which they were seated. If their Master had habituated them to the practice of giving something to the poor from their common purse on any special occasion when He sat down to a meal with them, in that case—and only in that case—could they suppose that Jesus sent out Judas, the purse-bearer, with something of the nature of a reproach for neglecting the duty to the poor, "That which thou art bound to do, do more quickly[1]."

On another occasion, Luke represents Jesus as saying "Now do ye, the Pharisees, cleanse the outside of the cup... but your inner part is full of ravening....Only *give ye the things that are inside [the vessel] as alms*, and behold, all things are pure unto you[2]." Here the meaning might be taken to be, literally, "send out some of the food in the dish to the poor and then all that is in the dish is pure." The parallel Matthew has "*Cleanse first the inward part of the cup*," shewing that this literalism ("send out to the poor") would not represent the meaning[3]. Yet it may represent a part of the meaning. Luke's version may represent a fact, namely, that Jesus was in the habit of giving to the poor either a portion of the meal at which He presided, or else a gift of money in lieu of that portion where the poor were not present in person. This would be a way of teaching the duty inculcated by Isaiah "Draw out thy soul to the hungry, and satisfy the afflicted soul[4]."

In view of these passages and of what Philo tells us about the common meal of the *Therapeutae*, we ought not perhaps to put aside the above-quoted grotesque extract from the Acts of John with a mere negation: "Of course there was nothing like this." Of course there was nothing "like this" literally. But

---

[1] Jn xiii. 27 τάχιον "more quickly." See *Joh. Gr.* **1918** and Index.

[2] Lk. xi. 39—41, see *Son* **3362** (iv) *a*.

[3] Mt. xxiii. 26.

[4] Is. lviii. 10, on the interpretations of which see *Proclam.* p. 312 "It is not to exclude, but to accompany, material giving."

are we not in danger of failing to realise that there may have been something "like this" spiritually, even before the Eucharist was instituted? Even at the house of a Pharisee where Jesus was but a guest, the disciples might be made by Him to feel that He was still their King, and that "in the light of the king's countenance there was life[1]," and that in His doctrine there was the living bread. Much more would this be the case where Jesus was Himself the host and the breaker of the bread. It seems antecedently probable that Jesus would have put into the breaking of the bread, and into the blessing of God over the bread, something beyond the formal Jewish meaning, something that was of the nature of a sacrifice.

In one of the Psalms, what is called by our Revised Version *"the sacrifice of thanksgiving,"* is called by the Authorised Version, more simply and more literally, *"thanksgiving"*; and Aquila, too, renders the precept "Sacrifice unto God *eucharist*[2]." The next Psalm says "The sacrifices of God are a broken spirit; a broken and a contrite heart, O God, thou wilt not despise[3]." To such a sacrifice Jesus seems to have pointed in His story of the publican who would not so much as lift up his face to heaven but stood afar off saying "God be merciful to me a sinner[4]."

Sorrow for wrong done to one's neighbour goes hand in hand with love and sympathy for one's neighbour; and the awaking consciousness of one's own sins awakens kindness towards others. Jesus is represented by Matthew as twice quoting from Hosea the words "I desire kindness and not

---

[1] Prov. xvi. 15. See above, p. 156.

[2] Ps. l. 14 Aq. θῦσον (זבח) τῷ θεῷ εὐχαριστίαν (תודה) (LXX θῦσον τῷ θεῷ θυσίαν αἰνέσεως). See Gesen. 393 a. *"Acknowledgment"* would be, in many respects, a good rendering of the Hebrew word תודה, since it could include "confession" and (Gesen. 392 b) *"thanksgiving."*

[3] Ps. li. 17.

[4] Lk. xviii. 13, peculiar to Luke.

sacrifice[1]," and by Mark as endorsing the saying of a scribe—
that to love God and one's neighbour is "better" than sacrifices[2].
Some early Evangelists may have argued: "We, too, we
Christians, have a sacrifice. Jesus did not mean that God
really desired no sacrifice. The words 'I desire kindness and
not sacrifice' are misleading if interpreted apart from the
doctrine of Christ as a whole." This may be the reason (or
one of the reasons) why Mark and Luke omit the quotation
from Hosea, and why Matthew and Luke omit the Marcan
tradition. Nevertheless it may be taken as certain that the
omitted passages represent Christ's fundamental thought.

§ 36. "We all partake of the one loaf[3]"

One more remains to be added to the allusions inherent in
early traditions about Christ's Doctrine of Bread, and about the
acts accompanying it. It comes to us stamped with Pauline
authority, but very difficult (one would suppose) for Greeks to
understand without some knowledge of Jewish customs[4].
Speaking to his Corinthian converts about the Christian
Eucharist Paul says "We all partake of *the one loaf*."

This assumes that "the one loaf" was the emblem of unity
and that the Corinthians understood the assumption. There
is nothing in Greek literature that points to, or explains, any
such notion. But we learn from Maimonides and from a
Talmudic tract called *Erubin*, that is, *Communions* or *Mixings*,
that the Jews had such a notion and a practice based upon it.
The scribes carried it back to Solomon, and the language used
by Paul indicates that it was at all events an established
practice of the Synagogue in Corinth during the first century.

---

[1] Mt. ix. 13, xii. 7 quoting Hos. vi. 6.
[2] Mk xii. 33. [3] 1 Cor. x. 17.
[4] Acts xviii. 7—17 shews the important part played by the
Corinthian Synagogue in connection with the foundation of the
Corinthian Church.

Maimonides tells us, in effect, that it is forbidden to neighbours to go [on the sabbath day] from one house to another "unless all the neighbours on the sabbath eve enter into communion (*lit.* make an *Erub* or Mixing)....But how is that communion made? They communicate in one food, which they prepare on the eve of the sabbath, as though they would say, We all communicate, and we have all one food[1]." Then he adds that this communion must be made with a whole loaf. Portions, however large they may be, of large loaves, cannot replace the one small loaf however small it may be: "They do not consort together in courts save with a whole loaf[2]."

The Teaching of the Twelve Apostles contains a brief Eucharistic ritual in which what Paul calls "*the loaf that we break*" is briefly called "*the broken* [*thing*]," or "*this which we are breaking*[3]." This is said to be a unique use of the word *clasma*, which in the Gospels and elsewhere means "fragment." Certainly it does not mean "fragment" here. For the ritual continues "As this *clasma* existed [once as seed] scattered abroad (*or*, widely sown) on the hills, and having been gathered together, became one, so let thy Church be gathered together

---

[1] See *Hor. Heb.* on 1 Cor. x. 17.

[2] The quotation continues "Although the bread of the batch be a whole *seah*, if it be not a whole loaf, they do not enter into consortship with it. But if it be whole, if it be no more than an *assarius* only, they enter into *consortship* with it."

"How do they enter into κοινωνίαν, communion, in the courts? They demand of every house which is in the court one whole cake or loaf, which they lay up in one vessel, and in some house which is in the court, although it be a barn, or a stable etc. And one of the company blesseth, and so all eat together," etc.

The phrase for "a whole loaf" is פת שלימה בלבד "a loaf complete by itself." Apparently the blessing and breaking would take place over one of these "whole loaves," one representing the whole number.

[3] *Didach.* ix. 3 περὶ δὲ τοῦ κλάσματος· Εὐχαριστοῦμέν σοι...follows πρῶτον περὶ τοῦ ποτηρίου· Εὐχαριστοῦμέν σοι, implying that "the broken" was a Eucharistic term as familiar to the readers as "the cup."

from the ends of the earth into thy kingdom[1]." This passage, and the Jewish practice of "communion by means of the one loaf," indicate that the word "bread (*or* loaf)" conveyed to Jews suggestions of unity that would be unintelligible to Greeks without explanation.

In the first passage where "bread" is mentioned in the Bible the LXX represents God as saying to Adam "In the sweat of thy brow shalt thou eat thy bread[2]." But the Hebrew omits "thy," and the Targum takes the meaning to be, in effect, "Thou shalt be permitted to eat bread, the food of man, instead of eating the herb of the field, the food of beasts—which was at first the sentence pronounced on thee." The Jews appear to have discerned in a loaf—prepared by the hand of man out of many particles through many processes, sowing, reaping, threshing, grinding, kneading and baking—a unity not apparent in a heap of grass or herbs. This unity seemed a fit symbol of the unifying power that converts individuals into a community, congregation, or church. When and whence this notion came into their literature is perhaps not ascertainable, but that it was current among the Christians of the first century is certain. We ought therefore to be prepared to find a trace of it in the Fourth Gospel.

§ 37. *"Jesus...taketh the loaf and giveth to them[3]," in John*

The Fourth Gospel concludes with a description of Jesus giving a meal in the morning to seven of His disciples who

---

[1] *Didach.* ix. 4 ὥσπερ ἦν τοῦτο τὸ κλάσμα διεσκορπισμένον ἐπάνω τῶν ὀρέων καὶ συναχθὲν ἐγένετο ἕν, οὕτω συναχθήτω σου ἡ ἐκκλησία ἀπὸ τῶν περάτων τῆς γῆς εἰς τὴν σὴν βασιλείαν. The position of ἦν shews that it is best taken by itself and not as part of a pluperf. "had been scattered." See p. 138, n. 2, for Jerome's saying "seminarium fit ciborum," and see *Son* **3606** *a* for the metaphor of "sowing" Israel.

[2] Gen. iii. 19.

[3] Jn xxi. 13 ἔρχεται Ἰησοῦς καὶ λαμβάνει τὸν ἄρτον καὶ δίδωσιν αὐτοῖς. On Jn xxi. 9 A.V. "fish...bread," Westcott says "Rather, *a fish...a loaf*.... Compare *ib.* 13 *the fish...the loaf*. The thought of unity

have been fishing. The food is first spoken of thus, as being seen by the fishermen disciples who have been fishing: "So when they got out upon the land they see a fire of coals laid and a fish laid thereon and a loaf[1]." No mention is made of the source whence the food came. Nor are the fishermen at once invited to partake of it. First they are bidden to draw in the net. They had caught nothing all through the night. But at the dawn, having been instructed to cast the net "on the right side," they have at last caught a draught, and the "*at last*" is emphasized in the command "Bring of the fish that ye have *now* taken." When this duty is performed they are invited to the morning meal, and then it is said that Jesus "cometh and taketh the loaf and giveth to them and the fish likewise."

Why and whence is Jesus described as "coming"? Is He to be regarded as now coming from a distance although at the beginning of the story He "stood on the beach" and the disciples have now "got out upon the land"? This seems impossible. "Coming" seems superfluous, if taken literally. But it may be taken as the act of "Him that Cometh[2]," like the Light that "cometh into the world," coming to all the seven collectively and to each individually. Then it becomes intelligible.

Similarly as regards the "taking," we are not to regard the word literally as signifying that He went to the fire and

---

seems to be distinctly presented." In Jn vi. 11, W. H. read διέδωκεν (Tisch. ἔδωκεν) but here δίδωσιν (D εὐχαριστήσας ἔδωκεν). In Jn xxi. 13, SS has "and Jesus took [the] bread and [the] fish and blessed [God] over them and gave to them."

[1] Jn xxi. 9 βλέπουσιν ἀνθρακιὰν κειμένην καὶ ὀψάριον ἐπικείμενον. R.V. omits κειμένην, or paraphrases it by "there." But in view of John's use of κεῖμαι elsewhere and the contextual ἐπικείμενον here, it seems desirable to render the two participles "*laid*" and "*laid hereon*." See below, p. 166 foll.

[2] On "Him that Cometh" as a name of the Messiah, see *Joh. Voc.* **1633**, *Son* **3239—41**.

took off the loaf[1], either once for all the disciples, or seven times for each of them. He "takes" it as the father of any Jewish family might "take" bread in his hands before blessing God and breaking it. In the Feeding of the Five Thousand Jesus is described as "giving separately" or "distributing." Here He simply "gives." What He "gives," whether a part of the loaf or the whole, is not made clear. It would have been easy to make it clear. But the writer leaves it in doubt—with what looks like deliberate purpose—as if to lead us to say "After all, what does it matter? Jesus comes. This must mean He comes to each. He gives. This must mean He gives to each. And what else can He give to us as our bread except Himself? We had a foretaste of this truth in the sign of the barley loaves; and the truth itself is now set forth in this homely farewell breakfast given by the Lord to prepare the disciples to labour for Him after His departure."

If words that at first appear superfluous in this narrative are to be regarded as symbolical or allusive, what symbolical meaning are we to attach to the *"fire of coals laid"*? Why is the word *"laid"* inserted—a word so superfluous (seemingly) that it is left untranslated by our English Versions? And what allusion, if any, exists in the rare word "fire-of-coals"? The Greek for "fire of coals" occurs nowhere else in N.T. except in the Johannine account of Peter's denials. There it is said that the servants of the High Priest had "made" the *"fire of coals,"* but here no "maker" or "layer" is mentioned. A supernatural origin is however suggested, like that of the " coals " by the side of Elijah whom "an angel touched," and "he looked, and behold, there was at his head a cake *baken on the coals*[2]." The Hebrew there rendered "coals" occurs no-where else except in Isaiah "Then flew one of the seraphim

---

[1] Apparently the loaf is on the embers. So Nonnus takes it, calling the loaf νέον, "new," and the fire μαραινομένην, *i.e.* dying down.

[2] 1 K. xix. 6 *"coals,"* marg. *"hot stones."*

unto me having *a live coal* in his hand," where the touch of
the coal purifies the prophet's lips and prepares him to deliver
his message[1]. An ancient Christian commentary calls attention
to the coincidence that Peter "denied and confessed near a
coal fire[2]." Are we to suppose that it is more than a coincidence, and that the coal fire represents trial or temptation
of two kinds:—first, in the High Priest's palace, temptation,
for evil, proceeding from men, secondly, by the Sea of Tiberias,
temptation, for good[3], proceeding from God?

This is perhaps too subtle, even for the author of the Fourth
Gospel. But if such a representation were intended we could
the better understand that this fire is regarded as "laid,"
"set," or "appointed." The Greek word is the same as that
used in the sayings "The axe is *laid* to the root of the trees[4],"
and "This [child] is (lit.) *laid* (R.V. *set*) for the falling and
rising up of many in Israel[5]." It is also used by John in connection with the sign of the wine at Cana: "Now there were
there stone water-vessels, six [in number], in accordance with
the purifying of the Jews, *laid* [*ready*]," that is, *prepared for
use, or for Christ's sign*[6]. And the same apparent superfluity
and latent mysticism is to be found in the account of the
vinegar at the Cross: "After this, Jesus,...that the scripture
might be accomplished, saith, I thirst. *A vessel lay* [*ready for*

---

[1] Is. vi. 6 "*live coal,*" marg. "*hot stone.*"

[2] See *Son* **3369** *a* foll.

[3] Yet where is the "temptation for good"? May we see it in
the question "Lovest thou me *more than these?*" as if it meant
"Wilt thou still *set thyself up above the others*, and say, *Though all
should stumble yet not I?*" In his reply, Peter does not now give
prominence to "I" but to "Thou." That is to say, he makes no
profession directly about himself, but appeals to Christ's knowledge
("thou knowest that I love thee").

[4] Mt. iii. 10, Lk. iii. 9.   [5] Lk. ii. 34.

[6] Jn ii. 6 ἦσαν δὲ ἐκεῖ λίθιναι ὑδρίαι ἓξ κατὰ τὸν καθαρισμὸν τῶν
Ἰουδαίων κείμεναι. The *Philocalia* of Origen § 12 (Lomm. xxv. 14)
paraphrases this as αἱ ἐπὶ καθαρισμῷ τῶν Ἰουδαίων ὑδρίαι κεῖσθαι λεγόμεναι,
but that is only a paraphrase.

the soldiers, or for the fulfilment of scripture] full of vinegar[1]."
Similarly here the meaning may be that the "coal fire" was
"laid" by the hand of God, the sign of that fiery trial through
which the soul is to pass into communion with Him. This is
a new revelation not given to the Five Thousand. They took
the bread of the barley loaves and were filled with it as cattle
with fodder. But this bread, or rather this one loaf, comes
"*laid above*" fire; and the fire itself is no ordinary one, but
fire as from the altar in heaven, "*laid*" by the hand of God.

It should be noted that after Peter and the rest have
partaken of this food baked on the coal fire, Peter is warned
that he himself will "follow" Jesus on the way of the Cross,
dying by crucifixion. If that is to be his fiery trial, the question
arises whether in early Christian literature there are any traces
of a comparison between martyrdom and the baking of bread
baked on the coals. There is something of the kind in the
account of the martyrdom of Polycarp. He was burned alive,
and the martyr's body is said to have emitted a fragrant odour
like that of "*bread that is being baked*[2]." Eusebius omits this;
but there can hardly be a doubt that he omits it, not as a
corrupt reading but in fear that the detail might shock his
readers. The fear was (doubtless) well grounded in the days
of Constantine. But when the Church was not yet established,
and while it was still being watered with the blood of martyrs,
passionate metaphor was natural and necessary. Clement of
Alexandria not only uses language resembling that rejected by
Eusebius, but also applies it to Christ Himself. Commenting
on the words of Jesus "The bread that I will give is my flesh,
which I will give for the life of the world," Clement implies
that the "*flesh*" must be prepared by "*fire*" to become the
food of the world. Then, playing on the double meaning of

---

[1] Jn xix. 29 σκεῦος ἔκειτο ὄξους μεστόν. Nonnus "there was
ready (ἑτοῖμον ἔην)."

[2] *Polyc. Mart.* § 15 ὡς ἄρτος ὀπτώμενος (v.r. ὀπτόμενος) is omitted
(Lightf.) by Eusebius.

the Greek *puros*, i.e. "fire" or "wheat," he introduces the thought of the wheat rising up in a kind of resurrection, and likens it at the same time to *"bread that is being baked*[1]*."* Aesthetically such language may be repellent, but it will be of use if it leads us to think how very much is implied by the author of the Fourth Gospel, for himself and for those who are in sympathy with him, by the vision of "the fire of coals" and that which was "laid thereon."

§ 38. *Christ's "leaven"*

This loaf that is seen, along with the fish, on "the coal fire[2]," is it to be supposed to be leavened or unleavened? The same question applies to the "one loaf" that the disciples had with them when they were told to "beware of leaven[3]." Tertullian implies a connection of "leaven" with fire through the "oven" in which bread is baked[4]. He is referring to Christ's saying that the Kingdom of God "is like unto leaven, which a woman took and hid in three measures of meal till it was all leavened[5]"; but he does not explain to us the nature of this "leaven," or its relation to "the leaven of the Pharisees." Ignatius recognises a *"new leaven"* as appertaining to Christ[6].

---

[1] Clem. Alex. 125 ἐνταῦθα τὸ μυστικὸν τοῦ ἄρτου παρασημειωτέον, ὅτι σάρκα αὐτὸν λέγει καὶ ὡς ἀνισταμένην δῆθεν διὰ πυρός, καθάπερ ἐκ φθορᾶς καὶ σπορᾶς ὁ πυρὸς ἀνίσταται, καὶ μέντοι διὰ πυρὸς συνισταμένην εἰς εὐφροσύνην ἐκκλησίας ὡς ἄρτον πεπτόμενον.

[2] Jn xxi. 9.   [3] Mk viii. 15.

[4] Tertullian *Adv. Marc.* (on Lk. xiii. 21) "fermentationem quoque congruere...regno Creatoris quia post illam clibanus vel furnus gehennae sequatur." See context. Is he referring to Hosea vii. 4?

[5] Mt. xiii. 33 ὁμοία ἐστὶν ἡ βασιλεία τῶν οὐρανῶν ζύμη ἣν λαβοῦσα γυνὴ ἐνέκρυψεν εἰς ἀλεύρου σάτα τρία ἕως οὗ ἐζυμώθη ὅλον, sim. Lk. xiii. 21.

[6] Ign. *Magn.* § 10 ὑπέρθεσθε οὖν τὴν κακὴν ζύμην τὴν παλαιωθεῖσαν καὶ ἐνοξίσασαν, καὶ μεταβάλεσθε εἰς νέαν ζύμην, ὅς ἐστιν Ἰησοῦς Χριστός. On this, Lightf. quotes 1 Cor. v. 7 "purge out *the old leaven*," but gives no instance of *"new leaven."* He adds "On the metaphor generally see the note *Galatians* v. 9." In that note, he says "The

Justin Martyr recognises a *"new leaven"* as the opposite of the *"old"* Egyptian *"leaven,"* which was to be superseded by the *"new,"* after the brief interval of the week of unleavened bread[1]. It is possible that this aspect of Christ's doctrine— implying an antithesis between "old leaven" and "new leaven," between "bad leaven" and "good leaven"—was overshadowed by the Pauline antithesis between "leaven" and "the unleavened[2]." At all events it is a significant fact that in the writings of the early Christian Fathers and Apologists the words "leaven" and "unleavened" do not occur except in

---

leaven of Scripture is always a symbol of evil, with the single exception of the parable (Matt. xiii. 33, Luke xiii. 20, 21), as it is for the most part also in rabbinical writers: see Lightfoot on Matt. xvi. 6 and Schöttgen on 1 Cor. v. 6."

But "for the most part" would be misleading if it led the reader to suppose that either Lightfoot (*i.e.* the author of *Horae Hebraicae*) or Schöttgen quotes, from "rabbinical writers," a single instance of "leaven" in a good sense. Nor does Wetstein quote one. Nor is any alleged in the Biblical Dictionaries of Black and Hastings ("Leaven"). Dr A. Büchler informs me that he has been unable to find any such instance.

[1] Justin (*Tryph.* § 14) is bold enough to say to the Jews "Wherefore also, *after the seven days of eating unleavened bread*, God commanded you to knead for yourselves *new leaven*, that is to say, the doing of other works and not the imitation of those that were old and vile." He has previously said (*ib.*) "For this is the symbol of the unleavened, [being intended] in order that ye may not do the old deeds of *the evil leaven*."

[2] 1 Cor. v. 6 foll. "Know ye not that a little *leaven* leaveneth the whole lump? Purge out *the old leaven*, that ye may be a new lump, even as ye are *unleavened*. For our passover also hath been sacrificed, [even] Christ; wherefore let us keep the feast, not with *old leaven*, neither with *the leaven of malice and wickedness*, but with the *unleavened bread* of sincerity and truth."

If Paul had been asked "But what are we to do during the rest of the Christian Year, after keeping the Christian Passover? Are we never to partake of the bread described by our Lord as 'wholly leavened'?" he would doubtless have replied "Yes." But he deals with a different aspect of the metaphor, as if Christians were always keeping their Passover.

the two passages quoted above from Ignatius and Justin Martyr, and in one other instance where Justin says to the Jews "If ye eat *unleavened* bread ye say that ye have fulfilled the will of God[1]." Perhaps one reason why the doctrine of Christ's leaven fell into the background was that among Gentiles, as well as among Jews, there was a feeling that leaven was corrupt and impure[2]. Another reason may have been that Christ's doctrine was obscured by superabundant allegorism[3].

---

[1] Justin *Tryph.* § 12.

[2] See Lightf. on Gal. v. 9, "Plutarch, *Quaest. Rom.* 109 (p. 289 E), in answer to the question why the Flamen Dialis was not allowed to touch leaven, explains it, ἡ ζύμη καὶ γέγονεν ἐκ φθορᾶς αὐτὴ καὶ φθείρει τὸ φύραμα μιγνυμένη."

[3] Jerome, on Mt. xiii. 33, gives three explanations of it, and says that he has not space for others. Many of them might deal with the allegorical meaning of the "three measures of meal," on which see Clem. Alex. 694. The N.T. ἐνέκρυψεν εἰς ἀλεύρου σάτα τρία might invite comparison with Gen. xviii. 6 (Aq. Sym.) τρία σάτα σεμιδάλεως (al. exempl. τρία μέτρα ἀλεύρου σεμιδάλεως) καὶ ποίησον ἐγκρυφίας, on which Philo has much to say. Clem. Alex. 693—4 (following Philo) connects Gen. xviii. 6 ἐγκρυφίας, "cakes hidden [in the embers]" with a mystical "hiding," and subsequently quotes Mt. xiii. 33 ἐνέκρυψεν, referring to the threefold nature of man.

The doctrine of "good leaven" and "bad leaven" seems to imply the pre-existence of a food that can be assimilated to good or evil. Elsewhere Jesus speaks of a "good eye" and an "evil eye," and of an antagonism, or want of harmony, between "the flesh" and "the spirit," and implies (Mk xiv. 38, Mt. xxvi. 41, but not Lk.) that man can control the evil or the weakness. Some of these expressions may be illustrated by a very ancient Jewish doctrine about a "good" and a "bad" *nature* in man. See *Aboth* iv. 2 "Who is mighty? He that subdues *his nature* (יצרו)" (Taylor's note). The Heb. *yetser* (Gesen. 428) meant "*form, framing, purpose,*" occurring for the first time in Gen. vi. 5 "every *imagination* of the thoughts of his [man's] heart was only evil." It means, in New Heb., "*impulse*" or "*tendency*" (Gesen. "good or bad tendency in man"). Levy gives abundant instances of the New Heb. use, and (ii. 258) of the fem. יצירה meaning the earthly and the heavenly shaping ("Bildung") of man. *Inter alia* it quotes *j. Jeb.* iv. 5ᶜ "zwei *Bildungen*

And yet is it not in accordance with the simple homeliness and restfulness of Christ's doctrines that He should have raised a protest for leaven as an emblem of quiet and unobtrusive growth, and for leavened bread as a homely and pleasant gift of God? Luke places the parables of leaven and mustard seed after the sabbath cure of the "daughter of Abraham." The ruler of the synagogue reproved the act. Jesus said to him and his abettors, "Ye hypocrites[1]!" He implies that they were defiled with "the leaven of the Pharisees,"—a hypocritical zeal, a sin against the light, in placing the literal prohibitions of the Law of Leviticus above the dictates of natural humanity. God, in Nature, works not so much by repressing as by developing. And this Jesus proceeded to shew by the parables of the mustard seed, and of the leaven fermenting in the loaf. The leaven was kindness, divine kindness, passing from the Father in heaven to His children and from His children to one another.

An instance of what Paul might have called *"the leaven of the Pharisees"* may be found in the record of the proceedings

---

des Menschen, näml. zuerst innerhalb dreier Tage nach Empfang des Samens, und dann nach 40wöchiger Schwangerschaft."

Ign. *Magn.* § 10, after the words *"new leaven* which is Jesus Christ," continues, *"Be salted* (ἁλίσθητε) in Him, lest any one among you grow putrid (διαφθαρῇ) since from your savour ye will be detected (ἐλεγχθήσεσθε)"—which alludes to Mk ix. 49—50 (comp. Mt. v. 13, Lk. xiv. 34) "for everyone shall be salted with fire." On the other hand Justin Martyr (*Tryph.* § 14) before mentioning *"new leaven,"* discourses on *"baptism,"* and *"the water of life"*—not the "living water" that satisfies spiritual thirst, but the "water of life" regarded as washing away spiritual defilement. Both writers illustrate the variety of metaphor with which early Christians, following the earliest traditions of their Master's words, inculcated the doctrine of spiritual regeneration, and they lead to the conclusion that this doctrine was very much more in His thoughts than we might have inferred from the Synoptic Gospels, and from the absence of any continuous discourse about it in the Double Tradition of Matthew and Luke (commonly called "Q").

[1] Lk. xiii. 15.

of the Council of Jerusalem. After the admission of un-circumcised Gentiles to the Church by Peter, in accordance with a revelation from the Lord, "There arose up certain of the sect of the Pharisees who believed, saying, It is needful to circumcise them, and to charge them to keep the law of Moses[1]." Paul did not speak on this occasion. But, had he spoken, it would probably have been to this effect: "In Christ Jesus neither circumcision availeth anything nor uncircum-cision, but faith working through love....This persuasion [cometh] not from him that calleth you. *A little leaven leaveneth the whole lump*[2]." This "little leaven" is leaven in a bad sense. Why cannot we point to mentions of "*a little leaven*" in a good sense? Perhaps because this metaphor was too cosmopolitan for many Jews and too homely and original for many Gentiles. But these very reasons are reasons for believing that it originated from Jesus Himself—more alive than His disciples to the quiet and unobtrusive influences of beneficent Nature.

These considerations indicate that the whole of the Mark-Matthew comparison between the Feeding of the Five Thousand and that of the Four Thousand may have been omitted by Luke, not because he disbelieved that there had been such a comparison, but because he believed that it referred to a period after Christ's resurrection. The disciples may have received at that time some revelation about the admission of the Gentile element into the Church, such a revelation as Peter received at Joppa. A voice may have come to them from Jesus, warning them against the "leaven" of "the Pharisees," the leaven of exclusiveness and unkindness, and reminding them that all alike, Jews and Gentiles, must feed on a bread that was not unleavened but was leavened with the "new leaven" of "faith working through love." The cir-cumstances of the two acts of feeding were different, but the

---

[1] Acts xv. 5.   [2] Gal. v. 6—9.

principle was the same. As the Apostles, when ministering to the twelve tribes of Israel, received correspondently twelve *cophinoi* of fragments, so, when ministering to the multitude of the Gentiles, who came from the four quarters of the world, they received seven *sphurides*, a number that would correspond to "the seven Spirits of God" and "the seven Churches," mentioned in Revelation. The "five loaves" of the Law were broken for the former; the "seven" loaves of the Spirit for the latter. But the loaves were broken by one and the same Lord. The difference did not prevent the recognition of the fact that all alike, Jews and Gentiles, partook of the "one loaf."

§ 39. *The passionateness of the Eucharist*

In the foregoing investigation the main object has been to ascertain, not what was the fact, but what was believed to be the fact by the Evangelists, and especially in those narratives where Luke omitted or altered something that was in Mark. And we have been led to the conclusion that Mark contains traces—not found in Luke and rarely found in Matthew—of early Eucharistic doctrine taught by Christ before the institution of the Eucharist. John appears to have cleared away what obscured those traces so that they shew something like a path, which he has broadened and lengthened into a highway running right through his Gospel. But this path or highway may guide us to the actual and historical fact.

Among the Jews it was customary for the father of the family, at the commencement of a family meal, to take up a loaf and to bless God over it and break it. This practice Jesus appears to have adopted, breathing into it a new spiritual meaning and a passionateness of His own. It was not enough, He might say, to lift up and break the loaf. We must, as Jeremiah said, "lift up our heart with our hands unto God in the heavens[1]," and the best way to lift up the heart to God

---

[1] Lam. iii. 41.

the Father in the breaking of bread was to do something from one's heart for His children that had no bread. This something was not to be the mere giving of alms for the sake of reward. Such alms (Jesus declared) the Pharisaean formalists gave. They allowed a conventional religion of rules to drive out the natural morality of the conscience. They encouraged a son to withhold a *Corban* from his needy parents in order to give it to God. But Christ's religion was to be of the heart, and His almsgiving was to be a "drawing out" of the "soul" to the hungry[1], a suffering with their sufferings, an action that partook of the nature of sacrifice.

It is not definitely recorded that Jesus ever carried out these precepts in a literal way by summoning the poor to His table and giving them food, or by sending them food or money before sitting down to table[2]. Jesus had no house, no "table," that He could call His own. But all the Evangelists agree that on one occasion, out in "the wilderness," He (so to speak) extemporised a "table" for a hungry multitude. Mark and Matthew add that He did this on a second occasion. John relates that He did this, after the Resurrection, on a third occasion. In the apocryphal Acts of John it is said that He did this habitually for His disciples even when He and they were in the house of a stranger.

There is a striking difference between Mark and Luke in one of these traditions about Jesus and His disciples at their common meal. Whereas Luke represents Jesus as saying to His disciples "Who is greater, he that sitteth at meat or he that serveth [at table]?....But I am in the midst of you as he that serveth [at table]," Mark represents Him as saying "The Son of man came not to be served [at table] but to serve [at table], and to give his life (*or*, soul) a ransom for many."

---

[1] Is. lviii. 10.

[2] See, however, p. 158 foll., on Jn xiii. 29 "that he should give something to the poor."

Also the occasions differ. Luke places the words much later than Mark, as being actually uttered at table, during the Last Supper[1].

John deals with these traditions in a simple, concrete, and dramatic way. Perhaps he knew that Mark's noun "servant [at table]," *diaconos*, or "deacon"—omitted by Luke—was liable to be confused with the Christian official "deacon[2]." At all events he first uses the noun concerning the "*servants [at table]*" in Cana who draw the water that becomes wine[3]. Then he uses the verb concerning Martha's literal, homely, waiting at table "Martha *was serving [at table]*[4]." Then, in the Temple on the morrow, when Jesus has heard that "certain Greeks" desire to see Him, there is a noteworthy change in the use of the word. The Law of the spiritual Harvest, and of Life through Death, is proclaimed as if it were also the Law of the Feast, or Joy, or Table, in Heaven, at which Table no soul is admitted to feast until it has first "*waited*," or "*served*," and he that desires thus to "*serve*" must be willing to lose his life: "He that loveth his life loseth (*or*, destroyeth) it, and he that hateth his life in this world shall keep it unto life eternal. If any one *is bent on serving me [at my table]* let him follow me, and where I am there also shall be *my servant [that serves at my table]*. If any one *is bent on serving me [at my table]*, him will my Father honour[5]."

This is the last Johannine instance of the *word* "serve [at table]" either as noun or as verb, but John proceeds to dramatize the *thing* by representing Jesus as actually "serving [at table]," during the Last Supper, girding Himself with a towel and washing the feet of the disciples. This no other Evangelist has related. In previous parts of this series the

---

[1] Mk x. 45, Lk. xxii. 27. [2] *Proclam.* p. 404.
[3] Jn ii. 5, 9.
[4] Jn xii. 2. Comp. Lk. x. 40 "Martha was distracted (περιεσπᾶτο) about much *serving [at table]* (διακονίαν)."
[5] Jn xii. 25—6. See *Joh. Gr.* **2552** c.

question has been discussed whether John's narrative of this particular act of "serving at table" can be accepted as literally true in spite of its omission by the Synoptists, and the opinion was expressed that the event was probably historical even if it did not occur on that particular occasion[1]. This opinion has been confirmed by further study revealing, through many sources, but especially through Mark and John, traces of early passionate feeling, expressed in passionate words, concerning the Sacrifice of the Eucharist and details connected with it. Some of these expressions might be omitted or softened in later days.

§ 40.   *The " kiss of love"*

It is of the utmost importance that we, Christians, should recall as far as possible this Christian passionateness, so far as it came from Christ Himself. The details of the Miracles of Feeding—the "taking" and "blessing" and "breaking," and the question whether the "breaking" may be metaphorical as well as literal, meaning the dividing and distribution of the word of God—are all subordinate to the realisation of the spirit of the common meal which we call the Eucharist, and to the question of the origin of that spirit.   Hence, in conclusion, a few words of apparent digression from the Miracles of Feeding in the Gospels to the thought of the Eucharist as it is discerned in the Epistles, may really be no digression at all, but a return to the essence of our subject.   Now among the accompaniments of the Eucharist (or of Christian gatherings) most frequently mentioned in the Epistles is the "kiss."   Paul speaks of "a holy kiss," Peter of "a kiss of love" wherewith Christians are to salute one another[2].   Whence did this spring?

---

[1] See *Son* **3276** *a* (and Index, "Washing") and the references there given.

[2] Rom. xvi. 16, 1 Cor. xvi. 20, 2 Cor. xiii. 12, 1 Thess. v. 26, ἐν φιλήματι ἁγίῳ (and comp. 1 Pet. v. 14 ἐν φιλήματι ἀγάπης).   The meaning might be "with *the* holy kiss," or "*the* kiss of love."   The long article on "Kiss" in Smith's *Dict. Antiq.* ii. 902—6 contains

We find nothing alleged from Jewish or Gentile practice that explains it[1]. It is true that Jesus is represented as saying reproachfully to a Pharisee at whose table He is sitting as a guest "Thou gavest me no kiss[2]"; but no commentator (so far as I know) shews that the kiss was a mere courtesy among the Jews—a courtesy expected by guests from their host as a matter of course. Has Luke been misled by the special practice of Christians? Did Jesus introduce it among His disciples as a sign that they belonged to the Family of God?

It was a practice open to obvious abuse. Only the earlier Pauline Epistles and the first Epistle of Peter contain the precept to salute after this fashion. Clement of Alexandria complains of the abuse of it between the sexes[3]. Athenagoras is said to quote an apocryphal precept of caution about it[4].

---

no mention or suggestion of any Jewish or Gentile origin or precedent for the Christian rite.

[1] On Rom. xvi. 16 (on which Wetstein and Schöttgen give no help) Fritzsche has a long note, and Lightfoot has one on 1 Thess. v. 26. But they give no illustration from Jewish usage. Nor is there any light thrown by Hamburger i. 685, or Levy iii. 453—4 where different kinds of kisses are distinguished.

[2] Lk. vii. 45. On this *Hor. Heb.* is silent, as also on 1 Cor. xvi. 20 "a holy kiss."

[3] Clem. Alex. 301 "The shameless use of the kiss, which ought to be mystic, occasions foul suspicions and evil reports."

[4] Athenagoras *Apolog.* § 32. This is important because if (as the translator in Clark's translation suggests) Athenagoras is quoting "probably from some apocryphal writing," the testimony takes us back to a period even earlier, and perhaps much earlier, than A.D. 177: "For the Logos again says to us 'If anyone kiss a second time because it has given him pleasure [he sins],' adding, Therefore *the kiss, or rather the salutation, should be given with the greatest care* (οὕτως οὖν ἀκριβώσασθαι τὸ φίλημα μᾶλλον δὲ τὸ προσκύνημα δεῖ)...." Here the correction of "kiss" into προσκύνημα, implying an act of homage or "worship" (in the old English sense), and the precept to "be precise about it (ἀκριβώσασθαι)," prove that the author of this early saying is referring to what Paul and Peter call "the holy kiss" or "kiss of love." He seems to regard it as almost equivalent to an act of homage or love to Christ, as the Lord and the Beloved,

Athenagoras is defending the Christians against the charge
of practising promiscuous intercourse, and he declares that,
so far from doing this, they recognise fellow-believers as being
spiritually blood relations according to age, sons or daughters,
brothers or sisters, fathers or mothers; and he bids us recognise
"the kiss or rather the obeisance" as the symbol of family
affection. Similarly the Jews, excusing the "kiss" given by
Jacob to Rachel, added to the three lawful kinds of kissing a
fourth, namely, the kiss between blood relations[1]. Now the
Synoptic Gospels tell us that Jesus introduced as it were a
relationship of blood between all His disciples, including them
in His own relations when He said "Who is my mother and my
brethren? And looking round on them that sat round about
him, he saith, Behold, my mother and my brethren! For who-
soever shall do the will of God, the same is my brother, and
sister, and mother[2]."

The parallel Luke—which has been discussed elsewhere[3]—
omits this last phrase where "sister" is added to "brother."
John has nothing of the kind verbally. But if, by "brother"
and "sister," we mean "beloved as a brother" and "beloved
as a sister," then we may say that by implication John did
not shrink from including sisters as well as brothers in the
newly instituted Family of Christ. He does this as usual in a
dramatic and concrete form. The sisters of Lazarus, he says,
"sent to Jesus, saying, Lord, behold, he whom thou lovest is

---

paid invisibly to Him when paid visibly to the brethren and sisters
who are members of His Body.

[1] See Gen. xxix. 11 and *Gen. r. ad loc.*, also *Exod. r.* on Exod. iv.
27, and Levy iii. 453 *b*. The other three lawful kinds were (1) "the
kiss of magnifying (נדולה) or glorifying," given by Samuel to Saul
(1 S. x. 1), (2) "the kiss of meeting [after long absence]" (Exod. iv.
27), (3) "the kiss of separation" (Ruth i. 14).

[2] Mk iii. 33—5, Mt. xii. 48—50, comp. Lk. viii. 21.

[3] The exact details of the parallelism are somewhat complicated.
See *Proclamation* p. 470 foll.

sick[1]." Then he adds, "Now Jesus loved Martha and her sister and Lazarus"; and he represents the tears of Martha's sister as preceding, and in part causing, tears from Jesus, and thus as preceding (and perhaps preparing for) the raising of Lazarus[2].

Lucian is the only writer of literary Greek quoted in the Thesaurus as using the expression "salute with a kiss," and the context shews how bad an impression the connection of such a phrase with Christian worship might produce on Gentiles[3]. Philo would certainly not have approved of it, for he expatiates on the frequent falseness of this "superficial welcoming," and is at great pains to distinguish the Greek, *philēma*, "kiss," literally "act of love," from *philiā*, "love" (or "friendship")[4]. Thus no Greek source presents itself for this Christian custom. And we have seen above that no Jewish source presents itself either, except in special conditions. We are driven to the conclusion that in some way one or more of those "special conditions" was fulfilled. Now one of these "special conditions" was blood-relationship. That, as we have seen, Christ might be said to have introduced among

---

[1] Jn xi. 3.

[2] Jn xi. 5, 33 foll.

[3] See Lucian ii. 248 *Alex.* § 41 φιλήματι ἀσπάζεσθαι, and οἱ ἐντὸς τοῦ φιλήματος, *i.e.* "those who were included in [the circle of those honoured with] a kiss," about a monster of sensuality, named Alexander. Possibly Lucian regarded Alexander as having borrowed from the Christians (though Alexander was opposed to them) this detail of their worship, and as having perverted it. A preceding chapter (*ib.* § 38) says that Alexander began his "mysteries" by proclaiming "Out with the Christians!"

Reasons of seemliness may have combined with textual reasons to induce John to omit the Synoptic tradition that Judas "betrayed with a kiss (נשק)." See *Son* 3326 c, and add Ps. cxl. 7 "day of battle (נשק)," explained (Levy iii. 453 a) by some as "*arming*" against the Messiah. This is more probable than the Greek corruption suggested in *Paradosis* 1365.

[4] Philo i. 478—9 φίλημα δὲ διαφέρει τοῦ φιλεῖν. A "kiss" he calls ἐπιπόλαιον δεξίωσιν.

His disciples. Another condition was consecration. This, too, might be regarded as proceeding from Christ's lips when He was present in the Eucharist. Another was either parting or return after absence. This would be fulfilled with special reality when Jesus, after the Resurrection, fulfilled His promise, "I will see you again, and your joy no man taketh from you." When He came thus to "see" them "again," it is said by John that He "breathed into them" and said "Receive ye the Holy Spirit[1]." Perhaps this might be regarded as, in some sense, the "kiss" of Christ. According to Jewish tradition, God "kissed" Moses when He drew forth his soul in a peaceful death[2]. That might be called a kiss of parting, the work of life on earth being over. But the name might also be given to the kiss of return, when the Lord prepared His disciples for the work of the Gospel, touching their lips and comforting their hearts with the kiss of the Holy Spirit. And the disciples, having once received this kiss from their Master at their first Eucharist after the Resurrection, may have henceforth passed on the salutation from one to another at every Eucharist, as being the kiss "of love" and "holy[3]."

---

[1] See *Son* **3623** *g—j* on Jn xx. 22 ἐνεφύσησε.

[2] Deut. xxxiv. 5 Jer. Targ. Miriam also (*M. Kat.* 28 *a*) died by "God's kiss," Abraham (*Test. Abr.* §20) by kissing the hand of the Angel of Death.

[3] The thought of the *philēma*, or "kiss," as proceeding from Jesus leads us to the thought of the title *philoi*, or "friends," used by Jesus about His disciples. Luke is the only one of the Synoptists who represents Jesus as using it thus:—

Mt. x. 27—8	Lk. xii. 3—4
"What ye hear in the ear, proclaim upon the housetops; and be not afraid of them that kill the body...."	"What ye have spoken in the ear in the inner chambers shall be proclaimed upon the housetops; and *I say unto you my friends*, Be not afraid of them that kill the body...."

In the Fourth Gospel, Jesus explains (Jn xv. 13—15) what He means when He says to the disciples "Ye are *my friends*." Friendship may imply dying for one's friend ("Greater love hath no man

Even if we reject this explanation some of us may be benefited by being compelled to confess that there is beneath this ancient Christian rite something that needs to be explained. The explanation, whatever it may be, appears to involve the recognition of a personality in Jesus even more marvellous than we had supposed. Many believe easily enough in Christ's material miracles who do not realise His spiritual, social, and (so to speak) revolutionary miracles wrought on human nature. This "holy kiss" seems to represent a kind of high-water mark, reached at one rush by the religion of Christ during the period that followed His death, and perhaps to be reached again, after an interval of many centuries hereafter, but in a different way. Then it was reached by a visible Presence and an audible Voice. Hereafter the Presence may be not visible, and the Voice not audible, to the bodily sense. But in either case the Spirit will be the same, human yet divine, cosmopolitan yet homely, the Spirit of the Family of God breathed into God's children by God's Son[1].

---

than this") but such death is not a condition: "Ye are *my friends* if ye do the things that I command you." The term "*Caesar's friend*" was known to the mob (Jn xix. 12) in Jerusalem. Epictetus uses it repeatedly in his lecture on Freedom (iv. 1. 8—95) bidding his pupils not to seek freedom by gaining admission to the circle of "*Caesar's friends*" but (*ib.* 98) to "attach themselves to God." Luke's tradition, taken with the context ("kill the body") enables us to understand that there would be a tendency in the Christian Church to call the martyrs "*Christ's friends*" in a special sense.

The conclusion of the Fourth Gospel (Jn xxi. 15—22) neutralises such a tendency. It shews that Peter, the future Martyr on the Cross, had no precedence in the matter of friendship, over the silent disciple "whom Jesus loved." The proof of Peter's affection demanded by Jesus is not expressed in an imperative "Then die for me," but in "Feed my sheep." In 3 Jn 14 (15), the expressions "*The friends* salute thee," and "salute *the friends*," are probably to be explained (from Jn xv. 14) as meaning "*the friends of the Lord* [*with me*]" and "*the friends of the Lord* [*with thee*]" (not "my friends" and "thy friends").

[1] Attention has been called (*Joh. Voc.* **1697**, and Index) to the

§ 41. *"Testament" or "Covenant"*

The last two sections bear less directly on the miracles of
feeding than on what appears to be their outcome. What
follows will depart still further from the miracles and will turn
itself toward the Eucharist. Not that we must permit ourselves to discuss so important a subject here out of its place.
But in fact all the preceding forty sections have been leading
us up, through the words "Give ye them to eat," to the
question "What was Jesus Himself preparing to give us to
eat?" Consequently, in taking our leave of the miracles of
feeding, some reply to this question seems demanded.

---

fact that Mark never uses the word ἀγάπη. Hermas, who frequently
resembles Mark, mentions ἀγάπη as a virtue thrice, twice connecting it with "understanding (φρόνησις)":—(*Sim.* ix. 17) "Having
therefore received the seal, they had *one understanding*, and one
mind, and their faith became one, and their *love one*," (*ib.* 18) "the
church of God shall be one body, *one understanding*, one mind, one
faith, *one love*." But he also uses it as a proper noun to denote the
last of the Angels that build up the Church (*Vis.* iii. 8 (*bis*), comp.
Sim. ix. 15). And here he regards it as proceeding "from Understanding," called Ἐπιστήμη. Ἀγάπη is called by the Greek Thesaurus
"a mere Biblical word (vox mere biblica)." In LXX it is almost
confined to Cant. and almost always has a sexual significance, but
the Wisdom of Solomon applies it to man's love of God (iii. 9) and says
that the beginning of wisdom is the desire of discipline, and (vi. 18)
"the care (φροντὶς) of discipline is *love*, and *love* is the keeping of her
laws (ἀγάπη δὲ τήρησις νόμων αὐτῆς)." Comp. Jn xiv. 23 "if a man
love me he will keep (τηρήσει) my word."

The Fourth Evangelist does not mention the noun "love"
(Jn v. 42 "I know you, how that ye have not *the love of God* within
you") till he has prepared his readers for it by connecting the verb
with God as loving (iii. 16, 35) "the world" and "the Son." After
that one mention of the noun, it is not mentioned again till the
night before the Crucifixion where it is, in effect, defined (xiii. 34—5,
xv. 9 foll.) as a unique love personified by Christ. The Gospel
manifests not only a spiritual struggle to express an inexpressibly
divine emotion, but also an intellectual attempt to rescue the word
ἀγάπη from its Old Testament associations.

We have seen above that John omits the words "Give ye them to eat." But we have been led to the conclusion that they were part of the earliest form of the narrative. If that is so, Jesus (we may suppose) was, even in those early days, training the disciples to "give" to the multitude, as, later on, He Himself was destined to "give" to the disciples in the Eucharist. What was that "gift"? As to part of it, all the Synoptists are agreed. They all tell us that He "gave" it with the words "This is my body." About this we shall say nothing here, since there is no disagreement. But as to another part there is a difference. Mark and Matthew indisputably represent Jesus as connecting the words "my blood" with a word (*diathēkè*) variously translated by our English Versions "covenant" or "testament," so that Jesus says "This is the blood of my *covenant* (or, *testament*)[1]." Luke, in one version of his text, the one adopted by our Revised Version, has "This cup is the new *covenant* (or, *testament*) in my blood." But Westcott and Hort place this (and some of the context) in double brackets, as not being a part of the original text[2]. Thus we are led to narrow down our question about the "gift" to a question, in the first place, as to the meaning attached by Jesus to the word *diathēkè*.

In LXX, the word *diathēkè* occurs for the first time in connection with the deluge by which God purposed to destroy mankind but to spare Noah: "Everything that is in the earth shall die, but I will establish my *covenant* with thee[3]." The

---

[1] Mk xiv. 24, Mt. xxvi. 28. Or the meaning may be (as R.V.) "This is my blood of the *covenant* (or, *testament*)." The Greek is τὸ αἷμά μου τῆς διαθήκης.

[2] Lk. xxii. 20. Curet. omits this. SS combines xxii. 17, 20 thus "...divide it among you; this is my blood, the new *testament*." For "*testament*," SS uses דיאתיקא, a Syriac form of the Greek διαθήκη, which is regularly used for "testamentary disposition," "will" (*Thes. Syr.* 873). The word for "covenant," *e.g.* with Noah, Abraham, Israel, etc., is represented by Syr. קימא = Heb. ברית (*Thes. Syr.* 3534).

[3] Gen. vi. 17—18.

Hebrew for "covenant" is *berîth*, meaning "compact," "alliance," "league," "agreement," "pledge of friendship." This is often well expressed by "covenant"—as when Joshua made a "covenant" with the Gibeonites at the time when he was purposing to destroy the Canaanites[1]. But in the case of Noah's *berîth*, as also often elsewhere, Aquila and Symmachus both substitute *sunthēkè* for *diathēkè*[2]. And they appear to be justified. For *sunthēkè*, in Greek, regularly has the meanings of the Hebrew *berîth*, that is, "compact," "agreement," etc.; *diathēkè* has not. The regular meaning of *diathēkè*—outside LXX and outside writings influenced by LXX—is "*last will and testament*[3]."

---

[1] Josh. ix. 6—16, see Gesen. 136.

[2] They also substitute συνθήκη for LXX διαθήκη in Gen. xvii. 2 (the BERÎTH with Abraham). There Jerome says "Notandum quod ubicumque in Graeco *testamentum* legimus, ibi in Hebraeo sermone sit *foedus*, sive *pactum*, id est BERÎTH." Field, on Is. lvi. 6 (one of the very few instances where Aq. and Sym. are recorded to have used διαθήκη), says "Pro διαθήκην juxta usum binorum interpretum requiritur συνθήκην."

[3] The only instance known to me of διαθήκη meaning "*agreement*," in Greek outside the sphere of LXX influence, is one quoted by Wetstein (on Mt. xxvi. 28) from Aristophanes (*Av.* 439). This is mentioned by Lightfoot (on Gal. iii. 15) as one of "some few exceptions." Westcott, who writes later, does not add any of these "exceptions" in his very long note on *Diathēkè* in *The Epistle to the Hebrews*. He says merely (p. 301) "The more general sense of 'arrangement,' 'agreement' is also found (Arist. *Av.* 440)." But Steph. *Thes.* gives no instance of "the more general sense" except the one from Aristophanes.

Josephus (*Ant.* xvii. 3. 2, xvii. 9. 7, *Bell.* ii. 2. 3) not only uses *diathēkè* several times for a "will," but also avoids using it in the phrase "the ark of *the covenant*," as, for example, in describing the passage of the Jordan by Joshua, and the capture of Jericho, where the phrase recurs frequently in Scripture. Justin Martyr, in his Dialogue with the Jew, where he frequently quotes LXX, uses διαθήκη more than thirty times; but in his Apology, addressed to Greeks, he does not use it once; *De Monarch.* ii. 3 quotes from the *Diathēkai* of Orpheus, apparently regarded as meaning "*last instructions*"—a testamentary recantation. Hermas never uses *diathēkè*.

Philo affords conclusive evidence that the LXX application of the Greek *diathēkè* to the "covenants" of God with Noah and Abraham caused difficulty to students of the Greek text. Unfortunately his Greek comment on the *berîth* with Noah is lost. When referring, however, to the *berîth* with Abraham, he says "*Diathēkai* are written for the sake of those who are worthy of a free gift, so that a *diathēkè* is a symbol of grace[1]." Then he says "About the whole subject of *diathēkai* I have written fully in two lectures, and I pass over the subject to avoid repeating myself." But he adds something that indicates (although briefly and obscurely) a connection in his mind between the *diathēkè* with Abraham and the "*inheritance*" promised to Abraham[2]. "To one class of men," he says, "God holds forth benefits through earth, water, air, sun, moon, sky, [and] other incorporeal powers[3],

---

[1] Philo i. 586 "a free gift (δωρεᾶς)." This appears directed against the view that the *diathēkè* was a "compact," or "agreement." As a fact, the Hebrew, *berîth*, does mean "compact." But the Greek διαθήκη does not.

[2] It should be noted that the Hebrew verb "*inherit* (ירש)" occurs for the first time in the Bible where God establishes His *berîth* with Abraham: Gen. xv. 3—8 "One born in my house shall *inherit* me... shall not *inherit* thee...he that shall come forth out of thine own bowels shall *inherit* thee...to give thee this land to *inherit* it.... Whereby shall I know that I shall *inherit* it?" In the preceding context, according to our R.V. text, God has promised Himself to Abraham (xv. 1) "I am...thy exceeding great reward." All this is above the level of "compacts" and "agreements" in the ordinary sense of the terms.

There is however no Hebrew noun—whether derived from ירש or otherwise—that represents the "bequeathing," or "testamentary disposition," of an inheritance. The Heb. verb צוה, "give [testamentary] instructions," is represented in Targ. by the Aram. verb פקד in 2 S. xvii. 23, 2 K. xx. 1, Is. xxxviii. 1; but the noun from פקד is not known to occur in Palestinian Aramaic, see below, p. 188, n.

[3] Philo i. 587. Comp. Gal. iv. 3 "We were in bondage under the elements (στοιχεῖα) of the world," where however στοιχεῖα probably means "elements" in a metaphorical as well as in a literal sense.

but to another class through Himself alone, *making Himself the inheritance of those who receive Him*." All this is based on the utterance of God to Abraham, which Philo reads thus: "And I, behold, [*am*] *my diathēkè* with thee[1]." He adds, as comment, "Now this suggests the following meaning. Though there are very many kinds of *diathēkè*, bestowing kindnesses (*lit.* graces) and free gifts on those who are worthy, yet the highest kind of *diathēkai* I MYSELF AM."

What Philo means—and especially what he means by "free gift" and "grace"—can hardly be understood unless we realise that by *diathēkè* he means, not "covenant" but "testament." By a "testament" a man may leave gifts and legacies to friends, servants, and dependants, but the highest form of it is that by which a father leaves "his real estate" to his son, who is to succeed him after the testator's death. God cannot die. Nevertheless God makes Abraham His "heir," and bequeaths to him, so to speak, His "real estate," His own personal presence, Himself. This conclusion as to Philo's meaning is confirmed by a Latin fragment of a comment of his on God's *diathēkè* with Noah: "In the case of men an inheritance transmitted by them is possessed [by the heir then, and only then] when the men themselves exist no longer but are dead. But on the other hand God, since He is everlasting, *concedes to the wise a joint participation in the inheritance that He transmits* [*to them while He is still living*], and He rejoices at their entering into possession of it[2]."

---

[1] Gen. xvii. 4 καὶ ἐγὼ ἰδοὺ ἡ διαθήκη μου μετὰ σοῦ. This may be variously punctuated. Clem. Alex. 427 quotes ἰδοὺ ἐγὼ (sic) ἡ διαθήκη μου μετὰ σοῦ as a proof that "Moses manifestly calls the Lord a *diathēkè*."

[2] Philo *Quaest. in Gen.* (on Gen. vi. 18 "I will establish my covenant with thee"). The comment concludes as follows: "Secundo ampliorem quandam largitur sapienti haereditatem. Non enim dixit *Ponam foedus meum tibi*, sed *te*: id est, Tu es justum verumque foedus, quod statuam generi rationali pro possessione ac decore quibus opus est virtutis." I am unable to explain this. The

In this last passage, about the *diathēkè* with Noah, we see Philo apparently influenced, partly by the natural meaning of the Greek word (namely, "testament"), and partly by the thought of the subsequent *diathēkè* with Abraham, so that he imports into the transaction with Noah a meaning that the Hebrew can hardly justify. As to the motives of the LXX in using *diathēkè* to render *berîth* we cannot speak confidently. It is possible that they avoided *sunthēkè*, the correct rendering, because the thought of God as making a "compact" or "treaty" with man seemed too anthropomorphic. In the illustrious instances of Noah and Abraham, the LXX may have felt justified in attempting to force into the Hebrew word some higher thought—taking *diathēkè* to mean not exactly a "*will*" but a "*deed of gift*." Then this precedent may have been followed by them in subsequent instances, for consistency's sake, where the Hebrew could not have that meaning.

At this stage, after these repeated mentions of "*testament*" in Greek, before we pass to the Gospels, it will be well to ask, "How would a Jew of the first century in Palestine express himself in Aramaic, if he wished to say 'This is my *last will and testament*'?" The answer is important and to some it may be surprising. The Jew could not possibly express this by "This is my *berîth*" any more than we in English could express it by "This is my *treaty*." He would have to say "This is my *diathēkè*," using a Hebraized form of the Greek word. Abundant instances of this use are given by Levy and Krauss. Babylonian Jews might have used another word (apparently of rare occurrence); but Palestinian Jews appear to have had practically no other[1].

---

heading of the comment is "Quid est *Statuam foedus meum tecum*?" The expression "I will give [*i.e.* appoint] thee for a covenant" occurs in Isaiah xlii. 6, xlix. 8; but Philo hardly ever quotes prophecy, and there is no various reading of *te* for *tecum* (or *tibi*) in renderings of Gen. vi. 18.

[1] See Levy, Levy *Ch.*, Krauss, and *Thes. Syr.* on דייתיקי or

Now coming to the Epistles we perceive that the Epistle to the Hebrews definitely says "For wherever there is a *dia thēkè* there *the death of the maker-of-the-diathēkè must of necessity have its course* (lit. *be brought*), for a *diathēkè* [*is as it were*] *based on dead persons*[1]." The Epistle to the Galatians takes the *diathēkè* with Abraham expressly out of the region of "law," and by implication out of the region of "compact," into the region of "heirs" and "promise" and "faith," when, after insisting on the unalterableness of a human *diathēkè*[2], it goes on to say " A *diathēkè* [such as that with Abraham] confirmed beforehand by God, *the law*, which came four hundred and thirty years after, doth not disannul, so as to make the *promise* of no effect....But before *faith* came we were kept in ward under the law....And if ye are Christ's, then are ye Abraham's seed, *heirs* according to *promise*[3]." In the light of these two passages we perceive that elsewhere, when Paul speaks of God's *diathēkè* with Abraham he not only does not include the thought of "compact," but excludes it and implies God's "free gift" (as

---

דיאתיקי used *passim* for "a will." Levy iv. 88 *a* gives one instance of the phrase "a writing of פקדתא," *i.e.* "a writing of last instructions," "a will," in *Git.* 50 *b*. But I am informed by Dr A. Büchler that this is in a discussion of Babylonian scholars and that he knows no instance of it in Palestinian Aramaic. Levy i. 404 quotes, *inter alia, J. Berach.* v. 9 *b*, where God is represented as saying that He gave the dew to Abraham "in a *diathēkè*," where Schwab has (p. 101) "C'est à *titre immuable* que j'en ai fait don à Abraham" (comp. Gal. iii. 15 foll. on the unalterableness of the *diathēkè* with Abraham). But it means "deed of gift" in *Gen. r.*, on Gen. xxiv. 10 "All the good[s] of his master was in his hand," where the comment is "This means a *diathēkè*," *i.e.* a deed of disposition by which Abraham, while still living, made over his property to his servant in trust for Isaac. This is exceptional. Neither here nor elsewhere do Levy's instances indicate that the Hebrew *diathēkè* was used to mean "bargain," "treaty," or "compact."

[1] Heb. ix. 16—17.
[2] Gal. iii. 15.
[3] Gal. iii. 17—29.

Philo does) and the thought of a Father bequeathing an inheritance to sons[1].

In dealing with the Law of Moses Paul labours under great difficulties. The LXX so frequently calls it a *diathēkè* that Paul is obliged to do the same. But he explains it as a testamentary disposition of an inferior character given to Israel for a time—almost as if he were Ishmael not Isaac— for "So long as the heir is a child, he differeth nothing from a bondservant[2]." This *diathēkè* is both old and new. Relatively to the Christian *diathēkè*, it is old and ready to be superseded. Relatively to the Promise, it is "new," but not in a good sense—being the *diathēkè* of Sinai, which "beareth children unto bondage," a novel though necessary makeshift. It cannot invalidate the ancient and unalterable *diathēkè* of God bequeathing Himself to Abraham His son and heir[3].

---

[1] Comp. Rom. ix. 4 "Whose is the adoption and the glory and the *diathēkai*," ib. xi. 27 "this is the *diathēkè* from me to them (comp. Is. lix. 21) when I shall take away their sins." The Epistle to the Hebrews (viii. 8—10) quotes Jeremiah (xxxi. 31—3) as predicting that God will make "a new *diathēkè*" for Israel, "I will put my law in their inward parts and in their heart will I write it, and I will be their God, and they shall be my people." This is in Paul's mind as the true *diathēkè*, the fulfilment of the *diathēkè* with Abraham and Isaac "the heir." The *diathēkè* of Sinai (Gal. iv. 24) "bearing children unto bondage" is represented by Hagar. That, too, is a legacy of a kind, since Ishmael is Abraham's child, but it is of an inferior kind.

[2] Gal. iv. 1.

[3] See 2 Cor. iii. 6—14 ἡμᾶς διακόνους καινῆς διαθήκης...ἐπὶ τῇ ἀναγνώσει τῆς παλαιᾶς διαθήκης. Eph. ii. 12 ξένοι τῶν διαθηκῶν τῆς ἐπαγγελίας, appears to mean "strangers to the *diathēkè* of the promise to Abraham in all the forms in which it was given to him and confirmed to his successors." For the remaining Pauline instance "this is the new *diathēkè* in my blood" see below, § 42. The instances in the Epistle to the Hebrews—where both meanings are intermixed—are too frequent to be quoted.

§ 42. *"Testament" in the Gospels*

Passing now to the Gospels we find that, apart from the narratives of the Eucharist, their evidence is almost entirely negative, since the word occurs but once, namely, in the Song of Zacharias "To remember his holy *diathēkè*, the oath that he sware unto our father Abraham[1]." Jesus repeatedly speaks of "the law," but never of the *diathēkè* of God, either with Abraham, or with Israel at Mount Sinai. Nor does any evangelist use the word, when writing in his own person.

In the accounts of the Eucharist the texts vary greatly. The Revised Version gives a longer Lucan text including a phrase that contains the word *diathēkè*, and closely agreeing with a Pauline passage that includes the same phrase[2]. Westcott and Hort give a shorter Lucan text omitting the phrase and containing no mention of *diathēkè*[3]. Also, in Mark and Matthew, Westcott and Hort reject "new" as applied to *diathēkè*. The Revised Version, although it says that "some ancient authorities" insert *new* in Mark, and that "many" insert it in Matthew, nevertheless does not itself insert *new* in either Gospel.

This omission of "new" makes all the difference in the interpretation of *diathēkè*. If "new" had been part of the text, we might have supposed the meaning to be "This is my blood of the New Covenant, or the blood of my New Covenant, as distinguished from the blood of the Old Covenant which was given to Israel on Mount Sinai." Even with the addition of "new," such a doctrine would seem abrupt and almost startling—especially in view of the fact that Jesus is not

---

[1] Lk. i. 72—3.

[2] Lk. xxii. 20 "This cup is the new *diathēkè* in my blood," comp. I Cor. xi. 25.

[3] W.H. pass from Lk. xxii. 19 "This is my body" to Lk. xxii. 21 "But behold, the hand... ," bracketing "that is given for you... that is shed for you."

recorded in any Gospel to have ever previously mentioned the word thus interpreted "covenant," either to the multitude or to the disciples. But, without the addition of "new," the meaning "covenant" seems quite impossible.

That being the case, we are led to accept, as probable, an explanation based on the demonstrated meaning of the Palestinian Aramaic word *diathēkè*, namely, "last will and testament." There may possibly have been some allusion to the *diathēkè* in Sinai[1]. But much more probably there was no allusion at all to that or to anything else in the Old Testament. It was an utterance of personal affection and of divine conviction. Using the language habitual in Palestine Jesus said to His disciples, "This is the blood that signifies my death and yet not my severance from you. This is the blood of my last will and testament in which, though dying, I bequeath to you my life and presence in perpetuity[2]."

Here we must add that although Mark and Matthew do not represent Jesus as speaking of a *"new diathēkè"* in connection with "cup" or "blood," they do represent Him as using the word *"new"* in connection with the act of drinking

---

[1] Comp. Exod. xxiv. 8 ἰδοὺ τὸ αἷμα τῆς διαθήκης ἧς διέθετο Κύριος πρὸς ὑμᾶς περὶ πάντων τῶν λόγων τούτων. These words Christians would naturally connect with Christ in after times, as they are connected in Heb. ix. 19, 20 etc. And the tradition peculiar to Luke and added by him a little later on (xxii. 29) κἀγὼ διατίθεμαι ὑμῖν...βασιλείαν (perhaps referring to the crown to be gained by the blood of martyrdom) may be an allusion to the διαθήκη of Sinai. But the words of Institution seem best interpreted as a simple, direct, non-allusive and personal utterance in which Jesus bequeathed Himself to His disciples.

[2] This conclusion—rejecting the word "new"—is compatible with a grateful acknowledgment of the value of the Pauline tradition (1 Cor. xi. 23 "received from the Lord") concerning the *meaning* of the Eucharist, as being something that was to be "done in remembrance" of the Lord, and also concerning the relation of it, as a "new" and higher "testament," to the old and inferior one. But the Pauline tradition has no claim to be regarded as more faithful than that of Mark and Matthew to Christ's original words.

from a "cup" at the Eucharist[1]. The parallel Luke, though in other respects closely similar to Mark and Matthew, omits "new[2]." John therefore is bound (according to the Rule of Johannine Intervention) to insert something about "newness," equivalent—from a Johannine point of view—to what Mark and Matthew have about "not drinking from *the offspring of the vine*" until Jesus shall "drink it *new*" in "the kingdom of God" (or, as Matthew has it, "the kingdom of my Father").

Starting, then, from the Synoptic "*offspring of the vine*," we ask for some equivalent in John. Origen, when commenting on "*the offspring of the vine*," in Matthew, asks "What vine?" He replies (from John) "That vine of which He Himself [*i.e.* Jesus] was the figure, saying *I am the Vine, ye the branches.* Whence He says again *My blood is truly drink....* For truly He '*washed His robe in the blood of the grape*[3].'"

---

[1] Mk xiv. 25   Mt. xxvi. 29   Lk. xxii. 18

Verily I say unto you, I will no more drink of the offspring of the vine, until that day when I drink it new in the kingdom of God.	But I say unto you, I will not drink henceforth of this offspring of the vine, until that day when I drink it new with you in my Father's kingdom.	For I say unto you, I will not drink from henceforth of the offspring of the vine, until the kingdom of God shall come.

The columns follow R.V., except in rendering γένημα "offspring" instead of "fruit." The formula for "blessing over the wine" was *Berach.* 35 *a* (Mishna) "Blessed [is] He that created *the fruit* (פרי) of the vine," and the usual Greek for פרי is καρπός. But in Deut. and Isaiah it is sometimes rendered γένημα.

[2] Luke has also a corresponding utterance of Jesus about "eating," peculiar to his Gospel (xxii. 16) "I will assuredly not eat it [where "it" refers to (xxii. 15) "this Passover"] until it be fulfilled in the kingdom of God." There, too, Luke omits "*new*."

The importance attached to "*the cup*" may be illustrated by the tradition in *Pesach.* 106 *a* "The Rabbis said that (Exod. xx. 8) *Remember the Sabbath* meant *Remember it over the wine.*" This "remembering" was a part of the "Hallowing of the Sabbath," a domestic rite known to have been practised before, and probably long before, the days of Hillel and Shammai.

[3] Origen *Levit. Hom.* vii. 2 (Lomm. ix. 292—3) quoting Mt. xxvi.

Now all would agree that the blood of Jesus represents His "love" ("greater *love* hath no man than this, that a man lay down his life for his friends[1]"). And the love of Jesus is regarded in the Fourth Gospel as a new kind of love. At the conclusion of His prayer to the Father for the disciples, Jesus says that He will make the Father's name known to them, "that *the love wherewith thou lovedst* me may be in them, and I in them[2]"; and He has previously defined this love in "a new commandment" to the disciples. Their love is to be like His love: "*A new commandment* give I unto you, that ye love one another—*even as I have loved* you, that ye also love one another[3]."

Does not this "new commandment," in John, correspond to the "new wine," in Mark and Matthew? That the epithet "new" is emphatic is confirmed, not only by the context, but also by the play on "new" and "old" in the Johannine Epistle[1], and by the fact that, apart from narrative, this is the only instance of the epithet in the whole of the Fourth Gospel[5]. Some may object that "commandment" implies constraint. "Love," they may say, "must not be commanded." That is not an objection that would be felt to be a serious one by John or by any spiritually-minded Jew, who would accept as God's gifts the two "great" commandments of the Law. God's commandments are affectionate imperatives, like the Pauline paraphrase "Be ye reconciled unto God[6]." They come to us

---

29, Jn xv. 5, vi. 55, Gen. xlix. 11. Comp. *Didach.* § 9 "First, about the *cup*:—We give thanks to thee, our Father, for the holy *Vine* of David thy servant (παιδός), which thou madest known to us through Jesus thy servant (παιδός)."

[1] Jn xv. 13.   [2] Jn xvii. 26.

[3] Jn xiii. 34.   There would be nothing "new" in the commandment "love your neighbours," or "love one another," but there was something "new" in the kind of love.

[4] The commandment was (1 Jn ii. 7) "not new" and yet (*ib.* 8) "on the other hand new."

[5] Jn xix. 4 "a new tomb" is the only other instance.

[6] 2 Cor. v. 20.

appealing for love—love toward God the Father, and love toward men the brethren. And, coming to us through the Son, they convey to us, if we will receive them in the Spirit of the Son, a power to respond to the appeal. Hence, in the Fourth Gospel, a "commandment" is regarded as something "given" by the Father to the Son, and even as being "eternal life[1]." The final mention of the word by Jesus indicates, so to speak, an appropriation of the Commandment of Love by the Son: "This is my very own commandment, that ye love one another[2]." By using "commandment" and not the ambiguous *diathēkè*, John avoids all notion of "covenanting" or "bargaining," And yet he also avoids any expressions that imply unconditional "giving" to those who are incapable of "receiving" the gift.

No Gospel inculcates more consistently than the Fourth the necessity of something real at heart and spiritually solid, incompatible with nebulous mysticism or inflated bubbles of profession. Conditions—of act as well as thought—are not only expressed but also reiterated. "If ye have love one to another," and "If ye do that which I command you," are but two out of many specimens[3]. Our expectation, then, that John would intervene—so far as concerns the Marcan tradition, certainly omitted by Luke, about the "newness" of the wine that was to be drunk by Jesus after His death—appears to be justified. We have no right to push our expectation further and to claim that John should intervene about the Marcan *diathēkè* to tell us whether it meant "testament" or "covenant." For, as we have seen, it is not certain that Luke omits this word.

Nevertheless we may say with confidence that, all through Christ's Last Discourse and Last Prayer, John is endeavouring

---

[1] Jn xii. 49, 50.
[2] Jn xv. 12. On the emphasis of ἡ ἐντολὴ ἡ ἐμή see *Joh. Gr.*, Index ἐμή.
[3] See ἐάν in Jn xiii. 17, 35, xiv. 15, 23, xv. 7, 10, 14.

to set before us the Son as playing (so to speak) the part of a Testator in behalf of the Father. In the Father's name, He is bequeathing Himself to mankind. The difficulty pointed out by Philo—that God the Father cannot die, so as to make a "testament" in the ordinary way—disappears in the Person of the incarnate Son. The Son could die. Since He could die He could make a "testament" as Mark and Matthew apparently say that He did. The difficulty for John, therefore, consisted, not in the actual words of Jesus, but in the interpretations of them by Christians, who might confuse "testament" with "covenant," or might give to both terms formal and unspiritual significations.

In the Fourth Gospel this danger is avoided partly by negative means—by avoiding the word "testament." But far more importance attaches to the positive means—the introduction of a substitute that could not possibly be reduced to the level of a technical term. This substitute—which reminds us of the promise to Abraham as interpreted above, "And I, behold, [am] my *diathēkē* with thee"—is a personal Testament, a Paraclete, an Alter Ego, or Second Self, who is to represent the Son after His departure and to recall the Son's acts and words and strengthening presence, with increased power. Thus, without hearing from His lips any such words as "This is my testament," we see Jesus in this Gospel standing in the midst of His troubled followers on the eve of His departure from them, and bestowing on them a Testament of a new kind, no less "new" than His love, a Testament indeed yet not a writing, a spiritual Friend to take His place in their orphaned hearts, and to breathe into them the assurance that although absent He is present and that they are not orphans in the comfort of His perpetual presence: "Peace I leave unto you, my own peace I give unto you, not as the world giveth give I unto you." "I will not leave you orphans, I come unto you[1]."

---

[1] Jn xiv. 27, 18.